Writing Your Doctoral Dissertation or Thesis Faster

Writing Your Doctoral Dissertation or Thesis Faster

A Proven Map to Success

E. Alana James

DoctoralNet.com
Walden University

Tracesea Slater

DoctoralNet.com

Los Angeles | London | New Delhi
Singapore | Washington DC

Los Angeles | London | New Delhi
Singapore | Washington DC

FOR INFORMATION:

SAGE Publications, Inc.

2455 Teller Road

Thousand Oaks, California 91320

E-mail: order@sagepub.com

SAGE Publications Ltd.

1 Oliver's Yard

55 City Road

London EC1Y 1SP

United Kingdom

SAGE Publications India Pvt. Ltd.

B 1/I 1 Mohan Cooperative Industrial Area

Mathura Road, New Delhi 110 044

India

SAGE Publications Asia-Pacific Pte. Ltd.

3 Church Street

#10-04 Samsung Hub

Singapore 049483

Acquisitions Editor: Helen Salmon

Editorial Assistant: Kaitlin Coghill

Production Editor: Brittany Bauhaus

Copy Editor: Karin Rathert

Typesetter: C&M Digitals (P) Ltd.

Proofreader: Dennis Webb

Indexer: Kathy Paparchontis

Cover Designer: Gail Buschman

Marketing Manager: Nicole Elliott

Printed in the United States of America

A catalog record of this book is available from the Library of Congress.

9781452274157

This book is printed on acid-free paper.

13 14 15 16 17 10 9 8 7 6 5 4 3 2 1

Brief Contents

Detailed Contents

About the Authors

Dr. E. Alana James received her EdD in educational leadership from Teachers College in 2005. Since then she has helped over 30 doctoral candidates in either educational leadership or business move through the process on to graduation. Working primarily as supervisor for a number of online for profit universities, but also sometimes in the role of committee member, she identified the key places and challenges that created extra stress and, unfortunately, sometimes breakdown. This book and her work developing DoctoralNet.com is in reaction to those difficulties and will, with adoption, increase graduation rates for those working towards a PhD or other type of doctoral degree. You can follow DoctoralNet on Twitter, Facebook, or Google +.

Dr. James also specializes in action research and has used that transformative process throughout the development of the techniques and strategies outlined herein. Information about her other books can be found on the website for SAGE Publishing.

A believer in the doctoral process as a rite of passage that releases the greatest potential in life, she reinvented her own life to move half way around the world from where she began. Living in Ireland with her partner, their two dogs and a cat she authors nonfiction work on health and wellness on her personal website at ealanajames.com where you can connect with her as a writer, a consultant or speaker.

Tracesea Slater, MA, is the director of strategy at DoctoralNet.com where she works with Dr. James to raise graduation rates by assisting doctoral students to finish their dissertations. Tracesea's main areas of research interest are education, disadvantaged populations, and youth development. Her research experience includes work as the manager of research and evaluation at a nonprofit serving homeless youth in Denver, Colorado. She also has done research and program evaluation in the fields of education and health care at a social research company. Tracesea's academic experience includes work as a sociology instructor at the University of Colorado and Colorado Technical University.

About DoctoralNet

DoctoralNet Limited, which employs both Dr. E. Alana James and Tracesea Slater, is an early stage technology startup based in Kinsale County, Cork, Ireland. The company's mission is to increase doctoral graduation rates around the world by employing web-based processes and delivering high quality modular support. This includes written, visual, and auditory content, as well as professorial help. DoctoralNet's goal is to provide on-demand services as doctoral students need them, ending the frustration and confusion that causes people to forgo their research. The company works directly with student members, as well as outsourcing their services to universities. All the staff who work with doctoral students have supervised at least 10 graduating theses for universities, as participating on committees is often the means by which we learn the intricacies of the outstanding dissertation or thesis.

Acknowledgments

All authors must acknowledge that no book is completed without the help and support of many people. Our editor Helen Salmon met us while completing our last book for SAGE on Action Research. We are grateful she offered us this opportunity because of our work with DoctoralNet.com. This book has been a joy to write. Without the universities that have trusted us to help guide their doctoral students through to completion, and most importantly, without those students, we would never have been introduced to the wild ride that leads up to successful doctoral graduation. We are blessed to keep many of the more than 50 graduates whose work we influenced as friends and colleagues—the world is a bigger, wider, and more interesting place because of the work you are doing.

We also wish to acknowledge the help and support of the other professors who reviewed the three main parts of this work. We gratefully recognize that it is only because of their help that this book is as polished as it is. Feedback is a gift that we all need, no matter where we stand in our academic careers, and we have worked to include most, if not all, of your suggestions. Thank you Ronald D. Valenti, PhD, St. John Fisher College executive leadership, EdD; Wesley T. Church II, PhD, associate professor and chair of the PhD program at the University of Alabama School of Social Work; Mark Monmonier, Syracuse University; John W. Presley, Illinois State University; Richard L. Wiggall, Northern Arizona University; Gretchen McAllister, Northern Arizona University; George W. Semich, EdD, professor/director of the Instructional Management/Leadership PhD program at Robert Morris University; and Paul J. Gerber, PhD, Virginia Commonwealth University. We want to especially thank Dr. Gene W. Gloeckner from the School of Education, Colorado State University. Gene, you made us laugh at the same time as you went to that extra effort to help our methodological, ontological, and theoretical discussions reach the top of their game. We are grateful and hope to work with you in the future. Likewise, we are grateful John Lesley joined the review team for the last segment. Using pithy comments, John held our work to the highest standard and helped the final section maintain the level of examples and so forth that will help our readers understand the points we hope to make.

We also need to acknowledge that we are qualitative researchers and the justice that we have been able to do for those working on the quantitative side of the house comes largely from my co-professor and colleague at DoctoralNet.com, Dr. Maria Sanchez Patino. She gave a lecture to our free Sunday web conference group on quantitative work that makes up the format for much of Chapter 12, and our reviewers praised its clarity.

The hard work after writing is covered in the copyediting and publication work. No book goes to press without people such as Brittany Bauhaus, Karin Rathert, and Dennis Webb in the wings. Thank you to all SAGE personnel before and after publication. You are a great company to write for, and we are delighted to be SAGE authors.

Introduction

Welcome to *Writing Your Doctoral Dissertation or Thesis Faster: A Proven Map to Success*. This book has developed over the last five years as we have worked with doctoral candidates, helping them through defense of proposal and on through their research to defending their final dissertation or thesis. Throughout those long journeys, we have blundered, watched some students fail, and ended up asking ourselves, how do we make this process better? How can we make it shorter? What can we do to make defense easier? What causes unnecessary delays? How could we have avoided that disaster? This book is our current best thinking on the subject, interwoven with research from others on the topic. We are also grateful to those professionals who helped us as we wrote through the peer-review process. Together, we believe this book will help all doctoral candidates move a little easier through the dissertation or, as they say in Europe, thesis, and on to graduation.

This book is written with voices from two points of view, Alana, who has mentored doctoral students, and Tracesea, who has a professional research background and who helps students on our website at DoctoralNet.com, but who has not yet begun a dissertation or thesis of her own. Throughout the book, we speak from time to time in our own voices so that our reader has an increased sense of the humanity involved in the dissertation process. We start off now with personal notes.

E. Alana James

I regularly tell students that writing your dissertation is a rite of passage, something I realized as a result of reading R. R. Clark's 1983 article "The Dissertation as a Rite of Passage" in The American Journal of Evaluation *when I was in your shoes. Doing doctoral level dissertation research is unlike anything most of you have faced before. I tell the students I work with that you have to take off your professional hat and put on the hat of a researcher. It is a treat to work in our own minds and see our critical analysis of the topic beloved to us develop. It also changes the way we see the world. I remember, and my recent graduates remind me, that you are also much more aware of what claims you have made and whether or not these are backed by data. This process will give you an assuredness in the world of how to approach difficult decisions and master strategic challenges in a way no other process can.*

A dissertation or thesis (depending on where you live in the world and what your university calls it) requires discipline as well as endurance and will test you in ways you cannot yet imagine. Yet, without having run that gauntlet and having finished my doctorate, I could not live the life I live nor write the book, or be the professional that I am. Therefore, I start off by wishing you all the best. May you find the communities you need to support your process, and whenever it is so difficult that you cannot believe you have the strength to go forward, may you find the inner resilience you need to do so. We write this book, and we support students through our business at doctoralnet.com because we personally believe that while extremely difficult, a doctoral level degree should be available to anyone who is willing to undergo the personal and professional transformation it requires. Keep at it. Perseverance and forthright dedication to the goal of finishing is required.

Cheers,
Alana

At the time of this writing, I have my master's degree in sociology but have not started my doctoral degree. As second author of this book, I will be keeping tabs on how well we are writing for those who may not be familiar with or are just starting the doctoral journey. I hope that my lack of experience will help me to ensure that the information presented here is accessible to all, no matter what your doctoral experience may be so far. I anticipate that my questions and confusion will also be yours, so I'll do my best to make sure those questions are answered and your path is clear.

Tracesea H. Slater

I have been working as a technical assistant and editor at doctoralnet.com for several years with Alana, and my favorite part of this job has been seeing the transformation that doctoral students go through. I have lived vicariously through their struggles and frustrations and watched them come out victorious on the other side. It is wonderful to hear stories of success and triumph from students as they earn their PhDs. One of the most exciting and inspiring things has been hearing about the new doors that have been opened for our students as they become doctors. As Alana said, getting your doctorate is a rite of passage, and I would add that it is also a pathway to new beginnings and increased opportunities. While completing your dissertation, you get a chance to really explore yourself and your capabilities. When you finish, you see a world of external experiences is now available for you to delve into.

I sincerely wish you the best of journeys, and may endless exciting possibilities await you on the other side. I'll see you there!

Cheers,
Tracesea

Questions Answered in This Section

1. I have friends that have been at this for years, what is the best way to ensure I finish faster?

2. How is this book laid out?

3. What is the easiest way to use it?

Do You Want to Finish Faster?

Do the difficult things while they are easy and do the great things while they are small. A journey of a thousand miles must begin with a single step.

– Lao Tzu

Speed Versus Quality: Efficiency or Sacrifice?

One of our reviewer's on this book asked whether finishing faster was the goal? We think that you, like the doctoral students we work with, would answer, yes! That being said, your professors might not agree but would challenge that the quality of work is the more important goal. This tension is understandable, and fortunately we have designed with both in mind.

You are likely a mature individual juggling a full life of responsibilities: work, children, taking care of aging parents, and other complexities. It is natural that you may feel stress and will be happy when no more of your time goes to studying. Professors likely graduated in the time when it was expected for their dissertation work to proceed over the course of many years. With that experience comes the belief that some of the maturity in thinking and understanding cannot be rushed. It is your responsibility to manage this process. To this end, you will see that in Chapter 1, we have included a section about time management. Hints and steps are presented to help your work be more efficient. Additional aid is included in pullouts throughout the book that are cross-referenced in the index.

On the other hand, we assume that most of you also would like to complete outstanding work. To this end, in Parts II and III we regularly discuss the qualities we have found in our mini meta-analysis comparing typical dissertations from the universities where we work to outstanding ones that have won awards all over the world.

How fast can I finish?

Alana says: *Perhaps when you entered graduate school you were told by your university that it is possible to earn your doctoral degree in three years. The wise student would ask, "What percentage of your students actually graduate in three years?" From my own experience and that of my students, graduating in three years is possible but difficult.*

We believe that you can finish your dissertation faster without sacrificing quality, but it's not likely to be easy. You will be up against several challenges. In our experience, some of the biggest obstacles include maintaining focus and persistence to reach your ultimate goal, finishing your research. Here are some ideas on how you can work through these challenges and achieve success.

Book Layout and Use

The purpose of this book is to give you, the doctoral candidate anywhere in the world, a comprehensive yet easy-to-follow map through the dissertation process. The authors' goal is to help you finish your degree. Because this is a large task, this book will lay out a map with three basic sections. These give you the basics and then suggest other sources to consider for the depth you will need in order to complete the work. The first section—designing your work prior to writing—is the longest.

Pragmatic in its intent and writing, the treatment for the book is practical, building on years of expertise as to what causes the dissertation process to stall or fail; not taking enough time, energy, and thought to the design is large on that list. While a restatement of existing knowledge, the fact that we have developed a map format helps illustrate the information in a new way.

Why does the planning, coupled with the proposal writing, take the majority of the book? We have found that the process is easier start to finish with this quality of care up front. Think of it in terms of inertia: You may not have done any research prior to this. Therefore, the start will feel like pushing a large ball up a mountain. By the time you have your research designed and proposal written, inertia works for you rather than against you, and the rest usually goes more easily. Nevertheless, there is one more push needed as you analyze the data you have collected and finish writing it all up. Therefore, unlike many texts, we spend some time in the last few chapters with those topics as well.

We have found that the ways in which universities approach the student's dissertation or thesis process generally follow variations on one of two themes. In the United States, as an example, students are usually required to do quite a bit of design work prior to asking for permission to do research. The proposal in this case is tight, methodologically correct, and no one can proceed without passing rigorous tests of that logic. On the other end of the continuum are countries (such as the United Kingdom) where students only need a general idea of their topic, some substantial amount of understanding of the context in literature, and an idea of how they will proceed. As a document from Cambridge University described it, "A research proposal is not a PhD." In this model you do not need to have all your ideas worked out or even enough concrete ideas to make a thesis, "just be able to give an indication that you know how to take the first steps" (Koprowski, 1972, p. 10). We have spoken with students in China, Nigeria, and Mexico, and all are working on some variation of these strategies. Nevertheless, the topics and logics that underlie the strategy of this book have been proven to be helpful to all. Following are two variations as to how to proceed, based upon these differences.

Please note: For the sake of ease of language, we adhere to U.S. spelling, language about research, and grammatical styles. When we have found tensions between these ideas and the successful completion of students on other continents, we describe the range of options dependent on our readers' context.

Design for the United States and the Countries Who Use That Model

Figure 1   The United States and many other countries require significant design work prior to asking for permission to do research.

Source: Brand X Pictures/Brand X Pictures/Thinkstock

There are three main sections in this book: **Part I: Designing Your Dissertation or Doctoral Thesis** deals with the concepts, ideas, and issues you must face before you do too much writing. Chapters 2 through 4 cover the three basic topics for consideration as you start: topic, literature, and methodology. Chapter 2 focuses on topic but introduces the considerations in tying it together with literature and methodology. Chapter 3 focuses on literature and helps you address what you have learned, musing about the logic of the proposal you will write and writing your research questions. Chapter 4 focuses on all the considerations of research design, including how these affect your thoughts on literature and topic. By the time you have finished the first section (and all the literature you will need to read) you will have a solid proposal in mind and will be ready to write. **Part II: Writing and Defending Your Proposal** covers standards of academic writing and what are generally the first three chapters of a finished dissertation or thesis. Each is covered in some depth with check-lists, probable headings, and the types of material you will be responsible to know. Finally, **Part III: Finding/Conclusions and Writing Your Final Dissertation or Thesis** lightly covers data collection and analysis issues while focusing on the troubles you face when writing your last two chapters and preparing final defense prior to graduation.

If you are just starting your dissertation process, then follow the map from the beginning. If you have collected literature, have a methodology in mind, and are writing a proposal, skim over all of Part I just to make sure there are no basic concepts you have missed and start with Part II. You will find the headings and subheadings in the table of contents useful to you as you catch up on the sub-tleties of the dissertation/thesis process that may still cause confusion or difficulty. If you have your data collected and you live in the United States, then we assume you have also your first three chapters in draft form from your proposal and you start with Part III. In all cases, since topic, literature, and methodology are covered throughout the book, as you delve into them again and again through-out the development of your dissertation/thesis, we expect that the index will be of great use in find-ing what you are looking for. Finally, if you are in a university working on the European model, then you may have your data collected but still be very unsure of methodology and a formal lit review, and we would suggest you read through Part I and II prior to moving to Part III.

This book will give you a solid map to follow through the spiral process following the most usual dissertation or thesis format. We assume you will write five chapters in total. An introduction to your study, a review of literature, and a methodology comprise what we usually call the proposal. After you gain permission and collect and analyze your data, you write the fourth chapter that is a neutral over-view of your findings and then the fifth that is your conclusion. While this book includes some expla-nation of research methodology, it is not to be relied on as a research text. We will, however, refer you onward through the Where to Go to Dig Deeper? sections in each chapter. Other thesis and dissertation forms and styles are discussed in Chapter 1, and we believe that most of the map can still be followed with some restructuring required when you superimpose the guidelines from your university.

Finally, we have come to believe that the sooner you write your methodology chapter the better in terms of long-term efficiency and success. This flies in the face of much of what is written and is based upon the assumption that you will do all the prep work in Part I before you start to write. Should your advisor or university insist you do your review of literature first, we do not disagree but suggest you read our chapter on the methodological choices you need to make, set a firm logic (see Chapter 4), and then proceed in the way that suits you best and also meets the requirements under which you work.

Design for the United Kingdom and the Countries Who Use That Model

Figure 2   Students in the United Kingdom or other countries following this model may need less concrete design work prior to starting.

Source: George Doyle/Stockbyte/Thinkstock

If you proceeded to collect data and to work with your advisor to advance your study prior to pinning down some of these concepts you may be in a position of retrofitting your reality to some of the logics described in this book. A good place to start may be a discussion with your advisor as to where your university and committee stand on the continuum from requiring a positivist versus a postmodern structure (see Chapter 5 for a definition of these terms and an outline of their parameters). Part I outlines all the basic sections of any research design, regardless of the methodological requirements of your particular study, and has proven to be helpful to students everywhere in understanding how the parts go together. Likewise, Part III is a discussion of data analysis, findings, and conclusions, and we find that students find it helpful as it sets standards that they can use as a measure of their own work. Part II is written with a standard of rigor in mind, and while not all students will need to have their work mirror this level of detail, they find that it is easier to consciously know what might be required and be allowed to leave it out rather than to not have an idea of the road map for writing. Finally, students who need to write a 10 to 20 page proposal early on may enjoy the detail in Part II as guidance for the ideas they might consider.

Figure 3 This book is designed to be useful for students going for all types of doctorate degrees.

Source: ©iStockphoto.com/zhudifeng

Designed for Multiple Types of Doctorate

This book is not just for PhDs! We have found that online and in social networks all doctoral students will converse under the heading of PhD, even when their degree may be an EdD for education majors, a DM for doctors of management, and so forth. We work with all types and requirements for doctoral work, from architects to social scientists, from educators to business people, for students who will be doctors working in all branches of business, from the public sector, the nonprofit or nongovernmental sectors, and into business. If and to the extent that research is required prior to graduation, you should find this book helpful to your process through to graduation.

Your First Challenge: Focusing on the Real Goal

These three tips should help.

Tip 1: Be Clear on the Reason You Are Starting and Why You Want to Finish

You may have entered the doctoral world for many reasons. You may want increased status in your community, you might see it as a terminal degree on a path you have traveling for a long time, or you might have concrete goals (frequently for some kind of advancement in your career). The reason you start and the reason you need to finish are often two separate things.

Alana says: *In my case, the place in which I was employed clearly valued people with that degree. You could say I started because of a desire to be valued more in my work. By the time I was moving towards the defense of my proposal two years later, I had a very different goal. I was on the path to moving to Ireland and that mattered more than anything I had ever wanted. I wanted it so badly that NOTHING was going to stand in my way. That turned out to be very helpful, because, although Columbia tells students they can graduate in three years, no one in my program ever had. To say I was pushing a boat upstream to get it done is an understatement.*

So why do you want to finish your degree? All of my students now agree that they want to finish, but those who take complete ownership of their own process have the greatest likelihood of getting it done. Why? Because it is the center of their focus, and they put constant and consistent effort towards completing the tasks at hand while looking ahead and sorting through roadblocks before they occur.

Tip 2: Be Aware of the Journey and Plan Ahead

You wouldn't go on a long journey without plotting your route ahead of time or programming your GPS. Also, while driving you would begin to look for the next gas station once you noticed your tank was below a quarter full. In a similar fashion, as a doctoral student you are responsible for your own path through the university, the defense of your proposal, your research, and then your final defense. Too many of my students put the responsibility on the university and never look ahead; this only slows them down and frustrates them.

What kind of roadblocks should you be aware of? Universities are conservative organizations. They do things in a certain way over and over and over again. Therefore, every step that involves permissions or requires other people to read your work ends up creating somewhere between two weeks and a month time lag. This is not an environment where, just because you are ready, they will help you to move on. From the university's point of view, too much is at stake. Research that is done under their auspices and is not well carried out could lead to liability issues. Researchers are ethically bound to proceed only after careful review. These roadblocks are put in place to protect others. Other times, you may rely on professors who are very busy and their time is not organized around the reading of dissertations, and so your work gets put on the back burner, and you wait for a while for feedback.

> *Be clear on the reason you are starting and why you want to finish*

Speaking of feedback, assume that your work will be torn apart and you will have to practically start over. If this is your assumption, when it happens you will not be dismayed and will not suffer from extended lack of motivation because of harsh criticism. If it doesn't happen, feel lucky. Too many go into a dissertation as though it was merely another assignment, and since you are generally good at school, you may assume your assignment will deserve good feedback. A dissertation is held to high outside standards and is nothing like any work you have done before. Sometimes your initial guidance about what to expect is weak, but even when it is strong, you still will not know what you are doing and may face serious rewrites.

Tip 3: Start Working on Your Dissertation as Soon as You Start at Your University

Alana says: *When I started a good friend of mine suggested that I had been in school a month and was therefore a month behind on my dissertation already. It was so shocking I still remember it, and she was right; it's a long process and you can't start too soon.*

It seems ludicrous, but in order to finish in three years you really must think about what your personal research will be from the time you get started. The work that makes a graduate a doctor, the task that is the rite of passage is the dissertation, and it demonstrates the ability to do personal research. This requires that you understand research methodology, you know how to phrase a question so it is researchable, you know how to collect and analyze data, and you can build a study that is valid and reliable. No matter what you are taught in your coursework, it is those skills that get you through to graduation. Don't lose sight of this fact.

Realize that no matter how good your university is in helping you define and work through your research practice, they cannot possibly tell you everything. In a nutshell, your advisor does not know what you don't know until you deliver a document that clearly shows your misunderstandings. Therefore, additional work on what goes into a dissertation, how they are written, how others describe each part of the process, and so forth will be well worth your time. I highly recommend you start early and read books on writing dissertations. In a similar fashion, find outside help. For instance, we run a website that offers guidance on all of the steps; other websites offer editing, statistical help, and support groups. All are good resources. Go look now for the help you need so that it will be there for you throughout the process.

Your Second Challenge: Endurance

A large percentage of doctoral students drop out or stall completely on the way to their defense of the proposal. This generally happens after they have stopped taking courses but before they are allowed to collect data. And on the other side of the same coin, several challenges cause people to fail the final hurdle once data are collected.

Unlike the other degrees you have finished, your doctoral thesis or dissertation requires a long body of independent work. It may be 100 or more pages when done, fully equal to a short book on your research. Along the journey many will offer, often without mincing words or being particularly nice, strong criticism and feedback. We recommend that from the very beginning you take on this challenge as though you were beginning to take on an endurance challenge for which you need to prepare at every juncture.

To avoid these traps keep the following tips in mind.

Tip 1: Your Relationship With Your Advisor Is Important

Prepare from the first and develop a great working relationship with your advisor, where you lead the conversations and keep the ball moving, but be prepared that you will get signals that cause you to stop and reconsider. Remember that the timeline you have in your head is not made of stone. Being persistent and flexible will help you to manage this important relationship.

Tip 2: Keep Emotions Out of Dissertation Relationships

Many people will say many critical things about your work as you go. You have to trust that they are doing so out of a concern that you can improve your work. Have a failsafe group in your home environment or personal life to whom you cry out your disappointment. Practice taking hard criticism without becoming defensive. As mentioned before, online support groups can be a great way to vent your frustrations and find a sympathetic shoulder to cry on.

Remember, when you have your degree it means that your university believes you to be a peer with all the doctors that have come before you. Think of those in your field whom you admire most—in education, John Dewey; in business, Chris Argyris or whoever is most frequently quoted in your particular field of interest. What does it take to be a peer with that person? This is the road you are on.

Figure 4   Developing a great working relationship with your advisor from the very beginning will be beneficial to your success.

Source: Photos.com/Thinkstock

Graduation Statistics

Across all the disciplines, on average and in most parts of the world, about 50% who complete all or most of their coursework or begin their thesis do not complete and graduate (Cyranoski, Gilbert, & Ledford, 2011; Kildea, Barclay, Wardaguga, & Dawumal, 2009). This is called "all but dissertation" or ABD. These are mentioned here, not to discourage but rather to toughen resolve. Maybe you have experienced some of this attrition. At the dissertation/thesis level, it is much more dramatic. The longer people take, the more likely they won't finish. The statistics vary on how long it takes on average for doctoral candidates to graduate, but we do know that business majors tend to be the group that finish fastest, with education majors lagging to as much as nine years before they graduate.

Of course, "life gets in the way," and many who are slower to graduate do so because of divorce, death in the family, raising children, changing jobs, and so forth. Every life transition brings with it a huge potential for dropping out of the race to finish. Life challenges cannot be underestimated as a reason many do not finish. One resource presents a very convisncing set of data outlining percentages of students who continue, opt out, or graduate. The norm is that, while as little as 3% graduate in three years, 12% have made it by five, and as the time lengthens to ten years in the humanities fields 49% graduate, 32% opt out, and 19% continue (Single, 2009).

Quick Note to Professors (Our Delimiters)

We realize that as this book goes to press, most universities in the United States still teach the sequence of writing a doctoral dissertation or thesis in a linear fashion. We feel strongly that this sequence leads to consistent challenges, the two most egregious being a review of literature that does not adequately support methodology and an introductory chapter that is hard to read and does not set the study (or the professor reader) up for success. We have seen, as have the professors in Europe and around the world who teach a focus on methodology as the core of the work, once the topic is defined and understood and the student knows "where they are going" and have their methodological design in place, their work and writing tighten accordingly.

Nevertheless, this book can easily be used by professors who teach the sequence in any order, as all approaches work when aided by a relationship that helps make the total logic clear. We have taken care that no matter in what order you teach the development of the chapters, your students will be able to start with that chapter and move through the sequence as you order the exercises.

What all readers and committees are concerned with and what we have tried to stress as we have written this text is that the doctoral candidate has developed a "golden thread" or cohesive argument throughout the design, implementation, and completion of their work. Where those threads develop, how they are laid out, and so forth is as obvious to those of us who have been doing this a long time as it is mysterious to our students. This book developed as we found ways to shine light on those dark places, and while for us that includes the focus on the development of methodology earlier in the sequence than some find comfortable, we understand it is not the only way to move forward that works and have tried to adequately accommodate both points of view.

Also please note that we do not advocate the use of any particular style manual, as we are writing for an international audience. While APA is common in the United States, the United Kingdom uses Harvard, and so forth; as well, many universities override all styles with their own considerations for publication. We have tried to suggest a middle ground between the common characteristics of style requirements in the writing and sending the doctoral candidate back to the specific rules of their university.

Features and Benefits

Distinct approaches to each chapter in this book include

- Use of an underlying map structure to guide you step-by-step through the dissertation process. A feature of this map is that you progress through the design phase in a nonlinear fashion, taking topic, literature, and research design into account together. The benefit of this "spiral" pattern of growth is that you develop an innate sense of how these elements are related— allowing you to build defensible logic early in the process.
- Chapter headings in the form of questions guide your understanding. The benefit is to help you find things easily once you have moved on from that section.
- Pages designed to enhance content for the visual learner.
- Pullouts and quotations that highlight important and interesting material, telling you stories of other student experiences and giving you tips to consider.
- Chapters that start with a list of the questions to be addressed from your point of view as a student. They help you prepare for the information you will learn about in that chapter and to quickly find topics of interest as you review.
- Checklists at the end of each chapter that help you check to make sure that you absorbed all the material presented and also allow you to bypass what you already know.
- Photographs and short paragraph stories that illuminate processes and let you see that the difficulties you are facing are within the norm. You are not alone!
- Illustrations used to demonstrate content and help explain concepts and processes.
- Additional resources that send you off to other locations to dig deeper into content areas while exercises and reflective questions give you personal experiences to test your understanding.

Taken together we intend that this book can be followed step-by-step in order but is also easy to leaf through to find "just the part you are looking for."

Ancillaries

As with previous books, ancillary materials including but not limited to PowerPoint slides developed for each chapter will be made publicly available through the author's websites and at **www.sagepub .com/jamesdiss.**

Questions and Checklists

Questions that will be answered in each chapter are listed at the beginning of that chapter. Checklists that you can use as a self-assessment will be found at the end. These are intended to help you move quickly to the exact information you need and to monitor your growth and understanding as you move through the process. Completing the checklists at the end of each chapter will not only keep you on track toward your goal, but can give you a sense of accomplishment as you make progress!

On your way now—it's time to begin!

All the best for a smooth yet exhilarating dissertation or thesis process,

Alana and Tracesea

PART I

DESIGNING YOUR DISSERTATION OR DOCTORAL THESIS

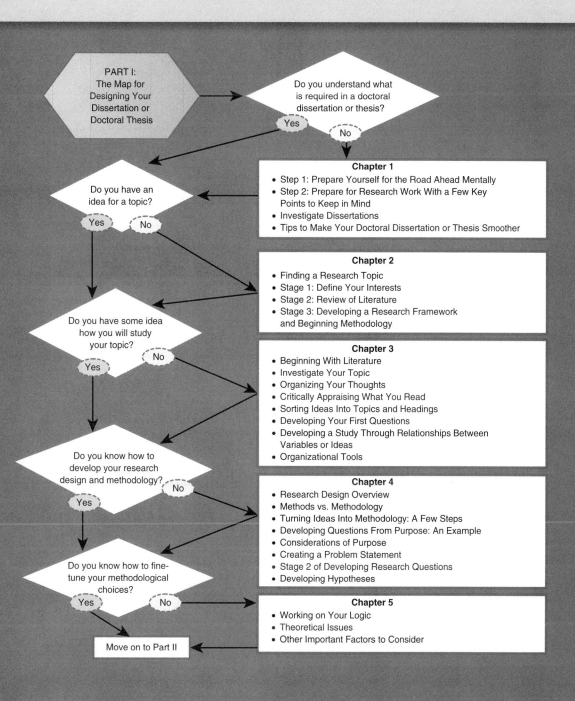

PART I:
The Map for Designing Your Dissertation or Doctoral Thesis

Do you understand what is required in a doctoral dissertation or thesis?

Yes · No

Do you have an idea for a topic?

Yes · No

Chapter 1
- Step 1: Prepare Yourself for the Road Ahead Mentally
- Step 2: Prepare for Research Work With a Few Key Points to Keep in Mind
- Investigate Dissertations
- Tips to Make Your Doctoral Dissertation or Thesis Smoother

Chapter 2
- Finding a Research Topic
- Stage 1: Define Your Interests
- Stage 2: Review of Literature
- Stage 3: Developing a Research Framework and Beginning Methodology

Do you have some idea how you will study your topic?

Yes · No

Chapter 3
- Beginning With Literature
- Investigate Your Topic
- Organizing Your Thoughts
- Critically Appraising What You Read
- Sorting Ideas Into Topics and Headings
- Developing Your First Questions
- Developing a Study Through Relationships Between Variables or Ideas
- Organizational Tools

Do you know how to develop your research design and methodology?

Yes · No

Chapter 4
- Research Design Overview
- Methods vs. Methodology
- Turning Ideas Into Methodology: A Few Steps
- Developing Questions From Purpose: An Example
- Considerations of Purpose
- Creating a Problem Statement
- Stage 2 of Developing Research Questions
- Developing Hypotheses

Do you know how to fine-tune your methodological choices?

Yes · No

Chapter 5
- Working on Your Logic
- Theoretical Issues
- Other Important Factors to Consider

Move on to Part II

1

Do You Understand What Is Required in a Doctoral Dissertation or Thesis?

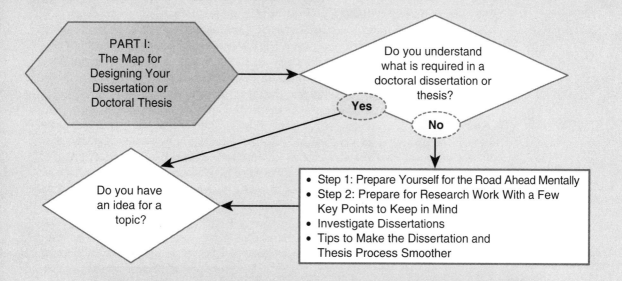

PART I:
The Map for Designing Your Dissertation or Doctoral Thesis

Do you understand what is required in a doctoral dissertation or thesis?

Yes

No

Do you have an idea for a topic?

- Step 1: Prepare Yourself for the Road Ahead Mentally
- Step 2: Prepare for Research Work With a Few Key Points to Keep in Mind
- Investigate Dissertations
- Tips to Make the Dissertation and Thesis Process Smoother

The Questions Answered in This Chapter:

1. What do I need to think about as I start?

2. What tools will I need to gather?

3. What is the general layout of a dissertation?

4. What is the underlying logic of a proposal?

5. What is required in a dissertation or thesis?

6. What can I do to make the process easier?

Introduction

If you live in the United States and you are in school to get a doctoral degree, chances are your university will require a "dissertation." If you live in other parts of the world that were more influenced by the English system of universities, they may call very similar work a "thesis." Both are seminal pieces of individual research and require the same skills in research, as they produce similar challenges and frustrations for students. We will go over variations in style later in this chapter and throughout the book, but for now let's discuss why this process is so challenging.

Step 1: Prepare Yourself for the Road Ahead Mentally

Whatever you call it, being required to design and execute a solid body of research is a rite of passage. If you leave your university unchanged, then those of us who are paid to help guide the journey have not done our jobs. What makes doctors different? The way we think—our ability to see the world, pick it apart and re-sort it in new ways—this is THE characteristic that makes us worth paying for a commodity that is priceless. This is not to say that all doctors are equally good at research or that a person without a degree is not skilled, only that the dissertation road is the only highway we know designed as a rite of passage that always ends in a change of worldview.

The part of this path that causes the personal transformation is the data collection and analysis portion. That is where our understanding of the world shifts and we are able to see more deeply. Therefore, one of the great travesties of higher education may be that some leave their dreams behind and finish "all but dissertation" or "ABD" and never make it to the place where they face that potential. Yet it is the dissertation proposal that holds a lot of people back. As one of our students put it, "it took me three years to realize that the dissertation or thesis is also teaching me how I have to be able to present things to other professionals."

We are positive that you will be successful in designing and writing your dissertation, but it is important that you realize you are embarking on something that many people fail to complete. This is an endurance test—never forget it. What do you do when things get really rough? Do you complain? Whine and give up? Don't kid yourself that this is hard—this is MUCH harder than merely difficult. There will be obstacles in your path, some of your own creation, some that are the faults of the people or systems you need to rely on, some technical (like losing all your data to a computer crash) and some personal (such as divorce, loved ones getting sick or dying, having babies, or getting married), all of which will assault you along the way. When these come it will be you and only you that determine your outcome and whether you will fall into the 50% that never earn the degree you are starting on.

Step 2: Prepare for the Research
Work With a Few Key Points to Keep in Mind

Know the Logic Behind the Dissertation/Thesis Proposal

To the extent you do that preparatory work and learn up front what it is all about, you help ensure a safe passage through the dissertation challenges. To use sports analogy, you do not want to be in a tight spot with your success depending on how well prepared you are or whether you have the right gear with you.

Your Research Needs to Address a Real Problem

Many students want to study a topic that interests them just because, from their view of the world, it is important. This may be acceptable if you are doing theoretical work, but if your degree is applied then think twice. You first will have to show that the problem you are studying has data that demonstrate the level of the problem. Unless your work addresses a real problem, you may work for years on a body of knowledge that has no "SO WHAT" factor. How your work is judged is determined by the problem it addresses. Who cares? Why do they care? What will they do about it once they hear your answers? These are the foundations of your work.

> ### Develop the 15-minute-a-day habit
>
> *The best thing you can do for yourself is not allow this process to seem overwhelming, instead develop the "15 minute a day" habit outlined by (Bolker, 1998). The idea is simple—like working out, a small bit all the time will do better for you than one mad rush every now and again. As our student A. J. says, "I would have quit a long time ago if I didn't have the 15 minute a day routine. It is the only thing that allows this work to go forward when my job and family life go over the top." Every task can be broken down into small segments. Do a bit in the morning before your family gets up, and you have started every day by building your dream!*

Think About Scope

Hopefully you are a creative and curious person and you wonder about the big ideas that propel our world. That does not mean you have access to them or the people who can give you the answers you need. We do not want to minimize the size of the task entailed in writing a dissertation. It needs to be big enough to push your limits, cause you pain, and force you to learn endurance, so that you will feel absolute success and accomplishment upon completion. Anyone who has earned their doctorate will tell you that all of these things are part of the journey.

Work On Organization

You may not understand the size of the undertaking and tackle your dissertation or thesis as though it were a normal paper. This results in sadness, unhappiness, and frustration when your doctoral advisor corrects you and sends the document back again and again for updates. Much of this can be avoided by understanding ahead of time what is involved and then preparing yourself for it. You would not climb Mount Everest in shorts and tennis shoes. In the same way, you do not write a dissertation with the same lack of preparation that you may have been able to use on every other college assignment.

Our students tell us the first level of organization is being able to concentrate when you sit down. This requires that you know your learning style and can quickly clear your thoughts and focus on the work. L. E. says, "I have to be in a quiet house or setting. Sometimes my house distracts me and I have to go to the library. I tested out several libraries before I found one big enough with a space in which I could concentrate." J. B. says "I put my ear phones on and play my music, this drowns everything else out."

Figure 1.1 You will need to prioritize your activities and possibly let go of things that were previously taking your time in order to make time for your doctoral work.

Source: Jupiterimages/Comstock/Thinkstock

Organization also requires that you let go of activities that have previously been taking your time. L. E. again says, "I have to guard my time. I have been very active within my community. I have not been able to be on committees and participate in my church as I used to. I have to allot how much time something needs and not go over it, in order to be able to meet my commitment to writing. I no longer open up my personal email everyday as it distracts me."

Once you start to write you will also need to organize how you take notes on what you read so that, often years later, you are able to recall the important references you find. This will be covered in detail in Chapter 3.

Gather a Few Good Tools

1. Guidelines from your university as to format and content requirements for your final document. If your university uses a rubric for judging your dissertation, then use it exactly as stated to form your topic headings. Write to these headings from the very beginning and as your content develops.

2. Several dissertations that you can use as models. Find one that is more or less on your topic, a second that uses a methodology you are considering, and a third that is engagingly written, where the author talks directly to you, the audience. More is written on this in the next section.

3. A few good dissertation books or website memberships. Our book is great to guide you through the writing process. You will also need several books on methodology—both general, such as John W. Creswell's *Research Design: Qualitative, Quantitative, and Mixed Methods Approaches*, and specific, which meet the requirements of the final methodology you choose (these suggestions will be listed in additional reading in Chapters 5 and 6).

4. The style manual required by your university. Your university will require that your final document follow a very specific publication style. Buy the manual at the beginning and if they are offered, take classes that clarify and illustrate the publication style required by your university. Taking your university's guidelines seriously from the beginning can save you days of time at the end.

Investigate Dissertations

General Layout

Whether you are required to produce the standard five chapters or some variation on that theme (one of the universities we work with has a five paper option), or even if you choose to elongate some of the thought process and develop seven or even nine chapters, these documents have more in common than you may notice at the beginning. You might want to investigate other references to hone in on a format that works best for you (Bryant, 2004; Garson, 2002; Krathwohl & Smith, 2005). In general, they all make use of the following five categories of discussion, each containing several components or building blocks upon which the section is constructed:

1. Chapter 1 Summary—A relatively brief (10–20 page) explanation of the problem to be studied, the context you are working in, and the methodology that you either are proposing or (after data collection and analysis) you used to answer the questions you raised.

Figure 1.2   You will be gathering, compiling, and analyzing a large amount of literature for your literature review chapter.

Source: Jupiterimages/BananaStock/Thinkstock

2. Chapter 2 Literature Review—a review of the research and/or theoretical literature into which your study will be embedded. This chapter helps your reader understand what work has gone before; it establishes the importance of the work in the field and uncovers either the gaps your research will address or discusses the work your study will replicate in a new setting. The reader also will understand how your methodological choices developed and lead to your study.

3. Chapter 3 Methodology—a discussion of your methodology and your research design. Depending on those choices, this writing will discuss some of the following: the problem you face, the questions you ask, of whom you ask the questions (or what documents you will study for them) and the form they take, how you will analyze your data (the answers you receive), how you will protect any human subjects who are involved, how your study design ensures accuracy and credibility in your findings, and its importance in your field and perhaps to your larger community.

4. Chapter 4 Data Collection and Analysis/Findings—a neutral discussion of your process, the data that developed or were collected, the way in which you analyzed these data and themes that were apparent in those answers. This discussion maintains its neutrality by including an equal discussion of all data that appear to differ from the majority findings.

5. Chapter 5 Conclusions—a conclusion that draws the study together and in which you get a chance to tell your reader what outcomes your work achieved, what it means to your field of study or your community of practice, steps you believe would take the work further in the future, and the limitations you see as you look back on what was done.

Each and every one of these components needs to be addressed from multiple angles, teasing the intellectual juice out of each topic (commonly known as displaying critical thinking). The difficulty in meeting this standard arises in that, until now, most of you have only been required to write up projects for class, or essays from a single viewpoint. A great dissertation is one in which the author looks at every building block of their study from multiple directions.

Does this seem daunting? In one sense that is good, it gives you a high standard to shoot for. In order to break your dissertation or thesis into manageable parts and begin to construct in your own mind how you will address both the sections and the building blocks, we recommend that you carefully examine how it was done in the model dissertations you will soon be collecting.

Dissertation Variations

There are many variations within the art form that is the thesis/dissertation. Some will be suggested as options or guidelines by the university, some you might suggest and get permission to use from your advisor. We recommend that you also ask them for a model of a dissertation they worked on that they felt was particularly well done. This will show you the standard that you need to meet.

Students writing for an applied degree are likely to study the development or evaluation of projects or programs that are ongoing in their or a similar work environment. Doctors of philosophy or any students focused on the theoretical components of their subject, on the other hand, may propose a new treatise and work to defend their ideas.

Pragmatic and applied degrees require scientific research with an outcome that moves the field of study ahead, perhaps developing new models for behavior or designs that will be implemented later. Evaluation studies rigorously research a project that has currently been implemented and generally include a design that includes different measures over time. Random control trials are within the class of experimental design and require a rigor, participant size, and so forth that is often held as a gold standard of positivistic research but is often outside the limitations of doctoral candidates. Science has moved on as well to consider complex adaptive systems, and measuring life as we find it requires research to be flexible in outlook and methodology. Action research forms another part of that continuum, is within everyone's grasp in size and scope, but is best used to solve a particular problem or to improve practice. In other words, this path will take you through many choices, each of which will have implications for the methodology you choose.

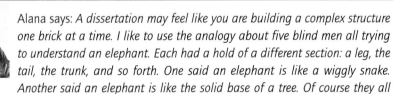

Alana says: *A dissertation may feel like you are building a complex structure one brick at a time. I like to use the analogy about five blind men all trying to understand an elephant. Each had a hold of a different section: a leg, the tail, the trunk, and so forth. One said an elephant is like a wiggly snake. Another said an elephant is like the solid base of a tree. Of course they all "knew" the elephant differently and they were all right! The books you read and the feedback that is given you are all like the separate men—seeing one section about which they comment. Your job is to know and build coherency between not only the main subject of each of the five sections listed above but also each of the building blocks within that subject, from each and every angle.*

How to Find Model Dissertations

Doctoral students sometimes find it challenging to find model dissertations from which to work. Part of this may be the relative strength of their university library. It may not be clear how one sets out to find

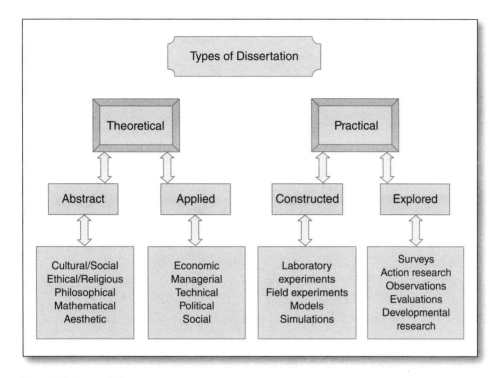

Figure 1.3   Types of dissertations.

Source: Reprinted by permission from Sage, www.sagepub.com/upm-data/9668_023128ch02.pdf

Note: This is where the author begins to sort out some of these complexities by looking at first theoretical versus practical considerations and then whether the research is either abstract versus applied or simulated/constructed or explored/evaluated.

one dissertation that matches your topic, one that uses your methodology, and one that is well written. This section will discuss the process of finding models in these three areas and offer suggestions.

Finding the dissertation that matches your topic area is probably the easiest of the three. ProQuest is the database most students use, but there may be others, all accessible through your university library. It may be as simple as typing in the keywords you yourself would use for your topic, but if that produces few results, then discuss your topic area with your professors, librarians, other students, or in an online forum. Others can help you expand your keyword search for both journal articles and dissertations. An example of this would be the many students who have, over time, wanted to study education for at-risk students. Discussing their interests with people who have worked in the field, they were able to expand their keyword search to include terms such as resiliency and strengths-based education and to search out the evaluation reports from programs funded through federal sources aimed at disadvantaged study participants. When you are new to a topic area, you do not understand the history it may have or how funding choices over time may have influenced where you will find the documents you search for. However, once you have a set of keywords that regularly produces journal article results, you can apply them to your dissertation search.

But is every dissertation a good dissertation? And what do the good ones look like as you search for one that is well written? One doctoral student we worked with addressed this issue by going to the research association's website in her field. Because the association held regular conventions and because they were supporting doctoral candidates or recent graduates, they sponsored a contest for the best dissertation published each year. This proved to be an excellent source for quality work.

Quality is in the eye of the beholder, and different configurations of professors will have a different influence on the final output of a dissertation. Therefore, assuming that you have one person on your committee who is knowledgeable about your topic area and another who knows your methodology, you can ask each of these people for examples of their favorite dissertations. These will give you a clear idea about what they are looking for. Some universities demand that final work is judged against a rubric—you would then use that as an additional guide regarding the quality they are looking for.

Many of our students tell us that this type of search actually netted them 20 or more dissertations that they found useful and that they printed and kept around while they were writing both their proposal and their final chapters four and five. Remember, you are not gathering these to copy or plagiarize someone's work but to use them as exemplars, models from which to work. Taken together they become a cookbook for the person who is learning to put a decent meal on the table and, along with books on writing dissertations, they will help steer you towards a solid, defensible piece of writing.

Tracesea asks: *Besides ProQuest, where can I search for model dissertations? Can I use Google?*

Answer: Quality methodology dissertations can be searched for in a manner similar to topic area work; so yes, use your web browser but also your local library resources. In the search fields, you simply enter your general field of endeavor and then use the Boolean search terms +*Qualitative*, or +*Quantitative*, and so forth. It is also wise to narrow the methodology as appropriate, such as +*Concurrent Mixed Method Design*, or +*Action Research*, or +*Narrative Inquiry*, and so forth. Don't forget to search online for award winning dissertations as well. You might as well see for yourself right away what makes a dissertation worthy of that level of accolade.

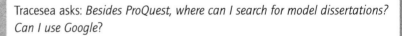

Activity 1.1 Three Model Dissertations

One of the biggest mistakes doctoral students make when they start to work on their dissertation is that they don't do enough background checking on what is involved in these documents. You have to read finished dissertations. This activity helps you establish a solid foundation of understanding about dissertations documents, which will aid you as you build your own. By the end, you will have gathered at least three model dissertations that can serve as a guide to how others addressed and answered the same issues you will face. Look for high quality dissertations that focus on each of the following areas, all of which are important for you to consider. At the end you will have at least one dissertation from each of these three categories:

1. Your topic

2. Your methodology

3. Your writing

When looking for dissertations focused on your topic area, do a broad search and then narrow it down. For your methodology, you want as tight a choice as is possible for you to find, preferably one that uses a similar population, instrumentation, data collection, and analysis procedures. If you can't find one that matches in all of these areas, find different dissertations, one that matches each portion. Finally, as you are looking through reading all these different dissertations, collect those that impress you because of the way they are written. You may like how engaging the story was told, the way the author used tables and graphic organizers, or any other number of reasons that would set the writing above others.

Students have suggested the following as avenues that have proven helpful for finding the models they needed:

- Award winning dissertations from previous years. Many professional organizations take entries and give awards for "best" dissertations or thesis of the previous year.
- Look for work within and outside your own geographic context. Different parts of the world hold to different standards, and you can learn from all of them. This is especially true as to how they approach both the style of writing and the methodology.
- Work sponsored by professors or writers working within institutions whose work you admire.

Remember, you're on the hunt for exemplars that you will use when the going gets rough and you can't think of how to do the section you're faced with writing. Remember, many others have done this way before you, the process is never simple, but examples of their finished work and the lessons they learned can help you.

> Dr. E. Johnson tells us that by the end she had 20 or more dissertations from others on a big stack on her floor. Each had been highlighted with the bits of writing she liked best and were well annotated with her notes as to how they transferred to her own work. Others in her class charted topics and methodologies, wrote them up in their bibliographic software, and so forth. While for E. J., a pile on the floor worked best, each student needs to develop a system that will work in his or her environment over the multiple years it will take to finish his or her research.

Figure 1.4 Searching for dissertations from all around the world will increase your understanding of the full range of possibilities.

Source: ©iStockphoto.com/Beboy_ltd

Tracesea asks: *Should I make notes of what I liked in these dissertations? I'm afraid I might forget why I kept a dissertation if I don't write it down somewhere. Do you have any suggestions or examples on how to organize the dissertations that I gather in this exercise so that I can better use them as I write my own dissertation?*

Answer: Make notes, write all over them, give yourself Post-it comments—whatever it takes so that when you come back to them six months to a year later you have some twig in your memory about what you are thinking today. In later areas we will discuss taking notes in your bibliographic software as well.

Throughout this book we will discuss what to look for as you go back and use these models in future activities. You'll start by comparing the headings they use in different chapters. The style and form each author uses, what you enjoy in their writing, how they use tables, all of these things will become important at different stages of your process.

Next, investigate dissertation/thesis author's use of headings and subheadings and how they guide the work. The next activity gives you multiple options for source material.

Activity 1.2 Pull Headings From Four Sources

This activity should, in our opinion, be the very first thinking/writing you do when starting your dissertation. Remember though, if your university has a rubric or some other means of directly assessing your writing, then those headings form the base of your work.

Source One

Appendix A has a proposal template—use it as an example of the headings that are frequently used for the first three chapters. Consider this the framework on which you will build.

Source Two

The second source will be at least two of your model dissertations or theses. You found these in the activity in the previous section. For now just look at their tables of contents and compare them to the headings in your basic list. Consider the importance of the flow of logic as determined by the way these headings nestle together.

Source Three

The third and often defining source is the set of guidelines from your university. Even if they offer a rubric or set of headings they expect you to follow, there will be some leeway for you to make changes with the approval of your advisor in order to better support the logic of your proposal. Of course, you have to include what they are looking for, but that does not preclude additions to it, and in some cases, rearranging their prescribed content areas. Remember, dissertations are an art form, and there are a lot of differences in the world regarding how they are done. If you cannot find guidelines for headings from your university then use those from several published dissertations from your university in this step.

Taken together, these sources will provide you with a clear framework on which to build your dissertation/thesis.

> What I found was that I needed to schedule time on a calendar for my family, myself, work time and then school work. This was very beneficial to me to stay on target for due dates and other commitments. I would suggest not letting one day go by without doing something that places you closer to the finish line. That may be just simply reading an article, but the more days you let go by without taking a step toward your tangible goal will make it that much easier to let another day go by (Dr. Brenda Finger, DoctoralNet, 2012).

Tips to Make Your Doctoral Dissertation or Thesis Process Smoother

Guidelines for a Smoother Process

Several guidelines will advance your dissertation process:

1. Work in a group. Often, groups outside of your university can offer you a range of ideas from people with whom you have no competition for resources. When you find your attention to detail or inspiration lagging, go find other groups. You can find online support groups for doctoral students all over the world. There are also many groups on Linkedin, Twitter feeds, or Facebook pages as well. Manage your process, set a firm timeline, and move ahead on it. Let your feelings be your guide—if you come away from an interaction not only happier but also more inspired to push yourself and do a great job, then it meets your needs for the moment.

2. Communicate. Let others know where you are in the process and don't be afraid to ask lots of questions. Solid feedback and answers to your questions help to move you forward more than any other means because both are targeted to your specific circumstances.

3. Know your university's process. Leave lots of time every time your work needs to be reviewed by others. Your professors are busy, but if they take over 2 to 3 weeks to return your documents with substantive comments then take this as an invitation to build a stronger relationship with them or to look for another relationship.

4. Be prepared to keep growing. Nothing is static, and you will make lots of mistakes,—so might your advisor. This is why having multiple sources of input will help guide you safely through these waters.

Figure 1.5 Spending a little time each day is often more beneficial than spending the same amount of time but only once a week.

Source: Digital Vision/Photodisc/Thinkstock

5. Work on your time management. Like any muscle we build, 15 to 30 minutes of work every day means a lot more than the same total minutes worked once a week.

Working With Your Committee

Your advisor needs to have enough communication with you to know you are not off track; on the other hand, they will get tired if they are asked to read your material too often. This is a challenging part of the relationship. Remember, they are not there to tell you what to do. You manage your own process with their advice.

The specific process of working with your broader committee is up to the protocols established by your university. Most call the second and third readers in to review your work only after your advisor has deemed it ready for their attention. Others have you submit to the wide group more frequently. Check with your university as to what is considered best practice and proceed accordingly. You can also use group input from your networks outside of your school.

As with all feedback, you have to judge for yourself whether and to what extent you will incorporate it. Even if your advisor is telling you a course of action to take, you should have negotiation power, as you are the one who best sees the entire context and understands the complexities you face in bringing your study to fruition. The worst mistake you can make is to work with feedback from this committee in the same way you may have worked with feedback from professors on single assignments, by simply doing what was required and moving on. With the exception perhaps of the ethical review boards, who set the standards for how you will interact with the public to do no harm, and even then, thesis work requires that you understand the reasoning behind the suggestion and can be counted on to apply that reasoning from that point on.

Alana says: *Generally, I have found that the students who are always telling me what they are doing are the ones most likely to get through the process quickly. Throughout this book, when appropriate you will find pullouts suggesting that, when the activity discussed in that section is complete, it will be a good time to discuss your ideas/work with your advisor or mentor.*

I recently was on a committee where the student's work was outstanding. I quizzed her and her advisor about their relationship,which had allowed and supported this level of creativity and excellence to develop. The section below summarizes their input.

Case Study Example of Advisor Student Relationship

Recently graduated Dr. Wakefield says:

My first introduction to David was when I opened up the 2001 narrative methods book, which is now a staple when I write. I was really green, naive, and steeped in the positivist mindset I had held for most of my life. I didn't like the book one bit. The reality was that I just didn't understand yet, was not sufficiently open to new ways of thinking nor sufficiently well read. I whined. A few days later, across the table at a faculty-student dinner, we had a tentative (for me) discussion about whether or not David had any students working on complexity theory. Again, I had no idea that David was a world expert in my newfound areas of interest, or that knowing him would forever change my mode of thought. A day later, he became my mentor and over the course of the next few years he opened my eyes and my mind to third order cybernetic thought, storytelling, and myriad other mind-bending ideas.

If I had to identify the greatest element of this lifelong partnership born of serendipity, I would have to say it's how David handled my more obtuse moments. Each time I would excitedly draw his attention to the obvious, including good ideas that had blossomed and withered years before, he would kindly indulge me. Then he would gently, with the utmost sensitivity, point me toward literature that would help me see my own folly and in the process open several new lines of inquiry. This art of guiding without dictating, shaping one's intellect without humiliating, and fostering life-changing growth, is the essence of good mentoring in my opinion. This gentle guidance built sufficient trust between us so that when I was on the verge of abandoning my early concept of fractal management theory, he was able to get me back on the path to seeing it through. I am truly grateful for that nudge.

Sure, there are the mechanical aspects of good mentoring that I was the happy recipient of as well. Quick turns on my writing, always with very good, thorough, actionable feedback were the norm. Deep answers to emails containing off the wall theoretical questions in the wee hours of the morning were typical. He even supported me for a good cry when I was terrified to quit a job where I was unhappy. Yet those are the ontic matters. Ontologically speaking, "Being" a mentor, and I use the word in the Heideggerian sense, involves an attunement to the student that goes much deeper than what is in the books. He knew my mind, believed in me (sometimes more than I did), and gave me the tools to make my own contribution to the body of knowledge.

These days, students often ask me questions about David's work. I tell them it's like Cognac. That first sip can knock you flat, but you soon develop a taste for it and it becomes a much sought after luxury.

Advisor Dr. Boje points out:

Tonya is one of those rare people you can depend upon to read the material, take it deeper, in new directions. In that case, a mentor can go deeper, make the challenges greater, loosen up and see where it goes. Tonya is also someone who expresses herself clearly in writing, and in oral presentation. With someone who wants to keep exploring, being a sounding board is part of the process. Lots of emails every day, keeping me informed, asking about how to play out opportunities in the dissertation. At one point Tonya got some feedback that made her doubt the direction of her study. It was early on as I recall. As she was trying out new ideas, she could have turned to an easier, safer topic. I am glad she stayed with it.

Alana says: *As I was finishing the writing on my own dissertation I visited a middle school in the United States. On the wall was a poster of a rock climber, spread an unbelievably long distance from one leg to the other and reaching for a handhold almost out of reach. In huge letters at the bottom was the word: ENDURANCE.*

Time Management

Old adages, such as "Rome wasn't built in a day" or "Every journey starts with a single step," bear on the daily grind of writing and rewriting, reading, developing new ideas, discussing, and then rewriting again—that is the process of dissertation or thesis development.

It is harder to stop and restart than to keep going—hence the importance of regular work, it builds a momentum under you that will help you past the rough spots. Specific tips that will help you develop and keep strong time management include the following:

1. Work every day! Get up 30 minutes earlier every day and do something that moves the work ahead.

2. Set up accountability structures. Work in a group; keep tabs on each other and how the work is progressing.

3. Keep in touch with your advisor. Set a timeline, discuss it with your advisor, and leave a copy with him/her.

4. Read dissertations and about dissertation writing. This keeps your creative juices on target to the task at hand.

5. Start with a template that illustrates the proper style as set by your university. Write every section with the whole in mind.

You are in charge of your dissertation/thesis; don't be afraid to be somewhat pushy, as it is appropriate to the role of project manager. Ask for and set appointments, share your agenda and the work you want to discuss before the meeting, keep asking questions until you either understand the answers or have been given resources to help you do so.

Alana says: *Of all the 50+ doctors who have graduated with my advising, those who drove themselves and the process finished faster and with less difficulty than any who did not. This does not mean they never faced having to go back and do it again, but they finished without stalling out or losing faith. There is a lot to be said for setting and keeping momentum.*

Emotional Support

Any life experience that is a rite of passage will, by definition, take us to our personal limits. It will feel traumatic at times, and the best way to soothe yourself past those moments is to preplan and make use of emotional support systems.

We believe you should look for three kinds of support:

1. Friends and family members who know you well

2. People who have already achieved the same goal

3. Colleagues who are facing the same or similar challenges at the same time

Friends and family can "cheerlead" for you, reminding you of other times you faced adversity and got through it. People who have their doctorates (no matter what the field) can share battle plans and stories from their experiences and help you feel as though the challenges you face are within the norm. They also can offer suggestions that may have merit. Colleagues, whether they are attending class with you or are working elsewhere, can offer a similarity of outlook and may also offer suggestions. Whether you take suggestions from any of these people is always your decision, but it will be nice to know your challenges and your feelings about them are not unique—they are just part of the process you have undertaken. Remember that the Internet is always a great place to connect with all three of these types of support. If you can't connect in person or on the phone, establish routine conversations with others online to ensure you have the support you need on your dissertation journey.

Figure 1.6   Family obligations can make it difficult to find time to work.
Source: BananaStock/BananaStock/Thinkstock

When I started the program, I had a 3-year-old and an 18-month-old. Midway through, I had another baby. Needless to say, my hands were full. As an adult, I realized that successful completion would require sacrifice and shuffling priorities. I worked full time at a regular job and then had family responsibilities. I had to carve out time within each day for school, which meant very early mornings and/or late nights. I took advantage of breaks and lunch periods at work and had my kids on a rest schedule that allowed a few hours during the day on weekends. Other than much-needed sleep, I sacrificed family fun outings for research and writing. I advise anyone beginning the doctoral journey to find his or her own groove. Observe your daily routine as if an outsider looking in. Determine the optimal time to devote to your studies, what you can delay/reschedule, and when to say "No." It sounds cliché but real friends will not be upset when you are not able to participate. Finally, for those with children, lean on your spouse, significant other, or other close family members for support. It's okay to schedule a date night where you are locked up in your bedroom, a library, or coffee shop with a very well-dressed laptop!

Dr. T. McNeal

Activity 1.3 Create a Backwards Planning Timeline or Personal Policy Option Brief

Elmore (1979) changed the face of NYC education by introducing backward mapping. You can change the amount of difficulty you will face in getting done in

Planning is a great time to begin to build a relationship with your advisor. Why not discuss Table 1.1 Backward Mapping Your Way to Doctoral Success with your advisor and make changes as they suggest?

the time frame you want by instituting it as well. Following is a general chart to help you get started. Other authors we suggest in our "dig deeper" section at the end of the chapter offer other suggestions as to specifics to consider as milestones (Brause, 2000; Mauch & Park, 2003; Roberts, 2004). Mimic the chart below, using the column to the right to fill in the dates of your expected graduation and the preceding deadlines. Fill in the chart by planning backwards from the day you want to graduate through to first items you must accomplish. Ancillary items for this book held on the doctoralnet.com website will also offer you a downloadable version to fill in for yourself. Then take it to your advisor and ask whether it matches their experience of student work at your university. Adjust to make your projected milestones match their experience. Be as specific on the dates as you can.

Table 1.1   Backward Mapping Your Way to Doctoral Success

Graduation date	Yea! You're done.	Your dates
Dissertation complete as per reader/committee requirements	One month to 6 weeks before graduation (this allows time for university requirements).	
Final defense	Your committee meets and decides to pass you with a few recommended changes (this is what happens to the majority of students)—approximately one month before you will finish those changes.	
Writing your conclusions (chapter 5)	One month before your final defense. This month presupposes that you are working with an editor in order to maximize the success of your writing to the minimum amount of time + add time for advisor review and revisions.	
Analyzing your data and writing your findings (chapter 4)	Two months before you are writing your conclusions + add time for advisor review and revisions.	
Data collection	At least two months, and if you have the time, three months	
IRB	Depending on the university, anywhere from two weeks to two months—check with your advisor on what to expect.	
Rewriting your introduction to reflect final drafts of your literature review and methodology chapters	This usually takes about one month + add time for advisor review.	

Graduation date	Yea! You're done.	Your dates
Rewriting your literature review and methodology so that they reflect a one-to-one correspondence of ideas or variables	This usually takes about one month + add time for advisor review.	
Writing your review of the literature needed to support your methodology	This can take students anywhere from one month to six, depending on their time and their literature search + add time for advisor review.	
Writing your methodology chapter	This usually takes a month or two, depending upon how much the student understands research methodology before they start, + add time for advisor review.	
Reading and collecting literature relative to your topic	Six months of regularly collecting three or more references a week + add time for advisor review.	
Writing your first draft of the introduction	You may want to start here, because this is an overview of what you intend to do, and you will feel as though you've accomplished something when it is done. This draft will have to be rewritten because you will have made many changes through the rest of the process. If you are short on time, I recommend you start with your methodology chapter while you are reading literature + add time for advisor review.	

Alana says: *One of our administrators at Teachers College had us add to Elmore's process by creating a "Personal Policy Option Brief," which I found to be a great way to look at the risks presented by dissertation work to my personal life.*

Activity 1.4 Personal Policy Option Brief

1. Looking over your relationships and support systems, identify the ones that will be greatly strained by you being largely unavailable for the 3 or 4 years it may take to write your doctoral dissertation thesis?

2. Who can you count on to be available for support?

3. What will you do if faced with a serious life transition or challenge, such as hospitalized loved ones, having children, enjoying marriage, or going through a divorce?

4. What pressures might derail this work, and how can you plan around them?

5. If you were to develop a personal policy that would guide when and how you used these resources to ensure that you would not fail—what would that policy entail?

6. If you are not 150% sure that you have the personal resources you will need, then begin now, when the pressure is not great, to develop those resources. Consider online support systems as well as in-person support.

Now you have options to fill in the help you may need before you need it. For example, you can have frank discussions with those people who will feel the greatest strain, working out compromises when necessary. The challenges you may face will seem less daunting if you have developed safety nets prior to their happening. Finally, you can see the importance of downtime and can begin to take the unnecessary components out of your schedule so that as the stress mounts, you will not have to make sudden adjustments.

Chapter 1 Checklist

Can You Say...?

- ❑ I've thought about what I need to do to be successful.
- ❑ I've gathered tools to support me.
- ❑ I understand the layout of the dissertation.
- ❑ I have found at least three model dissertations.
- ❑ I have examples of headings from four sources.
- ❑ I understand what I need to do to make the process easier.

Where Should I Go to Dig Deeper? Suggested Resources to Consider

Brause, R. S. (2000). *Writing your doctoral dissertation: Invisible rules for success*. London: Routledge. On pages 17 through 29, Brause discusses terms, stages, and the general process of doctoral research in the United States in detail.

Hadjioannou, X., Shelton, N. R., & Fu, D. (2007, March). The road to a doctoral degree: Co-travelers through a perilous passage. *College Student Journal, 41*(1), 160–177. Retrieved from ERIC Educational Resources Information Center website, http://www.eric.ed.gov/ERICWebPortal/search/detailmini.jsp?_nfpb=true&_&ERICExtSearch_SearchValue_0=EJ765415&ERICExtSearch_SearchType_0=no&accno=EJ765415 Hadjioannou et al. researched the value of their doctoral study team on themselves and their ability to finish.

Mauch, J. E., & Park, N. (2003). *Guide to the successful thesis and dissertation: A handbook for students and faculty.* New York: Marcel Dekker. On pages 13 through 23, Mauch and Park outline the qualities of a successful doctoral thesis.

Roberts, C. M. (2004). *The dissertation journey.* Thousand Oaks, CA: Corwin Press. On pages 18 through 30, Roberts discusses "What is a dissertation?" as well as going through the process in greater detail than allowed here.

Group Exercises

We find that groups developed around a specific goal have the best chance of helping all the members find success. Therefore we do not suggest you look for a group who will support you for the full writing process (although some members may continue that long), rather, we suggest groups form around specific goals and meet weekly for about a month to complete that milestone.

Figure 1.7 Form groups with other doctoral students around specific goals.

Source: Thomas Northcut/Digital Vision/Thinkstock

The challenge addressed in this chapter is getting started, figuring out your destination (a finished dissertation or thesis) and what it looks like, and gathering the support you need to give you a probable chance of finishing your work within the timeline you develop. To these ends, many people will work more efficiently than a person by themselves because a group can divide up the resources, proceed to investigate them, and bring back to the group a unique slice of knowledge or ideas. It is helpful if you have someone to facilitate and someone else to take notes, although those people need not always be the same each meeting. As an example, this chapter would start with a group who all discussed the ideas and made plans as to how they would cope. Group members could share the model dissertations they found. The group might even stay together through the next chapter, which covers your first attempt at coming up with a basic topic, set of research questions, and possible methodology.

2

Do You Have
an Idea for a Topic?

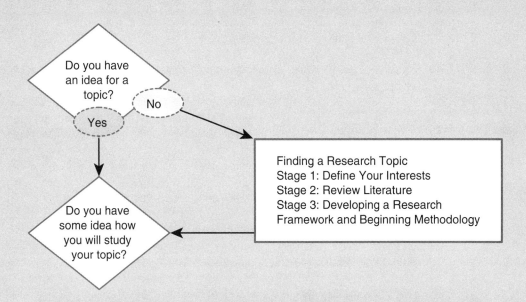

Do you have an idea for a topic?

Yes

No

Do you have some idea how you will study your topic?

Finding a Research Topic
Stage 1: Define Your Interests
Stage 2: Review Literature
Stage 3: Developing a Research Framework and Beginning Methodology

The Questions Answered in This Chapter:

1. Why is it hard to find a research topic?

2. How do I find a topic worthy of study?

3. What makes for a good topic?

4. How do I use literature already developed on my topical ideas?

5. Why do I need a problem and a purpose?

6. What makes for a good research question?

Finding a Research Topic

A quick perusal of forums and communities on the web will demonstrate that common issues for doctoral students include, "How do I choose my topic?" or the more desperate, "I need help deciding on a topic."

What makes deciding upon a topic difficult is that three things impinge on the quality of your ideas: (a) your passion for the general topic, (b) the literature amassed to date on this and related subjects, and (c) your context and whether you can pull off a research study on that topic from where you are. It's handy if you start the process of narrowing down a topic for your research as you begin your university work, allowing for you to keep it in mind as you go through classes and throughout all your reading. Discuss every idea you have, remembering that you are looking for a topic you have questions about—one you can research—and not one about which you feel a driving need to make a point or right an injustice.

There are several common ways for people to begin:

- It is not uncommon to continue work started during your masters, as appropriate and if it is still interesting to you.

> Identify a theme for each week and do something about it every day, just like taking vitamins (Dr. Ken Long, DoctoralNet, 2012).

- You may have an advisor or professor who is an expert in a topic of interest, and that person can help you find a subtopic or theme worth further investigation. You can also pursue a topic through interviewing someone of importance in your field and asking them for ideas (Bryant, 2004; Mauch & Park, 2003; Roberts, 2004; Rudestam & Newton, 2007).
- You may find a loose end or unresolved question that develops out of your course work or reading in the literature of your field (Bryant, 2004; Rudestam & Newton, 2007).
- Read other authors' dissertations. When they are of interest, pay special note to a common section in the last chapter called "Recommendations for Further Study" as it may contain an idea that you may want to take up for your work. You may want to pay special attention to dissertations that have won awards or been specialty noted by universities or during conferences (Bryant, 2004; Mauch & Park, 2003; Ogden, 2007; Roberts, 2004).
- Go to professional conferences in your field. Take the time to sit in many sessions where the abstract offered in the conference materials piqued your interest. Feel free to engage the presenter after their session and ask questions about what made their work interesting to them, what problems they had, and so forth (Roberts, 2004).
- There may be something in your personal experience that is interesting to both you personally and your wider field of study. Likewise there may be something of interest to your employer, a head of a local organization whom you know, or other stakeholder. Ideas from stakeholders generally come with access to their organization for data collection as well (Ogden, 2007; Rudestam & Newton, 2007).
- You might consider replicating a particularly interesting study by another person in your locale. While we are not suggesting this would make your journey problem free, as every locale requires adaptations and those always bring methodological decisions, this would

serve to give you instruments and a proven structure from which to work. Be sure to discuss this option with your advisor if you find such a study, as there may be university requirements involved. The difficulty will be in making it your own rather than just a carbon copy, so be very clear as to why and how these previously studied ideas fit your contextual needs (Roberts, 2004).

You may think that you will "choose your research topic" and that will be that—you'll move on, start reading your literature, and be comfortable that your topic is finished and complete. Not at all! This is a "work in progress," and when you are just about ready to defend your research proposal (usually chapters 1-3), you will realize how much your ideas have grown and matured aver the year or so since you made these first decisions.

We tend to see three main stages or times at which your dissertation topic will likely mature, and you will go through all three over and over again: stage 1—define your interests, stage 2—investigate the literature, and stage 3—determine the research ability of your ideas. Remember that in Chapter 1, we discussed a spiral growth pattern to your work as you design your study. This is the first part of that spiral, and in the next few chapters as your ideas progress, you will visit and revisit your topic, the literature, and the resulting methodology—each cycle helping your ideas mature and progress. Therefore, the short answer to how you find a research topic is that *you do the best you can at each stage (which we will discuss here in more detail)* and then allow it to mature along with your understanding of your field as you read what other authors have done. This chapter gives you an overview of the considerations that need to be woven into your choices, but don't worry if you can't take them all on right now. Do the best you can and the rest will sort themselves out at later stages in your designing and writing process.

Figure 2.1   Attending professional conferences can be a great way to find potential topics.

Source: David De Lossy/Photodisc/Thinkstock

> If you are a visual person you may want to make use a mind map and visually work out the relationships discussed in this chapter. There are several free programs available on the web.

Stage 1: Define Your Interests

It is commonly said that the most important thing in your research is that you really love your topic—after all, you will become the expert on it, you will spend three or more years of your life focused on it, and your professional life may revolve around or include this topic for the rest of your career. It is also true that you need to be practical; you cannot easily study things, no matter how interested in them you may be, if you have no access to the data that will be needed for your study (Rudestam & Newton, 2007).

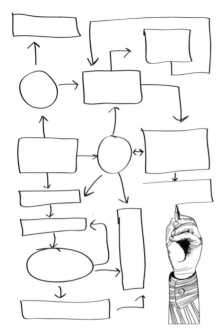

Figure 2.2   Mind mapping can help you develop your topic from your interests.

Source: ©iStockphoto.com/Booblgum

Main topic ideas will likely have several subtopics, and generally it is easier to develop a study and to become an expert on the subtopics than it is to focus on the larger field of study that contains it. For instance, organizational development is a good master's topic area but a daunting one on which to try to become a world expert. Within it, people could choose to study, write about, and develop expertise on a vast variety of subtopics, such as sustainability, global comparisons between similar organizations, organizational development within small, medium, large or multinational firms, and so forth.

Subtopics will break down into key ideas, variables, or themes of interest, and these can become components that you will measure. You may choose to study the relationship between these smaller components in relation to the subtopic you focus on. As an example, trust in multinational organizations might be used as a theme from which or through which to study change management and human resource (HR) policies. A researcher might measure professional development training for managers or employee relations or systems of communication as variables that develop out of the theme under study (trust in multinational organizations).

One way to begin your inquiry is to start with the broader issues and list the topics, subtopics, and themes of interest to you.

The following activity bridges the gap between your ideas and your work in Stage 2 as you review the literature.

Activity 2.1 Chart Your Interests as Potential Topics of Research

End Stage 1 by beginning a chart of possible topics. In Figure 2.3, we have laid out a basic chart that should work for most people/topics, but feel free to add columns depending on the intricacies of your ideas. Then you spend the next few months reading every study, every bit of research on everything you write in these columns. As you read the research of other authors, be sure to note what methodologies they used that you might emulate. You should constantly ask yourself, "Could I see myself doing this study? What would I need to do this study in my area?" Then you should be able to proceed with uncovering the purpose and questions of your research.

Topic	Subtopics	Themes	Data Collected From?	Methodology Used in Studies & Other Notes/Ideas

Figure 2.3   Chart your interests.

We'll use an example of a student we worked with because the confusion she faced is a common one. She wanted to study leadership, which is a worthwhile topic and one from which everyone could benefit, so on the surface it's a great topic for a dissertation. On the other hand, leadership is too broad. It is also an abstract concept and therefore impossible to research in a scientific manner unless it is rooted in a local context and problem. Scientific research models and design are all based on the idea that you have the equivalent of a laboratory in which to develop your study. Social sciences, education, business, and so forth all require that to study anything you need to be rooted in a location with a specific problem. The final problem she faced was that she wanted to study leadership because she had been subjected to bad bosses and she wanted to prove to others how bad it was—thus her whole thinking on her topic was full of bias. Research needs to come from a neutral position, and it is generally a very bad idea to choose a topic when you are likely to have a strong emotional response to the outcome (Bryant, 2004).

Frequently students express confusion around how the word "research" is used in a scholarly manner. Throughout your schooling, you were told to "go research" a topic, propelling you to read what was known about it, look for themes, and report back. Scientific research uses the same technique as part of the process in the literature review, but there the similarity ends.

 Alana says: *As another illustration, I'll consider my own journey to a disserta-tion topic. My degree is in educational leadership, and I knew that my passion and a good part of my career interest, lay in supporting at-risk students. The topic was students at risk of dropping out, and the subtopics were kids on drugs, afterschool programs, students experiencing homelessness, or mentor-ing at-risk students.*

Themes included academic achievement across all of the subtopics. I also considered the risk of dropping out of school, positive youth development programs to help students overcome the risks, or improving school climate. As I finished Stage 1 I had ideas, I understood my passions, but I had no clear passage to being able to design a study.

The final, precise topic and methodology only developed when I found a local situation (McKinney Vento distribution in Colorado) that required assistance. I did not know then what I know now: A topic is not a problem, and research develops from local problem situations.

Stage 2: Review the Literature

Your next step is to track down what research has been done on your topic in the past and what gaps may exist in that literature within which you might search out a problem situation. Right away you need to distinguish research from essay or scholarly writing. Many "experts" write on topics used in research, but at this point you need to compare your ideas in the realm of research. You are looking for scientific studies that used a particular methodology to study some aspect of your ideas. Why this focus? Because, you need to track down how others have approached the same problems you are

Figure 2.4 Finding a topic can seem difficult when you consider all the ramifications of your ideas.
Source: From Jorge Cham's *Thesis Topic Epiphany,* PhD Comic. Originally published by www.phdcomics.com.

> Look into the trade magazines for your industry. What do they consider the most important range of topics?
>
> Then go to your university library and look up what real research has been done on the ones that interest you most.

> The first consideration is WHY do you want to study this topic?
>
> What is the WOW factor for others?

facing and to organize their solutions in your mind to help you determine your best course forward.

It is during the examination of the literature that you should keep the idea of worthiness in your mind. What makes a topic worthy of doctoral study? It needs to have an element that is fresh, ideally adding to your field of study. On the other hand, this is your dissertation, not your book, which will come later. Therefore, consider what has been researched and find the nuances that may be worth exploiting for your doctoral study, which also might lead you to new arenas in your field over time (Roberts, 2004).

We were just discussing this phase of the work with a student in China. She complained that there was so much in her field (economics) that she had reams of articles and did not know how to cut through the work quickly. The secret to quickly reviewing the literature is that you need to be in control and aware of what information you are looking for and what parameters make for a good fit. Then you quickly go to the sections in others research, determine if they meet your parameters, and move on if they do not. In this case, in order to fill in the chart in Activity 2.2, you are looking for studies where the author describes his or her methodology as well as his or her outcomes or ideas.

Your field of study and the norms of research practice in your local context may require you to follow a different path as you develop your topic. Always remember that dissertation or thesis research is an art form rather than a set passage through which there is only one solution or process.

As an example, our student in China tells us that she was being pushed to do an empirical study, to gather economic data, and to figure out the precise topic for her study as she sees her findings develop. This is similar to many methods where theoretical understanding develops through research practice. The solution suggested by the Chinese professors would be the equivalent of doing a pilot study during which you would uncover the methodological challenges inherent in your idea. This student proceeded on an empirical study using longitudinal archival data to uncover (or not) correlations between inflation and employment. She continued by filling in the chart (activity below) with examples of other economic studies that met the general criteria she was searching for. Looking back, she found her spiral of discovery largely the same as the one described here, the only change being the immediate focus rather than any real substantive difference.

To make this process quicker and to help you bridge the ideas of the topics that interest you to potential methodology for your study, we suggest you continue with the previous activity in the following manner.

Figure 2.5   Knowing what you looking for and having clear parameters can help you review literature more quickly.

Source: Digital Vision/Digital Vision/Thinkstock

Activity 2.2 Add Others' Work to Your Chart of Interests

Add two new columns to your chart. For the first, as you find examples of the research of others who were studying topics or subtopics similar to those you are interested in, add a column for their reference information. The second new column reports the size or scope of their study. Read enough of their work to be able to fill in all the spaces and then set it aside for later if their study remains of interest. You may be fortunate to find a study that seems very close to your ideas, one whose scope you could replicate. It is always an option to take a previous study and build on it in a new location. This may be a discussion for you to have with your mentor or advisor.

Authors Reference	Topic	Subtopics	Themes	Scope (Size of Study)	Data Collected From?	Methodology Used in Studies & Other Notes/ Ideas

Figure 2.6   Add others' work to your chart of interests.

Stage 3: Developing a Research Framework and Beginning Methodology

In the next phase, you should begin to consider research design. You may want to go back to the best examples in your initial reading of the literature to take a look at how they did the following (each will be covered in detail in later chapters). Generally, there is a fulcrum of events that catapult you towards your goal of choosing your topic and taking the first steps in designing your study: (a) talking to others and defining the purpose of your study (maybe with the help of your employer), (b) getting a general handle on the methodological decisions you need to make (with the help of your advisor), and/or (c) developing a study through relationships between the parts of the topic you will study (with everyone's help). It is likely, if not completely necessary, that two or more of these will be at play as you work through each stage of designing your study and your research questions. The first ideas you should consider are discussed briefly below.

First Step: Define the Purpose of Your Study and/or the Problem It Revolves Around

If you are the type of person who desires to make a difference in the world, your field, or to your personal context, then purpose-driven work may make things easier for you. A strong purpose gives you a goal to reach for, but beware that it can also blind you to studies that are smaller, more concise, and would allow you to finish faster. You need to keep in mind that your dissertation is not your book or your life—just a means to advance both. Therefore, if you immediately think of a very big purpose, you may want to ask how that overarching idea might pertain to your local context.

You want a neutral purpose—so not to prove X relates to Y in some manner or to show how good (or bad) something is. Instead, plan to study whether and to what extent something that you believe might be true really is true when seriously studied.

The Problem Statement

If approaching a scientifically oriented study, you will need to have a problem situation that will help you define your topic in your locale. In the applied sciences you probably need to continue to define your topic and the variables you wish to measure. If X is the topic and Y is the context of your study, then you need to demonstrate either a problem or a situation in the Y context that makes X worth studying. If you are just discussing ideas, then you have not yet developed to a point where you can build defensible dissertation logic. This may be equally true in theoretical studies, although there you may create a hypothesis or treatise of ideas about X that can be studied or considered in a situation or through a kind of analysis that is Y.

> Dissertations and theses have career advancing potential.
>
> Consider who might be the stakeholders or audience you want to play to and discuss your ideas with them.

Second Step: Consider How Your Topic Evolves Into Research Design

We see too many people determine their topics without considering how they will evolve into research methodological choices. While you will come back to this topic at several future junctures during the evolution of your work, here are some early considerations you should keep in mind.

- Variables within the topic to study. As Rudestam and Newton (2007) point out: "Researchable questions almost invariably involve the relationship between two or more variables, phenomena, concepts, or ideas. The nature of that relationship may vary. Research studies generally consist of methods to explicate the nature of the relationship" (p. 11).

- The scope. You need a way to contain the size of your research, consider it your laboratory. Therefore, a big topic like leadership needs to be honed down to become leadership within a scope over which you have access and a certain amount of control. A dissertation editor online reminds us that "the narrower the focus the clearer the mission of the research" (Mauch & Park, 2003; Scott-Ladd & Chan, 2008).

> Don't forget to look up dissertations based on topics or using methodology similar to those of interest to you. Reading dissertations aids you in figuring out the relationships between topics and all the components discussed here.

- Access to data. In our most creative moments, all of us could design fantastic research studies about all the topics in the world about which we would love to know more. You will not develop these into defensible dissertation topics, however, unless you, as a principal investigator, have access to the data collection process on which your research hinges. Part of the access issue is whether your study participants might be considered vulnerable by institutional ethics boards. Key issues will be if you want to question any of the following: (a) people under the age of 18, (b) those adults for whom you have supervisory status, or (c) prisoners. A final consideration will be whether you enjoy direct contact with others. Many people do well using archival evidence from government or private sources and researching statistical significance of part or all of these data. (Ogden, 2007; Whitfield, 2012; Whitfield, Krinberg, & Zenhausern, 2012).

> Keep a separate personal learning journal for you to document just how you've changed day by day. You'll be amazed at your process of inner transformation at the end, and it's fun to have a record of the journey (Dr. Ken Long, DoctoralNet, 2012).

- An understanding of the analysis needed to build credible findings. While covered in depth in Chapters 4, 5, and 6, in general terms you might consider quantitative data collection when you have a problem that affects lots of people and about which earlier literature has established some findings worth testing in your situation. Think qualitative-data collection when you want to investigate the relationship of things

Figure 2.7 Think about the contribution your study will make to the world around you.

Source: Ryan McVay/Photodisc/Thinkstock

in the depth of human understanding or perceptions. Said another way, quantitative methods break data into easily analyzed numerical codes and are useful for questions on finite topics or larger populations. Qualitative methods of data collection allow you to comb through people's use of language to determine hidden depths of meaning about situations or experiences in their lives.

- An idea about how your study will contribute to your field, your community, or the world. Discussed as contribution, dissertations are long and arduous work, at the end of which you have the opportunity to advance your career into new and unexpected places. In order for you to reap the maximum benefit, you need to start with the idea of who cares about your topic and how you might use it to your benefit later.

Activity 2.3 Developing Problem and Purpose for Your Topic

Setting up a chart similar to the one below, fill in the spaces and keep drafting new versions and revising the content until all the relationships seem to go together in a manner that will allow you to envision being able to complete a study with these parameters.

Topic Idea	Problem/Locale	Scope of Research Data I Can Access	Type of Data/ Analysis	Contribution to Field

Figure 2.8   Problem and Purpose Chart

As an example, one of our recently graduating doctoral students would have filled out her table in the following manner.

Topic Idea	Problem/Locale	Scope of Research Data I Can Access	Type of Data/ Analysis	Contribution to Field
Early childhood analysis of difficulties in literacy and reading	A local school district shows that many students with literacy difficulties are not assessed until later in their education—making it harder for them to catch up.	Has access to teachers throughout the district as they come together for professional development activities	Quantitative survey mixed with interviews and focus groups. Questions would address what they know, how they were trained, and how they communicate needs to their district	May demonstrate need for increased professional development OR may highlight other areas of training or communication that need to be addressed

Figure 2.9   Problem and Purpose Chart, Education Major

To contrast this, a recently graduating business major would have filled theirs out this way.

Topic Idea	Problem/ Locale	Scope of Research Data I Can Access	Type of Data/ Analysis	Contribution to Field
The influence of marketing on professional musicians and their careers	The African American professional vocal artist	Knows several African American artists of renown in several genres of music	Qualitative interviews wrapped together to become narrative inquiry	May point out how musicians' artistic choices are dictated by business concerns OR may lead to training for new musicians to consider how to take their marketing into their own hands

Figure 2.10   Problem and Purpose Chart, Business Major

Once this chart is filled in you need to practice explaining your ideas to a few nonacademic people until you can easily discuss your ideas on what you think you want to do. At this point it would be a great idea to continue the conversation with your university advisor or mentor.

Activity 2.4 Keep a Personal Learning Journal

Personal learning journals or logs accomplish two things: First, they help you avoid becoming discouraged later in the process, as it allows you to celebrate at regular intervals how far you have come. Second, when life intervenes, and you miss a few days (or maybe weeks), a journal saves you time and lets you come back quickly to your last thoughts. The following framework helps with that process:

1. Start a new entry every day.

2. Include a list of the things you did. When you are working with literature, cite the author and year and keep track of the references in your bibliographic software.

3. Always end the day's notes with a line about what you hope to accomplish the next day.

4. Reread and notate your journal as appropriate with highlights, page markers, and so forth to indicate where in your dissertation or thesis proposal your ideas may fit.

Chapter 2 Checklist

❏ I have a good idea for a research topic.

❏ I know what problem I am focusing on.

❐ I can tell others the problem I am addressing with my research.

❐ I understand what the purpose is.

Where Should I Go to Dig Deeper? Suggested Resources to Consider

Borg, S. (2001). The research journal: A tool for promoting and understanding the researcher development. *Language Teaching Research, 5*(2), 156–177. A great article for the beginning researcher on how to use a journal. Found on the Internet.

Bryant, M. T. (2004). *The portable dissertation advisor*. Thousand Oaks, CA: Corwin Press. On pages 14 through 25, Bryant has great tips to consider as you determine your topic.

Glatthorn, A. A., & Joyner, R. L. (2005). *Writing the winning thesis or dissertation: A step-by-step guide* (2nd ed.). Thousand Oaks, CA: Corwin Press. On pages 29 through 30 and 63 through 68 the authors do a nice job of how to reflect, discuss, and analyze your first ideas as well as information on the pros and cons of working in groups.

Helmer, O. (1967). *Analysis of the future: The Delphi Method*. Santa Monica, CA: The Rand Corporation. This report on the Delphi Method goes back to its origins as it explains the methodology; it will be a resource for the group activity. Available on the web through the Rand Corporation.

Hsu, C.-C., & Sandford, B. (2007). The Delphi technique: Making sense of consensus. *Practical Assessment, Research, and Evaluation, 12*(10), 1–8. This article focuses on the considerations of using the Delphi method as a means of making sense of group ideas.

Ortlipp, M. (2008). Keeping and using reflective journals in the qualitative research process. *The Qualitative Report, 13*(4), 695–705. A more advanced article on the uses for a journal in a research process. This article takes the ideas of Borg to another level and is also available on the Internet.

Group Exercises

All of the sections in this chapter could be brainstormed either as an individual or collective basis. Garson (2002) points out that in a distance situation you could set up such a brainstorming session as a Delphi investigation. This is done by posing the first question, such as "What subtopics of interest to research cluster under topic X?" Then a number of people respond and you summarize their responses as you go on to pose the next question. These are done in a series until the group drills down to the range they can all agree on. Difficulties with the Delphi method are that people may not consistently respond or may take more time to do so than would give you expedient feedback. On the other hand you might engage professors or experts in the field in this manner.

3

Do You Have Some Idea
How You Will Study Your Topic?

Bridging Topic and Methods

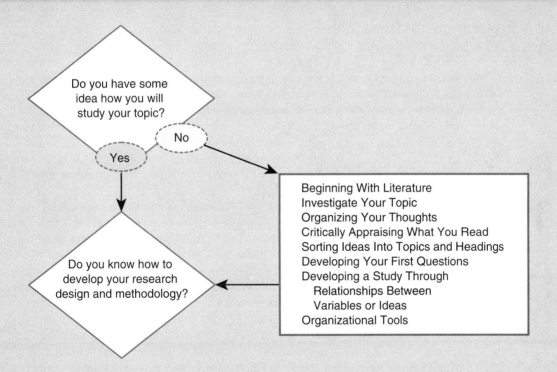

While the last chapter touched lightly on how topic influences other things, this chapter helps you sort out the work involved in reviewing the literature. Included here are instructions as to how you can dig deeper into what is known about your topic, including both expert opinion and research, the organizational basics of the review of literature, and the use of bibliographic software. We finish the chapter by visiting again how the choices you make as you develop your ideas influence methodology and vice versa.

The Questions Answered in This Chapter:

1. Now that I have a topic, where do I begin?

2. How can I best review and organize the literature?

3. What organizational tools will be helpful for me?

4. What is the logic upon which a proposal is grounded?

5. How do research questions develop my methodology?

6. How can I begin to develop my study?

Beginning With Literature

A concrete and in-depth understanding of your topic area form the foundation of your dissertation/ thesis. You will want to include how your topic has been researched in the past and which methodologies were used. You never begin research without thoroughly investigating what has gone before. Hart (1998) has a really good point of view as you consider what it means to you as a student to do a great job researching your topic area: "It takes time and a willingness to face challenges, acquire new understanding and have sufficient openness of mind to appreciate that there are other views of the world" (p. 11). Indeed the task of your review of the literature is to discuss the points of view that impinge upon your topic and lead you to the methodology with which you will study it.

Tip 3.2 Make the librarian at your university your new best friend, or at the least take every tutorial or attend every training offered by your librarians. They will offer numerous tricks to finding and using the most helpful keywords, to how to easily download to your bibliographic software, all of which are extremely helpful

(Roberts, 2004).

Part of the thesis process is to become comfortable with all of the standards of academic practice as they evolve from the literature on your topic area. In this chapter, we go through the review, offer tools you may find helpful, and go over the initial ideas you need to incorporate as you begin to develop the logic of your study. In the next chapter we discuss the basics of research design, developing problem statements and research questions. Finally, in Chapter 5 you put these beginnings together as you fine-tune the methodology you intend using in your study. It is our intent that by the end of Chapter 5, you will be ready to write serious drafts of your proposal. In the United States this would mean chapters 1 through 3 of your dissertation. In the United Kingdom and throughout Europe, a proposal includes less specificity but will be based on the same principles.

Investigating Your Topic

Reading academic material is often not easy, especially when you may have been out of the university environment for a while. Unlike reading for pleasure, reading academic material forces us to read and take notice of more components than just the content. From the viewpoint of the doctoral student who may be investigating this material as a potential for their dissertation and review of literature, several components need to be investigated all at once.

There are two basic types of academic articles: essays for explanatory works and research articles. In an essay or explanatory writing, such as this book, an author discusses their ideas that have been developed over the course of time and through a variety of experiences. Expert opinions, in order to be appropriate for a review of literature or as a basis for doctoral dissertation, need to be written by acknowledged experts in the field and peer reviewed. Research articles, on the other hand, are the outcomes of credible research techniques applied to a topic that give the article the expertise it needs for publication.

Universities require that articles used in reviews of literature come from peer-reviewed sources. Research journals are an excellent example of this, while magazines that frequently focus on a particular field or topic may not be. Books by some publishing houses will always be peer reviewed, while others may not. Books that fall under the peer-reviewed category generally have extensive references, glossaries, and often footnotes explaining particular ideas in greater detail. It is usually the case that the reviewers will be thanked by the author and the publishing house somewhere in the introduction or preface to the book.

You might consider five or six stages to your investigation:

1. Background search from textbooks, course work, and magazines from your industry.

2. Develop a mind map of your topic using the same sources while branching out to a few peer-reviewed books or journals to establish subtopics of potential interest.

3. Drilling down into the parts of your topic that capture your interest or are most relevant to your context by adding research literature.

4. Completing a detailed search across journals, books, electronic articles, government and educational databases, and so forth.

5. Consideration of the methodological implications of your ideas. This will be discussed in more detail later in this chapter.

6. A continuation of the investigation started above using secondary or tertiary sources (those referenced in the original search) delving into specifics that support your research methodology (Hart, 1998).

As you read, be sure in all of these cases to make note of the references in the reference list, especially when you come across ideas that are interesting to you. The first thing that you'll want to do is start a list of future reading that develops out of the reference sections of what you are currently reading. You will need to be able to track back to primary sources or the first people that came up with particular provocative or innovative ideas or research. Remember your topic is not "finished" yet. The more you look critically at both the ideas and the structure of other people's work, the easier it is to hone your own.

You will also want to note what keywords you used to find the article you are reading. Some universities require that you disclose these search words when you write your methodology chapter. Taking note of them will also help you hone the topics you will focus on in your review of literature, dependent upon your final methodology (this correlation and relationship will be discussed in

Figure 3.1 Organize all of your literature into reference software on your computer from the beginning to save time later.

Source: ©iStockphoto.com/Model-la

Chapter 5). The keywords that brought up particular content areas are also useful when you broaden your search through the Library of Congress, bookstores, reference libraries, and so forth.

It is also useful to write a few lines in your reference software about how you intend to use the article, what topic areas it pertains to, and/or identify its most interesting characteristics. When you read research, always note the purpose, scope (size and population), study participants, findings and conclusions, limitations, and contribution of the research. A handy seven-sentence structure that captures the specifics of research for later use involves writing one sentence for each of these topics. For example, "the purpose of this study was . . . ," "the size of its population was . . . ," "the methodology used was . . . ," and so forth.

Use of reference software, such as bibliographic software, coupled with the depth of the notes you take and the focus to which you capture all the elements in your references will make a difference in how much time you need to take at the end, tracking down details you no longer remember. Be sure to write citations for everything you read. Many students find that quotes and citations have been lost in the final hours when they could not track them back to their original source. Good habits in this regard are everything!

Secondary Information

Secondary information consists of sources of data and other information collected by others and archived in some form. These sources include government reports, industry studies, archived data sets, and syndicated information services as well as the traditional books and journals found in libraries. Secondary information offers relatively quick and inexpensive answers to many questions and is almost always the point of departure for primary research (Stewart & Kamins, 1993, p. 1).

Why are secondary sources important? The information age has made ever-increasing amounts of raw data available to the general public, and the people who have worked with those figures, analyzed them, and written essays on their meaning have done you a great favor and saved you time. Nevertheless, they did not collect the data themselves, nor did they do the primary research. Science is founded on the idea that in all human endeavors the further you are from the source the more likely ideas or facts will be misinterpreted. Therefore, it becomes necessary that you know what research (primary source material) is, and what are essays, reports, or some other form of secondary analysis. Scholarly research demands that the writer drill down to primary sources whenever they are available.

> You don't know when you're reading it how important it might be in two years to the dissertation, so take good notes, have a good recall and recovery system, and record your references each and every time (Dr. Ken Long, DoctoralNet, 2010).

Stewart and Kamins (1993) suggest you should ask yourself the following questions when evaluating secondary data:

- What was their purpose in writing the material?
- Who actually collected the material they are quoting and for what purpose?
- What does the actual data on which they are basing their ideas consist of?
- When was that information collected?
- How consistent is it with other things you have read?
- Looking carefully at their analysis of numerical ideas, do you agree with their interpretations?

The Debates Inherent in a Discussion of Your Topic

You will need to reorganize the ideas that come from reading literature into topics before you write your review. While you may read one author at a time, you do not discuss literature this way. Your discussion covers the subtopics that develop across groups of the authors you have read, as their ideas are considered en masse.

For instance, if your research is to ask people about their motivation to behave in a certain way, your subtopics might include both what is known from research about motivation and also the considerations of actions that impinge on the type of action you are interested in studying. One author may discuss two or three of these subtopics; another may discuss several as well, some overlapping. You will be required to write each subtopic in your own voice developing the conglomerate knowledge across authors and then use multiple citations at the end of the paragraph. Thus your writing becomes your understanding of the debates inherent within your field. Yet you are not speaking from only your own voice but that voice as it is backed up by others. You must digest what you are reading and re-sort each author's ideas into a new version of the whole fabric of your topic across the breadth of your reading.

Figure 3.2 You will need to absorb the many debates and ideas regarding your topic and then convey your understanding in a new version that demonstrates your voice as it is backed up by others.

Source: ©iStockphoto.com/qushe

Organizing Your Thoughts

Activity 3.1 Chart Your Reading

This activity presupposes that you are just starting your academic dissertation journey and that you have not yet taken many notes. It will help you set up the basic slots for organizational pulls that will help you capture the data you need. You will see in a later section that we strongly encourage the use of bibliographic software, and you can use the general spaces for notes, abstracts, and so forth in the lower sections of the database to record the information gathered in this activity.

1. Open a journal article that is a report on research done on your topic, and open the reference software or database/graphic organizer you will use to capture your references and notes for all of your reading.

2. Fill in all of the blanks if you're using reference software, or write about all of the necessary information so that you have your reference in the correct format as per the style of your university (for example, APA).

3. Capture as many of the seven concepts of research (purpose, scope, methodology, findings, conclusions, limitations, and contributions) as are evident from the article in one of your notes.

4. In another area, note if this research disagrees with other authors' works or points to gaps perceived in the literature on this topic.

5. Consider how this article works with what else you have read, and make notes in a different field of how you think you might use it.

Figure 3.3 Take notes in your personal learning journal as you go along.

Source: Jupiterimages/Comstock/Thinkstock

6. Whenever you particularly like the way in which an author addresses an idea, copy the text exactly for potential use as a quote. Always make note of the page number for direct quotations.

7. Read through the reference list at the end of the article and copy down a list of the authors and works that you intend to investigate later. Make note of these in your personal learning journal (Activity 2.4).

To the extent that you establish a routine where you adequately capture these details, you will be assured to have all the tiny bits of information you will need at the end of your writing process.

Critically Appraising What You Read

Tracesea asks: *How much literature do I need?*

Answer: This is somewhat complicated as it depends on your topic, how much it has been studied, and the complexity of ideas you wish to tie together.

Consider upwards to a hundred books and peer-reviewed journals that you will eventually use, as a minimum. This may mean you have to look over or read twice this many. Read into a topic/subtopic until (a) you know you have drilled back to the seminal authors on the topic (the ones everyone quotes) and (b) new articles seldom lead to any new information—you get a sense you have read it all before.

Can you discuss your topic with authority? Do you have the authors who most people cite and reference in your list (Bryant, 2004)? Are you confident enough to carry on a conversation or to ask questions of an expert? If you can answer yes to these questions, then likely you have done enough review.

A question came in from one of our students that is worthy of deeper consideration. He asked, "What is the best approach to critically appraise journal papers? Do you have any tips?"

Ask yourself the following questions:

- How interesting are their results? You might critically appraise the article as being very professional and the methodology impeccable, but if the findings and conclusions don't provoke new ideas, then this is an article that will, at best, be used as filler. Other articles you may find much more provocative, and you can keep track of these by separating them in your bibliographic software. As an example, you might consider pulling them into a special group where they can be found easily.
- How sound was their methodology? Did it make sense as you understand the constraints of that population? Were the results significant enough that you believe they would hold true over a wider population? Toss out any resources that are not methodologically and technically sound.
- Do these authors write in a credible manner? Is their research of a size/scope that seems appropriate to the number of stakeholders interested in what they are studying? Many studies are done that address issues close to yours, but when you look deeply their sample size may be small, their findings may not derive directly from their data, and so forth. Note your concerns about their studies in your bibliographic software notes as well.
- Do these authors discuss their work in a way that makes you respect their knowledge of their topic as well as believe in what they found or are trying to suggest? Researchers that have been around the block a few times write with a different voice than novices. Every sentence seems to have more behind it, and they casually reference other work as though they live and breathe these ideas (they probably do). Give a higher ranking and then go track down other things they have written—become conversant with them, as these are the authors on whose work/ideas you may base more than just this study. These may be the people whose work changes yours.
- Take robust notes in bibliographic software on every article you read. Have a ranking scale as to the likelihood of using them in

Figure 3.4   Rank the articles you read as to how applicable they are to your work and enter these assessments into your bibliographic software.

Source: Jupiterimages/Comstock/Thinkstock

your final work—even those that seem redundant can be used in multiple citations to give weight to the ideas on which all experts seem to agree.

- Don't forget to look up your DOI numbers and add them to your database—these are becoming very important if your university uses APA as its style manual.
- Watch for and make notes on the methodology used by authors studying ideas similar to yours. For instance, if they all seem to write about using quantitative methods over larger populations, ask yourself, "Why?". There may be peculiarities to your topic that make it common to use particular theoretical or methodological strategies. These are important questions as you define your own methodology.
- Is this research quantitative? If so, consider listing the statistical issues, such as effect size, p values, the actual statistics uses, and confidence intervals if appropriate.

 Tracesea asks: *Wow, that's a lot of stuff to keep track of while reading literature! Do you have a chart or a checklist that I can use to help me remember what I need to record from each piece of literature I review?*

Answer: Yes you will find one you can copy in Appendix B.

Sorting Ideas Into Topics and Headings

The work of a literature review will proceed more smoothly if you look into what sections are required and begin plotting your ideas as they fit that structure from the early days of your reading. This does not protect you from having to throw some things out and start over, but to the extent that your initial ideas follow through to the end, you will be well grounded in where they go and why.

> Use of a document map, navigation pane, accessed through the View menu on PCs or accessed via View/sidebar/document map on Macs helps avoid writing mistakes as you begin your dissertation. Each section refers to similar topics, at least in passing, and this system helps you jump around, find areas of redundancy, and avoid them.

Start by crafting a discussion that helps your reader understand the topic in general. This overview of the literature and of each subtopic as it nests within your study should be a few paragraphs long. Each topic is then discussed with a subheading that leads directly to the logic of the questions you ask in your methodology.

Next, start to develop specific discussions that lead your reader to the ideology and key ideas behind your study. Think of your topics and subtopical discussions as breadcrumbs, leading your reader through to the conclusions you want them to make. For example, they know your topic is X. Then you lay out five subtopics of importance, four of which are the main considerations or variables others have used to study X, and the fifth of which are the gaps between previous studies. Then it will not be a surprise to your reader when they come to your methodology that you are studying X using measurements relevant to those topic headings.

As mentioned, most reviews of literature include a later section/subtopic heading that covers the disagreements or gaps that exist in the research. If you have a number of gaps to discuss, list first those that lead naturally to questions you want to ask. Discuss gaps in the literature that position your study to become significant in your field. Outline these, making sure to note who else has mentioned them and any recent dissertations that may enhance the discussion in which your study will be embedded.

As you build a list of questions that you find most compelling, you will also be reading about methodology to help you decide how you will approach answering those questions. Many dissertations/theses discuss methodology as a topic in the review of literature. The advantage to this strategy is twofold: (a) you free up your writing in your methodology section to focus on your decisions and approach, and (b) you lead your reader to understand how this topic could naturally be studied in a certain way. This prepares the reader for your methodology chapter. Later in this chapter there will be a discussion on how to build research questions from your reading, which will then cycle back to influence your topics.

Sorting ideas into topics and relating those to methodology is a cyclical process. You are on the first cycle, you will come back to the relationship between literature and methodology several more times before you start to write the chapters of your proposal in Part II of this book.

The Logic Behind the Work

The review of literature, as we said at the beginning, forms the foundation for your study. Your methodology then is its heart. The two need to tie together with a specific one-to-one correlation. What we mean is that at the end, you will not include topics in your review of the literature unless you need them to back up, explain, or illuminate some aspect of your study. Put simply, if you are going to ask people about topics a, b, and c, in order to better understand how they relate in people's experience to x then a, b, c, and x need to be covered in the literature. While reviewing your literature, you may have found some interesting information about d and e, but since they turned out not to be directly related to your study, then they need to be left out.

We will come back to the full logic of the proposal in Chapter 5, but for now it will help you hone your literature review and to discard certain aspects of your reading. It is best not to spend too much time speeding down dark alleys only to discover that these very interesting studies are useless to you in the end. To that end, it is probably a good time for you to begin the first step in developing the questions around which your research will develop.

Developing Your First Questions

Let's first discuss the difference between a topic and a question. A topic is broad, such as "leadership;" a question pins down the aspect of your topic that you want to study and also the context. The question, "What makes for good leadership?" will not drive a research study. Neither will, "What types of leadership will the teachers at X high school respond to?" However, "What are the perceptions of the teachers at X high school about the recent push towards teacher leadership, and what are some examples they reference?" would be a good start towards a research question.

The wording, "whether and to what extent," works as a lead-in phrase, because it helps keep you away from a natural tendency towards biased questions. It is not uncommon for us to go into research believing we know what we will find. It's useful, therefore, to set up a wording that consistently reminds us that we may not find the outcomes we think we will find. One last little thing about research questions—you don't want too many of them. Depending on how quickly you want to finish, you don't want your methodology to set you up for an interminable amount of time and work. One of the universities that I work for restricts the data collection process to just eight weeks. It has proven to be very successful, flying in the face of what many academics thought was a requirement of three or four months. The more questions you ask, the more data you need to substantiate your answers, and a longer period of time is required to do the work you will need to do once you pass defense of your proposal. Don't begin your study with more than two or three questions without approval from your advisor.

Alana says: *Sometimes a general question works—I worked with a doctoral student who started with a list of 13 research questions. When we looked at them carefully, it appeared that many of them overlapped the same larger general question—that's the question she needed to be asking for her research. She was an education major, and many of her questions circled the general relationship between student engagement, motivation, and achievement. By asking an overarching question such as, "Whether and to what extent do students display positive outcomes when working with this computer program?" she was able to collect data on their engagement with the program, their motivation to work with the program, and the achievement they gained through that experience.*

Questions Bridge to Methodology

Your questions also tell your reader a lot about the methodology you intend to use. For an example, if you say you are comparing, you will be doing a quantitative study. If you query lived experience, it will be qualitative. These distinctions are subtle when you start, so we suggest you find work on your topic and compare both the questions to the methodology.

Figure 3.5 Do your questions lead to the methodology you intend to use?

Source: Stockbyte/Stockbyte/Thinkstock

Research questions morph and develop over time, as will the specifics of your study. One of the biggest areas of confusion voiced by doctoral students has to do with what makes up a solid and researchable question and how researchers know, just by listening to your questions, what methodology will fit. As always, it is useful to go to your sample dissertations and track how their research develops from their problem through their questions and on to their methodology. Understanding the logic helps you understand what makes for a good question.

The following points, delineated across qualitative, quantitative, and mixed methods, will help you craft the first draft of research questions.

They can then be inserted into your first full draft of the logic of your proposal. Once this is finished, we recommend you schedule a meeting with your mentor/advisor, as their expertise will help you go the next step or will ensure you are on a defensible path.

Broad Versus Focused Questions

Rudestam and Newton (2007) suggest starting to write questions as though you were observing your problem from multiple viewpoints. For instance, if your problem was on a movie screen and you, as the observer, were at a distance from it, what questions might you ask? What if your relationship to the problem was closer but still did not involve your life on a daily basis? What if it was having a huge impact on your life every day? Now look at your problem in relationship to other things that impact it—what questions can be asked about those relationships?

Questions That Lead to Methodology

Creswell (2009) delineates types of questions into the methodological considerations that support them. Look at the questions you are writing and see if they sort into the following considerations. Use these prompts to work out questions from your problem that might develop into a qualitative, quantitative, or mixed-methods study.

Qualitative Questions

1. Develop central questions—these will be broad and will ask for an exploration of a key or central phenomenon that is inherent in your problem statement.

2. Develop a series of potential sub-questions that develop from each central question you wrote. These narrow the broad focus of the central question but inquire about a specific aspect as it relates to the human experience involved.

3. Note which questions easily start with or can be rewritten to start with "how" or "what"— these beginnings indicate an emergent design (Creswell, 2009).

4. Reword or edit your questions until you can safely say that each has a single focus—delineating one and only one measurable aspect of some area of your problem.

Quantitative Questions/Hypotheses

Develop a series of questions that relate to your topic that inquire into the association or difference between two or more aspects of your problem (Morgan, Leech, Gloeckner, & Barrett, 2011). For instance they might do the following:

- Compare aspects of your problem.
- Investigate how aspects of your problem relate.
- Describe how one aspect of your problem may respond to another aspect of your problem.

Do you have a theory as to how these aspects compare, relate, or respond to one another? If so, then write a hypothesis that captures your assumptions or ideas. Please note that for greater understanding of descriptive, associational, or differential statistics and the kinds of questions you should ask, please refer to the Where Should I Go to Dig Deeper? section.

Prasad, Rao, and Rehani (2001) suggest that the commonsense approach to developing qualitative questions is to correlate the research question with the why of your research; you then develop a theory about the situation and suggest an answer. Then you identify variables that would measure the truth of that answer, establishing the how of your research design. What you expect becomes the hypotheses that you test while you collect data that measure those variables. "Hypothesis is a formal statement that presents the expected relationship between an independent and dependent variable" (Creswell, 2009).

Figure 3.6   Do you have access to the data you will need to answer your questions?

Source: ©iStockphoto.com/maxkabakov

Mixed Methods

Did you find the questions/hypotheses that resulted in both the qualitative and quantitative sections equally intriguing and easy? Consider advancing them all with a mixed-methods study. How they relate to each other and why will require further study.

Access to Data

Remember, questions have to be answered and analyzed. You are on the first wheel of the spiral of growth we discussed earlier, so the interaction between what you read, the questions you ask, and your methodology has just begun to develop. For now, think for a moment about who will provide the data you would need to answer your questions. Are those people readily available to you? Would they be interested in participating in your study? Stop now and reconsider if you answer "no" to these questions.

Other Question/Methodological Considerations

Other methodological decisions go hand-in-hand with the development of the questions that drive your study. For instance,

- Quantitative studies often test a hypothesis about how things are in the world. This automatically sets up a null hypothesis that says the variable or circumstance being studied does not prove true. Statistical measures then show the significance of the data proving the original hypothesis—or not. If there is no significant agreement then the null is not disproved and remains in place.
- Statistical analysis within quantitative work allows you to discuss the relationships or correlations between two or more variables you are interested in studying.

- Qualitative studies make use of people as data and ask questions, such as how do the people involved perceive the subject of your study, or what do you believe is involved in the situation, or what do you think it would take to build a positive outcome?
- Mixed methods are useful when you want a little of both of the above—through either concurrent or sequential use of qualitative and quantitative methods, a researcher asks a small population how they perceive a situation and tests a larger population as to whether they agree with the other assessment.
- Case studies are great for people who build relationships and have the time to follow a situation over time. A case study asks about how something develops or what factors are related to certain outcomes.
- Action research is used by people who want to make a difference as they go, testing their outcomes.
- Evaluation is used by people who already have something in place and want to test it in a rigorous manner.
- Narrative methods use qualitative means to ask what the story of the people involved is about the situation.

Tracesea asks: *What if I can see my ideas in none of these? Or maybe in several?*

Answer: Not to worry because you are just on your first round of developing these ideas. For now, make notes as to questions you want to ask and which of these methodological choices they may fit into. Discuss your ideas with fellow students, the professor from your research classes, and your advisor. Make notes in your personal journal and keep progressing through these ideas until, like a jigsaw puzzle, they begin to fall together.

Developing a Study Through Relationships Between Variables or Ideas

Sometimes how one thing relates to another seems the correct focus for your study. If, after reading deeply across your topics, subtopics, and themes of interest, it appears that two factors seem to have a relationship worth investigating, this may be a good focus. As an example, why youth from low socioeconomic backgrounds remain low in academic standards is a prevalent field of study for educational research in the United States. A variety of factors emerge, and a study could compare and contrast the effects of those variables on a local population. European systems have spent fortunes studying the qualities in teachers or schools that correlate with high test scores. Both of these examples focus on one issue through the relationship of two or more variables that seem to impinge on outcomes.

Tracesea asks: *Can you give me some examples of research questions in each of these categories: qualitative, quantitative and mixed methods?*

Answer: This is complex and beyond the scope of this book. When you are ready to drill down to the specifics of your methodology you will need references that can go into detail. Generally however and at a deep enough level to help you now, as you read, look closely at the questions in the research that comprise your literature. Look at their structure as much as for their meaning. Also look at our Chapters 4, 5, and 6 as well as at the other resources we suggest at the end of chapters for a more detailed explanation.

In short, qualitative questions generally dig deeply into human perception so you might ask how people felt about X or what their experience of X was. Quantitative questions are generally answered by ticking the box on a survey so you might break down the perception into 1, 2, 3, 4, or 5 possible answers or a range of responses. Mixed methods would use them both.

Your topic, questions, and ideas about methodology may seem like they shift and change with the wind as you start your search for the perfect topic on which to focus for the next few years in your doctoral research. Often they circle a central thread—for this reason, the following chart exercise can be very helpful, both for you to track your development and also as a talking document between you and your dissertation/thesis advisor. Don't worry if you can't fill in all the spaces at first—this too is a topic for conversation with other students in a study group and/or your advisor.

Activity 3.4 Iterative Planning

Your ideas regarding your research will develop over time. Use your research journal for this exercise so that you will later be able to track the iterative development of these ideas. Do not be concerned that at first you can only address one or two of these, the full frame develops with time.

1. Consider the drawing in the figure below and then list them in a column on a single sheet of your research journal.

2. Write a few words or a sentence for each. Some bubbles contain a group of ideas that cluster together as you design research. As an example, how you see the world, your theoretical stance, must be in line with the choices you make regarding methodology and methods. You will then employ those methods to uncover the type of data that will allow you to answer the questions that then, in turn, are pertinent to your theoretical point of view. Don't worry at this stage if much of these seem a foreign language, we will unpack the meanings as we go along.

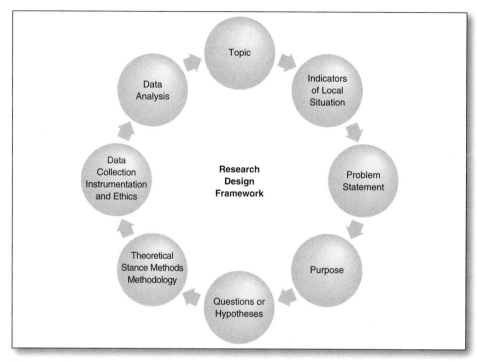

Figure 3.7   Research Design Framework

3. Date the page and be sure to include all the parts. As we just mentioned, at first, do not be dismayed if you have several blanks, and over time you may notice that, even if you have a pretty good idea of most of the areas, filling in a new position makes all the others change. Over time you will see the maturity of your ideas develop.

4. Periodically take these to your advisor and discuss the development of your methodological ideas.

Organizational Tools

This section discusses three organization tools that can be helpful in writing a dissertation: word processing software, bibliographic software, and voice dictation.

Word Processing Software

Depending upon your field of study, you may not have kept up with all the latest enhancements to the word processing software you use on a daily basis. We are surprised by the number of students who do not know how to make section breaks, use headings, or map their documents as they take notes and write. These will be discussed in more depth later as you move into writing your proposal.

Headings form the bones of the organizational pattern of any major work. They translate to the table of contents. We recommend students start to map out their ideas by

1. Finding a template for their final work.

2. Coming up with headings that map out the work required in each section. Some of these may be required by your university, others may mimic a published dissertation or thesis whose logic appealed to you.

3. Develop a document map or navigation pane as you write (this is terminology from Microsoft Word and is shown here in Figure 3.8). While different versions or manufacturers of software calls this option by different names, the headings allow you to see the relationship between sections, highlight them, and move them around as your ideas develop. It is handy to be able to find sections and move them around as needed, not to mention it makes your committee happier, as they can read your document more easily. See Figure 3.8 below as an example of a document map for this section of this book from when we were working on the draft.

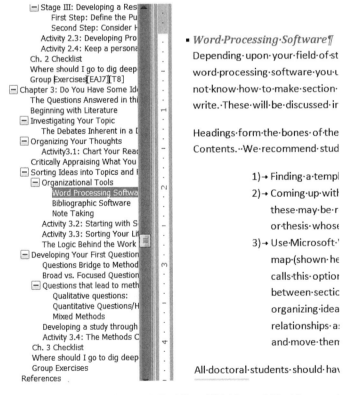

Figure 3.8   Scan of This Chapter in Draft Form With Microsoft Word Document Map/Navigation Pane

4. Upload your work to a server on the Internet. You will sleep at night much better knowing that you are not at risk of losing all your ideas, notes, references, and so forth. There are several ways to do this, depending on whether you are using a PC or Mac environment. Macs connect with iCloud and PCs can use Dropbox. Both have free options and keep your ideas, bibliographic libraries, and writing safe.

Voice Dictation

Voice dictation (voice to text) software has increased remarkably in its ability to capture what you say accurately. As such, it has become an excellent tool for writing and note taking. Many people can carry on a conversation with greater ease than they can write. Therefore, dictating ideas allows you to

> Use a voice recorder or index cards to jot down insights all the time and work those into your findings and personal learning journal (Dr. Ken Long, DoctoralNet, 2012).

quickly capture ideas without getting hung up in the mental challenges that may come while typing. It is important to reread what you write fairly quickly after you dictate it. Otherwise, if the software completely misheard a section, you may come back later to find that you have no idea what you meant at the time. Another advantage of taking notes using your voice is that you talk faster than you write. Some voice capturing can also be done on a mobile phone, later to be transferred to your notes.

As of this writing, what has not yet been perfected is recorded voice to text. When that comes about, many qualitative researchers will rejoice because the need to transcribe to text after interviews still is a cumbersome process.

Tracesea asks: *I'm interested in voice dictation software. What do you recommend? What do I need to consider when selecting this software?*

Answer: Dragon 12 or later. You need to consider that it takes some time to "train" the software to correctly interpret your voice. The more you work with it the more accurately it responds. We recently had a student rave about using the dictation capacity in Evernote, which is the online package we use. She said it did not require training, and that it worked for her voice immediately.

Bibliographic Software

Different parts of the world tend to use different bibliographic software, and new packages develop all the time. You will have to evaluate the different options and see which best fits your needs. One important feature you might consider is an online storage component, so that there is little or no chance that you might lose your library part way through your thesis work.

Bibliographic software is a database that has been set up specifically to organize reference information, including authors, year, title, publisher, and so forth. This software allows you to choose the style manual that you are required to follow, and then it formats the references in this style using the data that you entered.

Bibliographic software can do more than allow you to take notes, format citations, and create references. It can also be a structure through which you can easily sort and arrange your references into the subtopics you need for your literature review. You will have to learn how groups are formed in the particular software you use. Grouping the references into topics and subtopics makes it much easier for you when you come back to write your review of literature, as the authors and their work are already preselected per topic heading.

Single (2009) discusses the use of EndNote "citable notes." This author suggests that prior to starting your bibliographic database you decide what field you will consistently fill in with information.

 Alana says: *I am familiar with EndNote. With it you formalize a topic heading and add to groups in the left-hand column. When you finish filling in the database for a new reference and taking notes, you drag that reference into the group. Any one reference can be in multiple groups, as is appropriate, because some of your authors will speak largely to all the subtopics on which you write.*

Activity 3.2 Starting With Software

The following relates to manually entering your reference data into a bibliographic software program:

1. Open up your bibliographic software and choose the writing style required by your university as the way in which the references will be formatted.

2. To familiarize yourself with how to enter data, open up a new reference and transfer to it all the information from an article you read recently. Use a pull-down menu to indicate the type of reference: book, journal article, electronic article, and so forth. Fill in all the spaces or boxes in the allotted format.

3. Close out of the reference and check that it is formatted correctly when you preview it in the software.

4. Go to your word processing software and follow the path to insert the selected citation. Check the format of both the citation and the full reference from the test case you just completed.

5. Enter a few more references in this manner; include different types of writing so that you are familiar with the materials needed in each case.

The following relates to using the Internet to downloading data directly into a bibliographic software program:

1. Electronic entry requires that you are working out of an electronic database from which the reference will be pulled down into your software. As an example, many students used the Library of Congress to help them format all of their book references correctly. The software will search through the Library of Congress, and using normal database search procedures you

will find the reference you are looking for. The reference software then pulls that reference into your library in your bibliographic software directly onto your computer. Usually the entries are perfectly formatted, but you may wish to check; and you may note that there are some fields filled in which are not necessary for your work.

2. While reading references you have obtained through your university library database, you should be able to follow a series of links to download abstracts and sometimes full text to your bibliographic software. Frequently the library database will fill in all the reference data you need directly onto your library on your computer.

3. PDF files or other forms full text can also be added to your reference library database.

More specifics will need to be reviewed in the software directions. Each type of bibliographic software differs in the particulars used, but they all generally provide the same services. How to use automatic insertion of citations and automatic sorting of references will be covered in a later chapter when you're beginning to write.

Activity 3.3 Sorting Your Literature Into a Table of Authors and Topics

Not all sorting is best done electronically. Some of us need a graphic organizer to manually list our ideas as we learn about and more deeply understand our topics. To that end, this activity can be very useful.

1. Develop a table similar to the one below. List the authors or book titles that you have read on the first left-hand column.

2. Across the top of the table, list topic headings that you believe lead directly to your methodological choices or what you want to study.

3. Sort your readings into topic headings. You will notice that some authors, books, and articles are listed in many of the topic boxes, and others are related to just one.

Author (year)	Main Topic	Subtopic A	Subtopic B	Subtopic C	Methods Used	Findings	Notes

Figure 3.9   Literature Chart for Topics and Authors

You now have a list of how your literature sorts into topics. From this you may decide that you need to find more under a particular column. When it comes time to write up your review of literature, the work in the columns will guide your ideas.

Chapter 3 Checklist

❏ I understand the basic logic of the proposal.

❏ I have begun my literature review.

❏ I have a system for organizing my thoughts.

❏ I have a system for capturing the literature in meaningful ways.

❏ I have some idea of the methods that I will use in my study.

❏ I have beginning research questions.

Where Should I Go to Dig Deeper? Suggested Resources to Consider

Hart, C. (1998). *Doing a literature review: Releasing social science research imagination*. Thousand Oaks, CA: Sage. Chapters 5, 6, and 7 provides an in-depth discussion on how to construct meaning from multiple sources and build an argument as well as how to map and analyze ideas for a review of the literature.

Morgan, G. A., Leech, N. L., Gloeckner, G. W., & Barrett, K. C. (2011). *IBM SPSS for introductory statistics: Use and interpretation*. New York: Routledge Taylor & Francis Group. Appendix B on writing research questions and problems is thorough and easy to follow.

Robson, C. (2002). *Real world research: A resource for social scientists and practitioner-researchers* (2nd ed.). Oxford, UK; Madden, MA: Blackwell Publishers. Pages 54 through 61 do a great job of discussing developing your ideas from the questions, through the classification of the purposes of your study, and linking the two.

Single, P. B. (2009). *Demystifying dissertation writing: A streamlined process from choice of topic to final text* (1st ed.). Sterling, VA: Stylus. Chapter 4 goes into detail into the idea of citable notes and what can or should be included as you read literature.

Thomas, R. M. (2003). *Blending qualitative and quantitative research methods in theses and dissertations*. Thousand Oaks, CA: Corwin Press. Thomas goes in depth into the various considerations of a number of qualitative and quantitative methodologies and their requirements relative to data collection and analysis.

Group Exercises

Group work is particularly effective when it comes to provoking deeper thinking through reading and asking questions. A group of students might consider

- Reading through each other's bibliographic software asking each other about the themes, which authors seemed the most provocative and why
- Questioning how references influence understanding and the development of the methodology for the study
- Sharing bibliographic libraries and discussing how each organizes their literature, what they include in citable notes, and so forth

4

Do You Know How to Develop Your Research Design and Methodology?

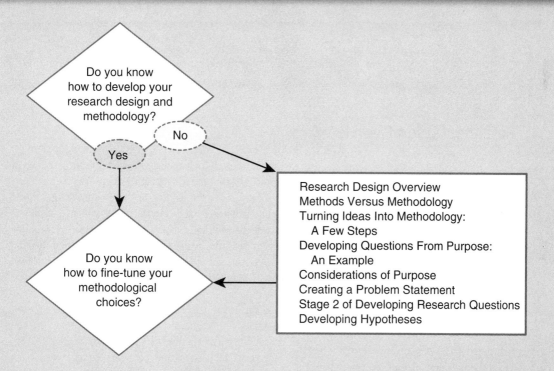

This chapter continues the cyclic development of your research through the discussion of parts of your research design, how they work together, how to determine what can be measured, and how to tie these to the purpose of your study. Since the scope of this book only allows an overview of these topics, further readings are extensively mentioned at the end of the chapter. We also discuss the purpose and use of theory along with the creation of a problem statement in which to root your discussion of the research design. We end this chapter by once again taking a look at your research questions.

The Questions Answered in This Chapter:

1. What is included in a research design?

2. What is the difference between methods and methodology?

3. What basic methods are there?

4. How do I begin to turn my topic ideas into methodology?

5. How can I create a problem statement?

6. How do I determine my purpose?

7. How can I develop research questions/hypothesis so that they can be measured?

Research Design Overview

For most doctoral students, the first attempt at research methodology is one of the scariest parts of the whole process. This book breaks that process down into a series of steps: (a) This chapter overviews the parts that you need to consider and takes you through the first steps in building a logical progression towards methodology, (b) Chapter 5 addresses the theoretical underpinnings, the contextual issues, and issues concerning validity and reliability, and (c) Part II, Chapter 6 is where we guide you through to writing a solid chapter. Nevertheless, the detailed and specific information that you will need to build a completely defensible design is outside of the purview of this book. While we present the overview, readers need to consult with their dissertation/thesis advisor and refer to the lists of outside resources at the end of these chapters.

Within every research proposal there is a chain of logic that needs to be addressed, and you will want to understand how that logic unfolds and the questions you need to answer for each section. Unfortunately, writers on topics of research tend to use slightly different words to describe the necessary components of the design process, and the research elements are described differently, depending on where you are in the world. Whatever specific methodological terms are used however, the following two parts should always be considered:

> Each and every one of these subheadings offers you an excuse for continuing to tease out your ideas in your research journal.

Part I

- Explanation of topic—gives your reader a sense of the issue and your investigation of it.
- Discussion of the context for the study—some specific data solidifies your readers' understanding of where/how the study will be done.

- Links or references to previous research—your use of citations and references demonstrate that you have deep knowledge of your topics, and all blunt statements are backed up by others' thoughts and research as well.
- Theory or point of view—it is clear you have uncovered the theoretical base that serves as a foundation for your ideas and your analysis of your topic.
- Rationale for the importance of the problem—you make a strong case that this subject needs to be studied.

Part II

- The logic of the design—from problem to question, to study participants, to methodology—is outlined succinctly for your reader.
- Questions and/or hypotheses develop naturally out of your discussion and are introduced.
- The methodological model to be employed makes sense and derives naturally from your discussion of context.
- Scope—quantification of number of participants, context for situation, focus of action, records to be accessed, time schedule—is adequate to build a credible study.
- Procedure(s) for data collection is outlined.
- Data analysis techniques are discussed in a way that demonstrates your understanding of the work involved.
- Statistical and narrative analyses are discussed as appropriate.
- Limitations of the study are discussed.
- Contribution or significance to your field is touched upon and is credible in its relationship to the size of your study.
- Your conclusion ties all the pieces together and models the norms of academic writing and is completed in the style proscribed by your university.

The specifics of how to write and what to include in all of these sections will be discussed in this book in Part II as you write your chapters. What is important now is that you begin to develop ideas and a general description of how each will be defined and how they add up to your whole study (Glatthorn & Joyner, 2005).

Within this series of logical steps, it is useful to remember that a practical or theoretical problem needs to be evident. What motivates you? The way you phrase your research problem leads to both your research questions and to your methodology. In a following section, we will help you begin to develop this foundational set of ideas. Some authors will tell you that the research question defines your study, but we believe that the problem and the context underlie that.

The research design can be thought of as having two parts, as mentioned previously. The first part sets up the problem, context, questions, and/or issue to be investigated, and it is like the first two wheels in the diagram in Figure 4.1 below. Your problem drives your questions, which then go on to drive the third wheel, your methodology, and as they develop they change slightly because no part is independent of the others.

As you start to move from your topic to your problem, consider the following questions: Why is your topic interesting to you? What causes the topic? When does it occur? What types of events or

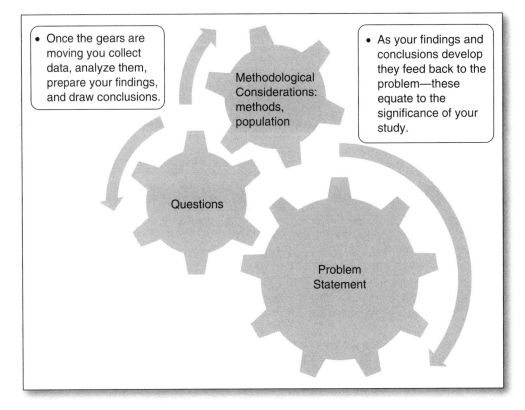

Figure 4.1   Interaction Between Parts of the Research Design

issues are there? How do various groups perceive these circumstances? Does it progress? If so, what stages does it have? What may make it better? What makes it effective, a concern, or dangerous? What relationship(s) does it have with other phenomena? (Glatthorn & Joyner, 2005).

For this section, we will consider the work of Sandy. She started out interested in whether a particular professional development (PD) program embedded in her school district was working.

The difference between a good and a great dissertation amounts to the size and importance of a problem that is being considered. A situation or condition occurs or exists, leading to undesirable consequences or costs. The bigger the problem or the bigger the segment(s) of the population that care about the problem, the greater its significance to your field; this does not mean though that smaller studies are discounted, only that the significance you claim needs to reflect whether and to what extent your context is only at the local level. Pure research improves the knowledge of a problem in the field (small population of those who care) but doesn't come up with a solution. Applied research is when a solution leads to improvement of a life situation and must be described (as a potential) in the problem statement.

If Sandy had chosen to just measure the outcome of this PD program in just one school, then the final significance would have been low. Instead, she decided to investigate whether or not it worked throughout the district. She studied the test scores of cohorts taught by teachers influenced by this design as opposed to those not involved. She captured the vision and support of the entire school district

It may seem self-evident that the purpose of your research is often to investigate or sometimes even to solve a problem, and in many qualitative studies this is true. On the other hand, sometimes the problem is enormous, and your purpose is to investigate a significant but tangential part of that overarching issue. Your purpose carves out the specifics you will address through your questions in your methodology, where sometimes the problem will not be solved by your study but your study will be a component of that solution.

In this manner Sandy could not have investigated whether and to what extent all PD was useful, not even how all PD was used in one school, rather the proper scope to maximize the significance of her study was a major effort across the school district. This was only possible because she caught the attention of the stakeholders and was given access to the data she needed for her study.

Tracesea asks: *In your example, Sandy had to extend her scope to include an entire district rather than one school. Is it possible to do a doctorate research study with a small scope, for example in just one or two schools? How can I know what the proper scope is to make my study significant?*

Answer: To a large extent this is up to your university. We recommend you discuss your plans with your advisor/supervisor/mentor and ask this person, "Is this enough to meet the standard for doctoral work here?" Your ideas will likely be considered by teams of professors and students, and you should quickly catch on to what others are considering and bring your study in line with that.

Methods Versus Methodology

You may be confused about the difference between the methods and methodology. Research makes use of three primary methods or tools for collecting data: quantitative, qualitative, and mixed methods. In general, methodology merges theoretical and contextual considerations with these methods and sorts them out in a variety of ways to best serve the researcher's needs. Specific details regarding the types and choices of methodology is beyond the scope of this book, but excellent resources are listed at the end of the chapter. We may guide general discussions, but you will need to consult many texts that specify subtleties before settling on your final choice.

Quantitative methods break data down into easily manipulated numbers and use statistics to develop an idea about the significance of results. Quantitative data are most appropriate for larger

Figure 4.2 Quantitative methods break data down into numbers and are useful for larger populations and very specific, well-defined variables.

Source: Goodshoot/Goodshoot/Thinkstock

Figure 4.3   Qualitative methods involve working with people to gather data, often in the form of words, and are useful when you want to explore the human experience.

Source: Stockbyte/Stockbyte/thinkstock

populations of people where you need to gather information around a relatively small and specific set of topics or variables. These data collection methods require a great deal of original work, building solid and reliable instrumentation through which you will gather data. Most doctoral programs strongly suggest that you use instruments previously developed, tested, and proved reliable. After data are collected, the mathematical tests can be run through software and take a relatively short time to analyze.

Sandy, from the previous section, decided to statistically analyze district-wide data, comparing the students who had been part of the PD she was studying as opposed to students from teachers who had not been trained in this manner. There had been thousands of data points to be analyzed from these students, and quantitative methods were perfect for her study.

Qualitative methods are most appropriate when your research issues or questions need to probe into the human experience. You may want to find out perceptions, feelings, or delve into historic memory about your topic and have to rely on people sharing as much as they can with you in order for you to understand your issue better. Here you will be working with words and human personalities, which requires you to be able to probe and make the most of the moment, to fully understand the complexities of your topic. Qualitative methods take very little upfront time, as you are working in a live situation with people asking questions and can probe more deeply when they don't give you the answers you are searching for. Quantitative analysis, on the other hand, takes a great deal of time because it requires that you look carefully at the relative weight or amount of data collected on each view of a topic. You will have to weigh its relative importance (as an example, to 25% of the people this was important, while to 75% it was not important), then you read and reread your material to pull out the nuances, and then finally sort then re-sort as you uncover hidden connections.

Had Sandy been forced to limit her study to one school or one cohort of teachers having been trained, she might have focused her study on their perceptions of what they learned and implemented because of the PD design. What she could investigate in this manner that would not have been available in the quantitative study would include the personal reactions of the teachers, stories about the specifics of what worked and what did not, and so forth.

Mixed methods make use of both types of data collection in order to test or further understand sections of the issue being studied. As an example, (a) you can ask people questions and then survey the larger population to see if they agree with the general answers you received from the first batch of participants, or (b) you can survey a large population and then interview key stakeholders to pull out the nuances or complexities of the original data. You know yourself best. Think about what strengths and weaknesses will make the data collection and analysis phase of your research drudgery. Some people do not enjoy the statistical analysis. On the other hand, to others the time it takes to read and reread huge quantities of qualitative data during analysis is daunting. Qualitative data collection and analysis can be fascinating for those who really enjoy people and stories, while quantitative might be more enjoyable for people who like to cut cleanly to the heart of the matter. If you enjoy the complexities of life, qualitative might be for you; if you prefer to see things in a more black and white manner, then quantitative might appeal. Finally, the world is a complex place, we are complex individuals, and mixed methodologies may often shed light where one or the other leave gray areas.

 Tracesea asks: *You mention that using previously developed, tested, reliable instruments is preferable when doing quantitative work, but what if I can't find any instruments to suit my purposes? Or what if I am not happy with the instruments I find? Can I develop my own instruments but base them on others' research?*

Answer: There are two university standards that come into play with this question. The first is your ethical review board, which, in some parts of the world, may simply no longer allow student-built instruments. On the other hand, if you are attending a university that has facilities to teach you the skills involved in building reliable instruments, then likely you can take an extra course on that subject and write, test, and prove the reliability of your own. A lot is involved in the process, and for the sake of expediency, many students choose an alternate route.

Again, if Sandy had not had access to the entire school district she might have been able to run a similar statistical comparison between test scores of students as in her larger quantitative study and triangulated it with interview or focus group data. Qualitative questions could probe the teacher's perceptions of their work and helped to uncover complexities within the educational setting, which the larger study will not show.

Activity 4.1 Table of Methods/Methodologies Begun

In this activity you will begin to sort the articles you read for your review of literature through the creation of a table that is focused on the methods/methodologies used in the research you are reading. Students have found this activity is useful because it creates a body of information through which to discuss ideas about the development of a final dissertation methodology with others. Be sure to consult notes from any research coursework that is applicable to bolster your understanding of these steps.

Start by beginning a 3 by 3 table. The first column is used for the reference of the article, book, or dissertation that you're reading. In the second column, you capture any words or descriptions of the methodology the researcher employed. Finally, the third column delineates the particular methods used.

Think of methodology as the umbrella under which your methods fit. There is no better way to understand research than to diagram the methodological designs of others as you read.

Please note that while this table has three columns of information that it catches, you may choose to expand upon this basic framework and sort your reading in additional ways. Additional columns you may consider would include the following: the research questions being addressed, the variables being researched, a description of the population, the theoretical or epistemological considerations discussed, and so forth. You will also want to keep a bibliographic reference library that discusses each reading in more detail (as discussed in the last chapter).

The following is an example from a student who was studying mentoring as a means of improving overall quality in teachers:

Reference	Methodology	Methods
Finkelstein, L. M., Allen, T. D., & Rhoton, L. A. (2003). An examination of the role of age in mentoring relationships. *Group Organization Management, 28*(2), 249–281.	Mixed methodology	Quantitative surveys backed up with a variety of qualitative: observational data, interviews, and so forth
Godshalk, V. M., & Sosik, J. J. (2000). Does mentor-protégé agreement on mentor leadership behavior influence the quality of a mentoring relationship? *Group Organization Management, 25*(3), 291–317.	First separated paired mentoring teams into three classifications and then surveyed regarding transformational qualities of mentors	Quantitative: multivariate analysis of variance
Dingus, J. E. (2008). "I'm learning the trade": Mentoring networks of black women teachers. *Urban Education, 43*(3), 361–377.	Qualitative comparative case studies examining mentoring networks	Interviews and qualitative surveys

Figure 4.4   Example of Table Resulting From Activity 4.1

Activity 4.2 Check the Logic of Your Methods

The purpose of this exercise is to process the learning developed in Activity 4.1 and transfer it to your own research design.

Procedure

1. Draw a table. In the first column list all your potential research questions.

2. In the second column list the people or documents supplying these data.

3. In the third column list how you will analyze the data derived from the questions in the first column.

4. In the fourth column list the ideas, specifics, and variables that you will measure and/or derive new information about through your proposed investigation. The following example comes from a student who wants to study corporate responsibility in small business settings.

List your proposed research questions	What populations of people are included in these data? Do you have access to them or archival data derived from them?	Are these data qualitative or quantitative in nature? How will these data be analyzed?	List the various topics or variables you are trying to measure and the methodological implications for each.
For example— to what extent do small businesses use corporate responsibility measures?	Small business owners would form the main population, with a possibility to ask for access to archival data from local small business associations.	Likely a survey to query business activities and overall knowledge of CRM. Data to be analyzed with simple statistics. Focus groups or Interviews/qualitative data to be open and selectively coded. If records were accessed, they might be either qualitative or quantitative.	Variables include practices in the following five areas: workplace, environment, marketplace, community, and company values. Methodology will probably be a survey with a random sample followed up by visits to the business site for observation.

Figure 4.5   Checking the Logic of Your Methods

Turning Ideas Into Methodology: A Few Steps

As shown in Figure 4.6 below, a research framework consists of many parts, each dependent on the logic of the sections before it. One section not in alignment logically with the others and the whole research design wobbles. The issue, problem, or set of questions starts the process, but how you think about the world (your epistemology) determines how you are inclined to investigate those issues, and likewise, your methodology must be in alignment with it. The ways in which you collect and analyze data develop out of the methodological considerations and must, at the end, address the issue, problem, and questions you set out at the beginning (Bryant, 2004).

Tracesea asks: *You mention that my epistemology is my worldview and tends to color how I am inclined to study my issues. Does this mean that if numbers and math aren't my strong point, then I shouldn't do quantitative research? Or, if I'm not exactly a "people person," then I shouldn't do a qualitative study? How much should my own perceived strengths affect my choice of methods?*

Answer: This is a really good question and there are two parts to it. First, epistemology is more concerned with your view of the world of what constitutes knowledge and how it is built. Outside of the scope of this book, we recommend you look it up on the web and engage in conversations with your supervisor about its place in your work.

The second part of your question though has to do with two things: (a) your natural tendencies and the role they play in your decisions and (b) what you consider "valid" information. Don't neglect a qualitative study if you are shy, but on the other hand if numbers and statistics overwhelm you, we would not recommend a quantitative study without professional assistance. If you discount the opinions of others, a qualitative study may not be meaningful for you.

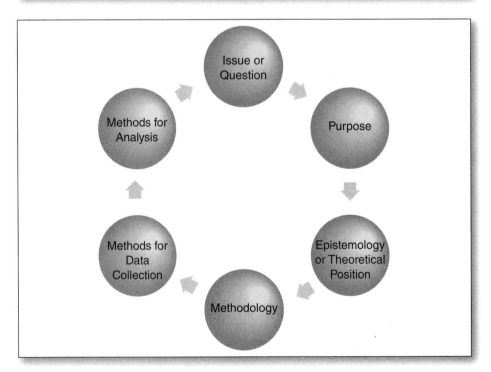

Figure 4.6   The Logical Cycle of Methodological Design

The logical development from topic idea to research design is not straightforward. To illustrate how many issues might come up in this section, let us consider an example from a student. Her first step was to organize her design ideas in the chart below. In Figure 4.7 below, she chose to look at her purpose, hypothesis, sample population, how she would collect data (instrumentation), and procedures. Notice that she compared her ideas to a model dissertation by someone else—this is smart because it gives her (and us) some points of comparison.

Purpose	Hypothesis	Sample Population	Instrumentation	Procedure
To research in-school suspension programs in schools and whether they are meeting the needs of students	The student academic progress slows or is halted by these programs.	Students, parents, instructors, and administrators	Survey and interviews	Survey everyone, comparing the frequencies of replies across the four subpopulations. Then interview key stakeholders about their perception of the differences in viewpoint between the groups.
To explore the social and personal characteristics of students who are referred to in-school suspension programs	Students are often sent to disciplinary action for relatively small or harmless infractions, such as tardiness or small incidents of acting up in school (Morris & Skiba, 2001).	78% of the total student population who had been referred to in-school suspension agreed to be in the study. N = 85: 78% male, 22% female.	Rating scale used to measure behavioral change. Sample populations from administrators, teachers, and students. Archival data—student referral forms	Students completed surveys when they first arrived in in-school suspension and a follow-up at end of school year with access to student records for confirmation.

Figure 4.7   Research Design Work

Now to start to fill in the research framework we see.

Developing Questions From Purpose: An Example

This student's topic is in-school suspension programs, and her preliminary data, as stated in her problem statement, suggest that assigning students who are tardy or misbehave to a room separate from their peers does not help them advance academically. From that she derives the purpose of her

Figure 4.8 If you plan to involve youth in your study be aware that there will be special considerations, such as parental permissions as well as issues of relationship, power, and influence.

Source: Jupiterimages/Comstock/Thinkstock

study: to research in-school suspension as compared to other alternative models as to how they meet the needs of students.

Her first question was, "Do in-school suspension programs meet the needs of students from elementary through 8th grades?" *Needs* from whose point of view? Teachers and students may have differing opinions on what the students need. A secondary question is whether other alternative models might work better. Again, point of view is important. Who is the stakeholder, and is she measuring her perception of what is true now against her guess as to what might work better?

What methods of inquiry could she use to answer these questions? If need was defined as academic advancement, then the first question about "meeting needs," might be addressed through archival school records—correlating the scores of students who had been assigned in-school suspension and their academic progress with students who had not been assigned this suspension. You can probably see right away that this is likely to be too complex an issue for that methodology. Students who have in-school suspensions may have an array of complex issues with school, any one of which might poorly impact their grade.

She could interview students and teachers and uncover a comparison between their feelings and opinions on in-school suspension and its efficacy as an educational policy. This same interview could probe into their ideas and feeling on other models as well, but those answers would only be conjecture if the participants had not experienced their effects directly. If her purpose is to investigate whether in-school suspension or other alternative models better meet the needs of students then, so far, she is not asking questions that lead to a methodology that will get her there.

Who is her population? It could be students in Grades 4 through 8, teachers, and/or parents. Is it all students or just those who have experienced in-school suspension (ISS)? Since her topic will have to pass an ethical review, she will find that students are protected because of their youth, and in order to question them she will need parental permission and student assent. In many universities, she might be discouraged from asking questions of students in her own school because it might produce issues of unequal influence where students would give her the answer they believe she wants to hear. In this example, she wants to ask everyone in the equation what they think of this policy as compared to other ideas. She will need to develop a means of questioning administrators, teachers, parents, and the instructors in the suspension classrooms.

Tracesea asks: *In your example, you talk about how the relationship of the research to the subject is important. You mention the issue of unequal influence where subjects might be giving the researcher the answers they think this person wants to hear. In that same example, couldn't a relationship also lead subjects to be more open and honest with a researcher who they trust? How do I decide if my relationship will be an asset or a detriment to my study?*

Answer: This is worthy of a discussion with your advisor/supervisor or mentor as it varies around the world. In some locations, an ethical review board will not allow you to conduct a study with certain types of relationships—for example, if you manage any of the subjects at work. A mediating factor may be both your gender and your relationship, as with one of our clients, a woman, conducting health research in Sudan. A stranger or a man could not have asked these women the questions she included in her interview.

She wants to survey everyone (meaning she will have to design the survey) as well as conduct phone and in-person interviews. This implies a mixed methodological study with the survey instrument as quantitative evidence triangulated against what she learns through interviews. She also could consider other qualitative methodologies: case study, phenomenology, narrative, or grounded. She does not yet know enough about research to know how or why she will put these together. Figure 4.9 is the resulting logic, with the darker circles representing holes that she still needs to fill.

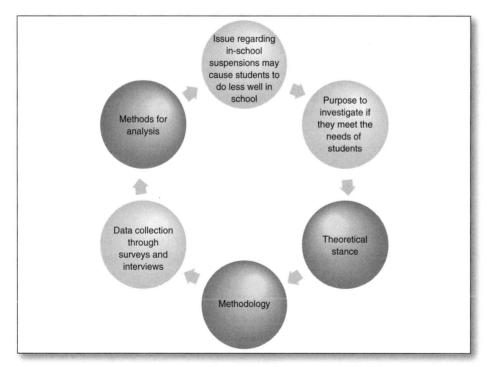

Figure 4.9   Student's Research Framework Partially Complete

We'll come back to this example as these topics develop.

Considerations of Purpose

What is the purpose of your research? A group of professors brainstormed research purposes, and the following list is the result:

- Understand
- Evaluate—over time or at a particular moment
- Investigate—current or archival
- Design new type of system
- Explain something not yet understood
- Influence policy
- Develop new approaches
- Deepen understanding of the minute
- Process investigation
- Impact analysis using statistical parameters (E. A. James, Sanchez-Patino, & Banerji, 2013)

There are both personal and professional purposes to your research, and perhaps they overlap. Consider what it means to everyone involved. To yourself it will be the culmination of your degree; it also may be the catapult you need to take you to the next level in your career; therefore, it must be interesting to others. Who are the people who control your next career move? What are the "hot" topics from their point of view? What do your stakeholders want and need to know?

Considering what others purposes might be critical to you receiving the permissions you need. We recently had a student who, right as he was defending his proposal, learned that he would not have access to the people he needed; permission had not been granted by the company. Quickly he scrambled to find a similar population, but when he did, he found out that these managers had very different concerns. This change led to a revision (for the better as it turned out) in his research design. You can see that your purpose must align with the desires of the stakeholders from whom you will need permission to do your study.

Purpose is your reason for going forward with (a) this particular research design and (b) in this particular context, so the way you state the purpose must match up with those concerns. It is also the reason that the participants you want to encourage to give you data may feel propelled to do so.

> The precise words you use to describe your problem are not static. As you read and critically appraise the work of other researchers, be sure to go back and revisit the way you state your problem. It should mature over the course of your thesis writing.

Purpose must also align with the methods—for instance, if you want to use qualitative methods, then likely your purpose will be to investigate some aspect of human experience in a somewhat subjective manner. In that same example, it would be unlikely that your context would be international, unless you were drawing on personal relationships to gather your data or had travel plans. If your purpose was to make people's lives easier, it is more likely that others will donate the time it takes to fill out your questionnaire or to answer your questions. If your purpose is to study a specific aspect of something, it is likely that only those who are also engaged with that topic on the same level will care enough to respond.

Finally, the statement of purpose as it will be written in your document needs to include two segments, according to Locke: "Why you want to do the study and what you intend to accomplish" (as cited by Creswell, 2009, p. 111). The purpose is a short section, as you will see in Chapter 6, and it should not be encumbered with the problem or the issue that lead to your choosing this topic (Creswell, 2009).

Creating a Problem Statement

So what is the problem statement, or "Statement of the Problem?" This section may be the one most important part of building a defensible research proposal, but it may feel to you as though you are entering a section as convoluted as the picture on this page. Your problem statement should merge the data from the context of your study together with the literature and turn out convincing reasons that your study is important. From a solid problem statement, the development of your purpose, your significance, and the ability to ensure stakeholder support all evolve. Functionally, to your reader it is a piece of writing that serves as a transition point in the logic between your literature review and your methodology. For you as the researcher, it is the underlying issue, as it has evolved in the context of your study that drives the reason for your research. Everything you think and write needs to ground here. Your problem statement succinctly sets up your particular study.

Figure 4.10 Molding your research design to address a specific problem will often make your data collection and analysis easier.

Source: ©iStockphoto.com/CurvaBezier

Not all authors on research design include a specific statement of the problem in their design. We have found though, that the students who have not considered these questions or molded their design to address a specific problem frequently find that finishing their data collection and analysis is harder. You may derive answers to questions, but if those questions are not based upon a problem to which they are related, then the final document can have a decided "so what?" factor. In essence, working your ideas until they also focus directly on a measurable problem gives your work uncontestable meaning and value.

Template for a Problem Statement

This situation in/within ____ (societal organization/institution/ policy, etc.) has created a problem____ (describe it in a few words). In ____(name the context of your study), this problem plays out and creates this situation ____(be specific and give data to quantify the issue). While it is being addressed in this manner ____(describe current activities), however, there is need for this study to ____(discuss purpose of study generally). This problem impacts ____ (name population) because ____ (describe impact). Literature discusses the following as being likely to impact the issue ____(describe variables and cite references). This study contributes to the body of knowledge needed to address this problem by answering the following questions ____(the research questions) (Creswell, 2012; Roberts, 2004).

Here is one example of how an award-winning dissertation successfully included all this information using a similar and equally concise format. We return to this topic as you write out your methodology in Part II.

> The wide variety of information in databases for biological model organisms has great potential utility for biomedical researchers, but only if it is of high quality. Human-curated annotations made in model organism databases are viewed as important links between an organism's underlying genomic data and the experimental literature. Gene Ontology (GO) annotations in particular are expected to provide significant value in reducing disciplinary fragmentation, and facilitating cross-organism information integration. As an organism-independent set of controlled vocabularies, scientists could use GO to cut across disciplinary boundaries to discover information relevant to their specialty. However, a common question associated with manually-curated knowledge bases (such as GO, model organism databases (MODs), and even PubMed/MEDLINE) is to what degree variation in human curators' annotations affects the overall quality of information in the resource. Information quality is a complex concept, with many facets that have interdependencies. While annotation quality is of great importance to the genomics community, very little is known about the types and amounts of GO annotation variation in MODs. Dolan et al. (2005) state that: "Since differences in application of annotation standards would dilute the effectiveness of comparative analysis, methods for assessing annotation consistency are essential. The development of methodologies that are broadly applicable for the assessment of GO annotation consistency is an important issue for the comparative genomics community. (i136; as cited by MacMullen, 2007, p. 1)

Specificity is important here, as is brevity. A problem statement should seldom be more than a half a page long. Specifically you want to develop a problem statement that

- Demonstrates the problem's importance with a compelling opening statement
- Explains the problem in the perspective of the larger field of study
- Shows how the problem generalizes to or across other issues/fields
- Limits the problem through its focus in/on your study
- Is brief
- Gives the reader a perspective on the whole study being proposed
- Sets the time frame and scope of the project (Krathwohl & Smith, 2005, p. 49)

> Remember that in the initial stages everything changes. Do not become too attached to any one question until you can be positive that it clearly leads to your methodology. These relationships will become clear in the next chapter.

Once you have completed a first draft of your problem statement, you can go back and ask what questions need to be answered? Of whom? What is the best way to ask them? These are addressed by the scope (population) and methodological choices you make, which we will discuss in Chapter 5.

Checklist for Problem Statement Sections

Note: Because of the brevity required in a problem statement, all of the following are given only one to two sentences. Your problem statement includes

- ✓ A smooth introduction that synthesizes past research
- ✓ A clear explanation of the local problem, which can be addressed through this research
- ✓ Evidence or data on which that problem is founded
- ✓ A clear explanation of the goals of the research; these may be stated as purpose and focus for the study
- ✓ The literature of the field making it evident that your study either builds upon or has the potential to derive new understanding in the field
- ✓ A clear explanation of the theoretical foundation is included
- ✓ Research questions or hypotheses around which the study revolves
- ✓ Objectives for the study or contributions to your field
- ✓ Potentially a statement for the implications for positive social change

Tracesea asks: *I'm having a hard time keeping my problem statement brief, there's just so much to talk about. What do you suggest to help me make it more concise?*

Answer: Have you ever noticed that the more expert you get in something the fewer words you use? There is no need to repeat in your problem statement any argument that has been discussed in other areas within your writing, a mention of it will do. As you consider your writing, remember that to be convincing your statements need to be only the central components of your arguments. One well-known professor at Columbia used to say that editing should take out half of the words, so be ruthless in your own behalf.

Stage 2 of Developing Research Questions

In your first stage of developing your research questions, you likely were focused on the topic of your study; in the second stage, you need to bring the wording into alignment with the other issues you have considered in this chapter. Let us return to the student who wanted to corporate responsibility measures (CRM) in small business environments. In the first stage of question development, this student was questioning the advantages and disadvantages of some of the CRM practices from the European Union (EU) on larger corporate entities. The research questions that drive his design are, To what extent do small to medium [-sized] businesses in the United States use CRM practices? Are there links between CRM, leadership, and profitability?

Figure 4.11 Make sure your instruments adequately address your research questions.

Source: ©iStockphoto.com/alexskopje

During the work in this chapter he (a) decided that his methodology needed to be comparisons of interview data between owners of small businesses across various sectors (a qualitative study), (b) the purpose of which was to uncover linkages between the values held by leadership and their sense of corporate responsibility, because (c) the stakeholders (small business administration executives who were giving him access to their databases) were concerned with whether and to what extent these practices continued in hard economic times. His questions then needed to lead towards business outcomes, meeting the purposes that were important to his stakeholders. As the questions developed, he was able to tie multiple considerations into how he collected data, using the EU survey as a starting place and designing a mixed methodological study.

The next step for this student and for you as you craft your research design is to revisit each of the research questions to ensure that you have an instrument (in quantitative designs) or interview protocols designed if your methodology is ethnographic, grounded theory, phenomenological, narrative, or a case study.

Developing Hypotheses

As you have continued to read the literature on your topic, do you believe that you now understand the dynamics that control the situation you want to study? Do you, in fact, believe that you know the answer to the questions you originally thought you wanted to ask? If that is the case, and if the population of people who would have knowledge of or opinions about the truth of those suppositions is large enough (say about 50 or more), then you might consider employing quantitative methods and testing your hypothesis.

While we will give you resources in the next few sections that will help you dig deeper into this possibility, in general, a hypothesis proposes that you understand a particular phenomenon. The corresponding null hypothesis says that you are wrong and that there is no evidence or correlation to support what you thought was true. You then set up a quantitative instrument (or find one that already queries similar issues) and statistical analysis of your data will either prove or disprove the null hypothesis. If it is disproved, then you can run further statistical tests as you probe your data for deeper understanding.

Chapter 4 Checklist

❑ I understand the basics of research design.

❑ I understand the difference between methodology and methods.

❑ I understand the different methods available to me.

❏ I have a problem statement.

❏ I have a purpose.

❏ I have developed some preliminary research questions that I believe are measurable.

❏ I have developed a hypothesis to test if my research is quantitative in nature.

Where Should I Go to Dig Deeper? Suggested Resources to Consider

Creswell, J. W. (2002). *Educational research: Planning, conducting, and evaluating quantitative and qualitative research*. London: Pearson Education. Pages 75 through 80 go in-depth and with great detail into the audience identification, explanation of deficiency of evidence, guidelines, justification for and writing strategies of problem statements.

Creswell, J. W. (2009). *Research design: Qualitative, quantitative, and mixed methods approaches* (3rd ed.). Thousand Oaks, CA: Sage. Pages 112 though 126 give several examples and a detailed discussion of purpose statements specifically targeted to a number of particular methodological formats.

Herr, K., & Anderson, G. L. (2005). *The action research dissertation: A guide for students and faculty*. Thousand Oaks, CA: Sage. The only book to date that considers constraints of action research for dissertations and thesis development.

Krathwohl, D. R., & Smith, N. L. (2005). *How to prepare a dissertation proposal: Suggestions for students in education and the social and behavioral sciences* (1st ed.). Syracuse, NY: Syracuse University Press. Part 2, pages 45 through 118 offer another in-depth look at the logics behind these same methodological design considerations.

Maxwell, J. A. (2005). *Qualitative research design: An interactive approach* (2nd ed.). Thousand Oaks, CA: Sage. Gives a good overview of various types of qualitative research methodologies.

Maxwell, J. A. (2012). *A realist approach for qualitative research*. Thousand Oaks, CA: Sage. Two excellent resources by one of the acknowledged great authors on qualitative research design.

Piantanida, M., & Garman, N. B. (1999). *The qualitative dissertation: A guide for students and faculty*. Thousand Oaks, CA: Corwin Press. Chapters 3, 4, and 5 cover similar design considerations from other angles and with more depth. This is an excellent secondary resource for consideration.

Robson, C. (2002). *Real world research: A resource for social scientists and practitioner-researchers* (2nd ed.). Oxford, UK: Blackwell Publishers. Pages 79 through 220 discuss methodological-design issues for social sciences and practical research in detail. General designs, fixed designs, flexible designs, and those for a particular purpose are all covered.

Thomas, R. M. (2003). *Blending qualitative and quantitative research methods in theses and dissertations*. Thousand Oaks, CA: Corwin Press. Pages 100 through 145 outline several specific types of studies targeted to fulfill a variety of social science issues. Included are evaluating teaching, political marketing, ESL curriculum, juvenile delinquents lifestyles, cheating, conducting a public opinion poll, and so forth.

Weiss, C. H. (1998). *Evaluation: Methods for studying programs and policies* (2nd ed.). Upper Saddle River, NJ: Prentice Hall. Outlines the specific research methodology appropriate to study a program or a policy that has already been implemented and is ready for review.

Group Exercises

Research design by its nature is an iterative set of steps: Consider problems, which lead to potential solutions, which then get shot down as others bring up issues you can't get around—then you go back to see what else will lead you to where you want to go. Because of its iterative and convoluted nature, it is wonderful to work in a group as the human dynamic takes the pressure off. An ongoing group exercise that we use at the DoctoralNet community site is to practice presentations of your research design with each other.

Procedure

1. Group designates who will be the speaker, the timekeeper, and the person in charge of leading the debate. Members also discuss how much time is to be allotted to the presentation (full proposals can go 15–20 minutes but generally forcing topics to be 10–15 minutes works best).

2. The presenter puts together a discussion of their research using presentation software. Planning for one minute per screen, the presenter goes through their research design, while the timekeeper helps them know when they have 7, 5, and 3 minutes left to wrap up. Part of the learning is keeping to the time, and many have difficulty with this on their first round. Note that you can reference the diagram in Activity 3.4 for the diagram of all the parts that should be included in the discussion.

3. The person in charge of leading the debate asks for positive comments first—what is this person doing well? What was intriguing? How does the group think this will be significant?

4. Then the group moves to what needs to be challenged and improved. Members are asked to respond to all the appropriate criticisms that they have heard from classmates.

This is a prewriting, design stage, so members should not expect to witness tight or necessarily solid research designs. It is helpful, however, to continue to work together on the redefinition of each part, to continue to ask questions, and so forth as everyone improves in their understanding through a dynamic process. If possible, gather questions from the group at the end of each section and see if you can develop a relationship with a faculty member to get these answered.

5

Do You Understand How to Fine-Tune Your Methodological Choices?

Moving From Basics to Getting Ready to Write

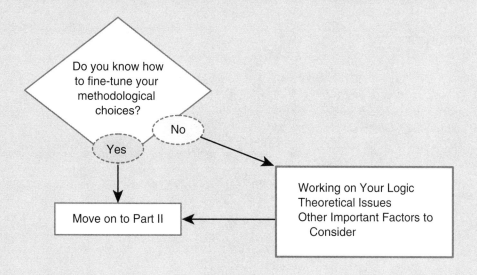

This chapter continues our discussion of the various parts of a research design by centering first on the underpinning logic that must flow between the parts. Theoretical issues are covered with further reading suggested at the end of the chapter. Finally, other important factors in your design are gone over: size and scope, local context, validity and reliability. By the end of this chapter and your subsequent exploration into further resources, you will have gone over the basic design considerations and, once you get a general approval on your ideas from your advisor, you will be ready to begin writing.

The Questions Answered in This Chapter:

1. I have a basic methodology—what else is needed?

2. Do I have the full logic I need to start writing?

3. What is the purpose and use of theory as I design my research?

4. How is local context important?

5. How are population, size, and scope important?

6. What are validity and reliability?

7. Why should I write my methodology chapter first?

Working on Your Logic

"I worked on my dissertation thesis for three years before I realized it was not completely an exercise in research, it is every bit as much an exercise in how to speak to other professionals—the logic is key." Dr. J. L. Newcom, DoctoralNet, 2012.

You may or may not find research logic makes sense to you; much has to do with how similar it may be to the logic of your professional field. As an example, we find that those who are trained in project development or curricular design often find the logic of research difficult. They are used to building things not measuring things. Don't be concerned if you find yourself feeling as though you do not yet understand the logic behind the work you are being asked to do, or if your grasp of this logic slips away at times. Just yesterday I was speaking with a woman who had gone on in this manner for a year, and now with only nine months to go, she was panicked because she still did not feel like she knew what she was doing. Research logic requires scaffolding these ideas and working and reworking your full research design as new elements are added.

Depending on the support you have at the university level, if your university is one that follows the doctoral program more similar to the United Kingdom (see the introduction for an explanation), then you may have already collected data and some but not all of these decisions are moot. Most research is written up so that all the components in Figure 5.1 (below) are listed and relate to each other as they do here. Many students find this system a very useful tool as they start to design their research.

In Activity 5.1 below, you will work through the diagram. As you build the components in order, you begin to see that the topics necessary for your review of literature relate in a one-to-one correspondence to the specifics discussed in Numbers 1, 2, and 3. In simple terms, your review of literature now needs to be cut down from a general overview of your topic and all that is known about it to just what your reader needs to know in order to understand your ideas and how you will proceed with your study.

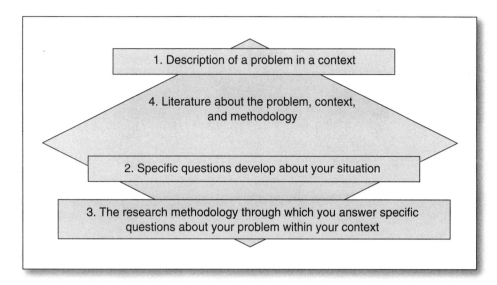

Figure 5.1   Basic Research Logic

As discussed in previous chapters, it all starts with the problem statement and continues as you develop a body of literature that addresses all aspects of that problem in your context. You follow these up with your research questions that tie the literature to the problem in your context.

Most students who have difficulty defending their research find that the problems arise because one or more elements in this logic are missing or are not in agreement with each other. For instance, you may set out wanting to research a particular topic and reading literature about that topic early on in your doctoral work, before you have been exposed to more in-depth ideas. As time goes on, you refine and re-refine your research questions and your methodology, but seldom do you want to go back and ask whether or not your literature continues to support your research model. Elements shift as your research progresses. Even a small change can cause the logic to topple, making Activity 5.1 a simple test to see if your work remains on track as your research evolves.

This logic is bolstered and supported by other aspects of research logic:

- A theoretical base that forms the conceptual foundation on which your design rests
- Specifics of the context in which you will work to help determine the population, size, and scope of your study
- Issues of validity and reliability that you build into your research design to help it measure just what you have in mind

If and when all the aspects of the design lead easily one to another, your efforts should bring credible results from which you will be able to draw the conclusions you need to address the problem you set. Any wobble in logic and the stretch from design to credible results becomes much more difficult. Figure 5.2 below illustrates this circle.

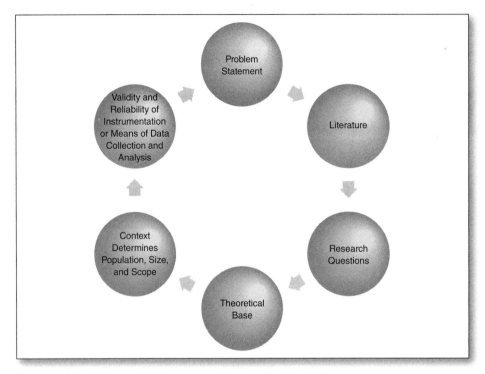

Figure 5.2   Simplified research logic as you write it—see also Figure 3.7.

Consider this example: First, the problem you are studying relates to transition of leadership in your organization. Second, your literature must include all that is known about the transition of leadership, hopefully in a context similar to yours. That literature will discuss several variables or factors that impinge upon success. In this example, those factors might point out that successful transition is more likely to happen if middle-level managers are empowered to go on about their work even when the top executives are not in place. This would evolve to the third component, a question about the extent to which the mid-level managers in your organization felt they were empowered in that way. Fourth, you decide your research question then could be answered by a survey, interviews, or focus groups addressing how much your individual circumstance agreed with previous research (Creswell, 2009; Garson, 2002; Kalmbach, Phillips, & Carr, 2009; Pease, 2009; Thomas, 2003).

Other students may approach the same issue slightly differently, developing their theoretical ideas as they research the literature, and from that foundation, developing their questions. The order is not specific, as diverse minds will develop concepts in different ways. This is one of the reasons that doctoral work is an art form rather than a prescription. The goal, however, remains the same: to build a logic that includes all the pieces in harmony and can be stated in such a way that others can easily follow it. Once these four components (problem, literature, research questions, and methodology) are in sync and seem to flow logically, then if you build upon a theoretical base that strengthens them and use valid and reliable tools, you will have a design that works. The next sections will discuss these additional components.

Activity 5.1 Tracking Your Logic

Working alone may be adequate for this exercise, but we have found that pairs or small groups work best, as frequently others see what we do not. This exercise builds on the relationships discussed in Figure 5.1 Basic Research Logic (Note: Appendix C is a student example of this activity).

Procedure

1. Write out the problem your research will address, then answer each of the following questions about the way you have expressed it.

    - Is the problem easily described in a sentence or two?
    - Is the specific context for your study mentioned in your problem statement?
    - Can you gather your answers from a specific set of people?
    - Do you have easy access to those people?

2. What questions do you want to ask?

    - Is there a clear relationship between the problem statement and your questions/hypothesis?
    - Do they address the problem from the same angle?
    - Do your questions address the heart of the problem?
    - Will you be able to find the answers?

3. How will you ask your questions and to whom? How will you analyze your answers?

    Are you comfortable that the analysis will give you the answers you need?

4. Now look at the relationship between Questions 1, 2, and 3.

    - Will the questions in 2 asked of the people and under the circumstances in 3 build a convincing argument to others?
    - Will this plan lead you to be an acknowledged expert on this topic?

5. What are the topics that are needed in your review of literature?

    - Do you cover the information needed to understand the context of the problem?
    - Do you discuss what others have researched around that problem?
    - Does your literature establish your questions as important?
    - Are your questions and your measurements discussed in your literature?
    - Does your literature show other researchers using similar methodology?
    - Do you discuss your methodological choices?

    Does each and every part of your literature link directly to something discussed in Questions 1, 2, and 3?

Figure 5.3   Reading your ideas out loud to others can help you uncover issues that you might not find when proofreading by yourself.

Source: Jupiterimages/Comstock/Thinkstock

Activity 5.2 Revising Your Logic

It is useful to double-check your work by reading your ideas out loud to others. When words are spoken in a group, it is possible to hear issues with language that might otherwise be overlooked.

Procedure

1. Discuss your 5.1 exercises within a small group.

2. Take turns reading your answers to Questions 1 through 5 out loud to each other.

3. Help each other wordsmith as necessary until all sentences are clean and precise.

Tracesea asks: *I want to do these activities in a group as you suggest. How do I find a group to work with? Is it important that the others in the group are doing similar research or in a similar field?*

Answer: You have several options, so first decide whether and to what extent you want your group members to be working under exactly the same constraints as you. If you do want a local group working under the same conditions as yourself then go to your supervisor or even the administrative offices of your university and suggest it. You may also consider notices in your university paper or up in your student area. It could be as simple as finding a room and posting a meeting time. On the other hand, if you would prefer being more anonymous and might enjoy an international group, DoctoralNet.com runs online groups for both people in the design and writing phases of the work. No matter where you work, holding group members accountable to come back with a certain amount done before the next meeting is key.

Theoretical Issues

Whether and to what extent a doctoral student understands theory and the purpose of a theoretical base when writing his dissertation/thesis may be largely dependent on the research training he has prior to the time they begin this process. How strong a theoretical underpinning needs to be is also variable, dependent on the research level of the university and the tastes of any particular advisor. This book lightly covers issues to consider and then gives additional readings that may be important for students who find their basic knowledge does not meet their needs.

Developing a Theoretical Base

When bouncing around dissertation ideas, doctoral students frequently come up with variations on a question, such as "How can my field make the changes that we need in order to succeed?" Unfortunately a "how can" question is rarely defensible as research; therefore, in order to move it into the research framework, you need to refocus and reframe your question. Any student on the road to finish their doctorate early will want to quickly develop defensible research methodology for their proposal. This section discusses how to develop your dissertation methodology by asking you to consider where your initial research topic ideas naturally lead your thinking? Are you making the most of the theories on which you are basing your work? The intent is to help you easily defend your proposal for your dissertation research (Roberts, 2004).

Figure 5.4   A theoretical base can help ensure your work will be defensible.

Source: ©iStockphoto.com/Osuleo

   The word theory has many uses across topics, and while we describe a theoretical base, other authors will discuss a conceptual framework. Consider these ideas as cousins to each other, and your task is to find those that you can work most easily from. This may make it hard on the doctoral student who is really just looking for some foundation on which to build the rest of his/her work. Some theories used by behavioral, social, and educational theorists, such as Gardner's theory of multiple intelligences, may not take us down a nice logical path to our epistemology and methodology like other theories that specifically deal with issues of measurement—for instance empiricism or positivism. A first question you may want to ask when investigating theories is, what structure the adoption of these ideas would influence, the practice in the field or measurement of results? Or both?

   Basic theoretical discussions usually include empiricism, positivism, postmodernism, critical theory, pragmatism, constructivism, and so forth, each of which has impact on research measurement in that they either discuss a belief about what, how, or to what effect things are measured (Creswell, 2009; Garson, 2002; Kalmbach, Phillips, & Carr, 2009; Pease, 2009; Thomas, 2003). Similar in some ways to constructivism, model-dependent reality fits the modern scientific discussions that include alternate dimensions or the variety of conceptual views being explored by math and science in our complex adaptive world (Hawking & Mlodinow, 2010).

Alana says: *Your theoretical stance is similar to the way the context works in a photograph. Your viewer might not pay that much attention to the background in a picture, but if something is "off" between the person and the foreground, she will notice. In a similar fashion, your theoretical stance may not seem important when you just want to get on with completing your research, but if it is off from your methodology, your reader will notice. As an example, I am a pragmatist. I use research as a means to understand and develop better outcomes. It would be a stretch for me to use a large-scale data set and analyze the elements statistically—there would just not be enough tie to the theoretical reasons I love research.*

Activity 5.3 Reflecting on Theoretical Implications

This is a reflective exercise aimed at helping you uncover the implications of the theories you think may be important to the conceptual framework of your study.

Procedure

Take out a piece of paper and put on the top of it a few theories that you are considering. Write the author's name and their focus, what the meaning of the theory is to you, what qualities you believe it instills, and any beliefs or ideas about the world that underpin it. Then answer the following questions:

1. Do you personally believe that you can know "truth" absolutely and without question? Is there a truth that is true under all circumstances? If so, how will you know it, what attributes will you search for? What philosophical theorists is this in line with? Is your belief about the nature of truth in line with the theories you have listed?

2. From this sense of your ability to know truth you can extrapolate whether and to what extent this knowledge comes from internal subjective experience or external, more objective experience. In other words, do you know that things are true or false because you have a certain feeling inside yourself that tells you? Or do you know something is true because of outside objective standards? Again, which theories and theorists are in line with your understanding of life?

3. What ethical issues come into play for you? For instance, pragmatism versus objectivism are ethical stances. Pragmatism believes that it is better to do studies that will have direct outcome on the improvement of practices. Objectivism believes that it is better to do pure science, standing at a distance and observing objectively. What do you believe and which of the theories you are considering is in closest alignment with your ethics? If you are in social science and studying a group, is it ethical to study a community without giving them power over what data are collected and how findings are reported? What else do you believe about how participants in a study should be treated? Are there other issues that help you position yourself along ethical dimensions?

4. Where do all these questions lead you when you consider which methodological choices make sense? Do any of the theories you are considering have methodological implications that are in agreement or disagreement with your ideas? As an example, an empiricist believes things can be finitely measured, which is not a great conceptual background for a qualitative study.

5. Would you consider yourself a constructivist? Do you believe that a new understanding of truth evolves with experience and new data? What effects does this have on methodological choices you may be making?

6. Is the essence of your work measurement of something that is true now? Perhaps you want to use this study to influence the future? Do you want to develop new theory out of current circumstances? Does your theoretical position support your desire?

Let's start by considering four main research theories: empiricism, pragmatism, constructivism, and grounded theory. There are many others; however, these three are instructive for our purposes. Empiricism basically says that the world can be measured, and it usually translates into a quantitative design. Quantitative methodology easily translates into numbers and graphs. Pragmatism, on the other hand, suggests that research should be practical and usually translates to qualitative methodology because qualitative methods help us understand how human beings perceive the issue we study from their point of view. Pragmatism is often a foundation for action research, as its focus on the practical lends itself to a study that wants to develop new solutions to a problem. Constructivism tells us that the world is somewhat relative, and that means that outcomes are derived from a series of events through which we construct meaning. You may consider mixed methodology in this case, because it allows the best of both the quantitative and qualitative world. These are postulated as examples only and are not meant to suggest that these methods only go with these theoretical bases or that these theoretical ideas translate to only one type of methodology. Finally, grounded theory builds new theoretical understanding of events and their consequence to people through the way in which you work with qualitative data derived from the populations you are studying (Creswell, 2009; Garson, 2002; James & Gunn, 2000; Pease, 2009; Thomas, 2003).

Alana says: *I graduated with my EdD from Teachers College, Columbia University. My program was based upon and the school has a historical tie to pragmatist John Dewey, who taught there. The program is also very proud of their work improving education, especially with disenfranchised populations, and so the university is very much in line with critical theory as well. My professors and my committee were much more interested in the thoughts behind my work and my findings that advanced education in the United States for students who were homeless than they were of whether each section of my dissertation was correctly written. My dissertation would not have come close to passing at any of the universities where I have taught, each being held to very high positivistic standards.*

Situating Yourself and Your University Theoretically

Because we work with an international base of students, we see the consequences that theoretical stances adopted in general within a local research community have on their students' dissertations and theses. As discussed in the introduction, one end of the continuum locksteps students through a rigorous logic, while the other gets students started with much less initial understanding, allowing them to develop methodology as they go. Students have told us that it is helpful to consider their university structure and the type of theoretical stance prevalent in their school as they write their own dissertation/thesis. Certainly there is no legal issue in suggesting a mode of research that varies from the logic of the school in which you study—BUT—it may be much harder going if you don't think about it first.

In general, much research is based on the ideas of a Newtonian worldview, which we know is now overshadowed in many disciplines. Everything will not be fully understood if we develop meaning from logical steps in a scientific process. Nevertheless, methodological rigor counts—internal and

Figure 5.5 Explore the theoretical leanings of your university and community and consider how this will affect your study.

Source: Jupiterimages/Photos.com/Think stock

external validity need to be considered, and then, in conjunction with your advisor and university, you need to design work that is both appropriate to your topic and that will allow you to graduate easily. We no longer assume that there is one worldview (Mauer & Githens, 2009; Volk, 2009).

Postpositivism considers lots of things to be research, as it does not believe that theory and practice can be separated. Also called postmodernism, this theoretical position is built on a theme that no knowledge, stance, or idea is neutral, and therefore this position is in direct opposition with some aspects of neutral scientific research. Postpositivism would question the role of the researcher in the research and has contributed ideas of liberation, justice, and freedom to the world of research in the social sciences. It assumes that this is a complex world with multiple worldviews and that passion and politics need to be taken into account (Pease, 2009; Volk, 2009).

The critical theories (critical race theory, feminist critical theory, etc.) discuss the disenfranchised populations whose opinions and worldviews were left out of the majority voice claimed by positivism. Theoretically interested in uncovering the part of reality as yet unaddressed and righting the wrongs created by not taking these positions into account as valid, critical theory considers inequity and proposes justice (McKenna & Deunstan-Lewis, 2004).

As mentioned before, when considering your dissertation/thesis research design it may be important or at least informative to discuss the overarching theoretical position of the university along these lines.

Tracesea asks: *What if I'm getting my doctorate at an institution which has more of a positivistic/empiricist slant, but I'm definitely in the post positivist/ postmodern camp? Will I be fighting an uphill battle? What can I do about this discrepancy?*

Answer: Within most institutions there will be professors whose personal views diverge from the overall slant of the university as a whole. Ask around and find the people that best fit with you for your committee. Then have frank conversations with these people as you go along about your concerns. Be willing to compromise where it is not as important so that you save your goodwill by standing up for just the issues that seem paramount to you being able to do the research you want.

Theoretical Justification for Methodology

The final set of considerations then, as you make your theoretical decisions for your study, are to take into account how your theoretical stance contributes to or contrasts with your desire to add significantly to your field? How do these translate to researchable questions? At a simplistic level, for instance, certain fields in some parts of the world would never take a purely qualitative study seriously. Or, in contrast, in other arenas if you did not ask the people affected by the problem for their experience, you would be discounted.

To deepen our example, we can imagine a doctoral student in business who wants to investigate how an organization can revamp their structure in order to be more innovative. Merging theory with a desire to have research make a difference develops in the following three ways:

1. We can imagine *empiricists*, surveying a large number of people, begin research with some ideas about the answers to their questions. These become hypotheses and null hypotheses. Therefore, if this student is investigating a realm of potential ideas, derived from the literature on the subject, then they will build these hypotheses about innovation, how people see it, and what impedes it. The student then builds a survey to test each hypothesis. The survey results should lead to a confirmation of potential strategies and lead to conclusions that help answer the question, how should we proceed?

2. The *pragmatist* would be concerned with being effective and, therefore, builds a methodology that develops from a series of qualitative methods, such as focus groups and interviews with key stakeholders. Whether the methodology would be narrative inquiry, case study, or phenomenology (to be determined by the ultimate purpose of the work and the specific questions being asked), the student asks a series of questions that pertain to both personal past experience around similar issues and for perceptions as to what people believe are the next logical steps. By the time these data are analyzed, the student begins to develop ideas that can lead to conclusions that help answer their questions or develop the narrative that is interesting to them. If the student wants to develop a theory about their situation and its probable best solution, then the application of grounded theory is appropriate.

Figure 5.6 A pragmatist would likely build a methodology using focus groups and interviews with key stakeholders.

Source: David Woolley/Digital Vision/Thinkstock

3. The *constructivist* point of view is that ideas and best practices are developed over time and are added to by each subsequent experience. Therefore, this researcher might choose a sequential mixed methods study where they survey the greater population and develop a snapshot of potential strategies, which they then investigate through personal interviews with key stakeholders. The opposite tack might also work, whereby the student interviews key stakeholders first and develops potential strategies, to be tested through the greater population using surveys to test the hypotheses. Either strategy will lead to conclusions that help answer the question, how should we proceed?

The important thing to note in these three examples is that in each case the student's desire for the research to make a difference in the field going forward is achieved. By the time the student collected and analyzed these data, the conclusions could be drawn that led towards the answer to the initial question, how can something be done? The theoretical stance invoked different specific questions and a different research methodology.

Other Important Factors to Consider

Size and Scope

Why are the size and scope of your study important? In general, they are important because if your study is too small, it will have little or no significance, and if it is too large, it will be more likely to bog down and cause you to fail. There are two sides to this issue—on the one hand is your desire for the best population and sample size that you can imagine with which to do a fantastic study—on the other hand are the practical matters as to how you will obtain contact and permission of the sample population you desire (Rudestam & Newton, 2007).

Below are some questions to consider about the ideal population:

- Who is affected by the issues/challenges or problems around which your study revolves?
- How much area does your study cover?
- What is the demographic makeup of that group in that area?
- Are there any particular considerations that make them special or unique from the wider diversity that surround them?
- Will the effect of the outcome of your study on this group be direct or indirect? It is merely of interest or will it create policy?
- If it will create policy, who will the policy affect directly and indirectly?

The following are some practical questions to consider:

- Who can you get access to and get Internal Review Board (IRB) permission to ask questions of, through which you will develop your results?
- To what extent does the smaller group you will ask questions of mirror the larger group who may be affected?
- If your population is large, how are you ensuring that you have enough credible evidence to ensure that your data speak to the issues of a large group?

Figure 5.7 Consider how much area your study covers and the demographic makeup of that area.

Source: Digital Vision/Digital Vision/Thinkstock

Figure 5.8 below demonstrates the nested relationship between the population who would be interested in or affected by the outcome of your study (its potential significance) to the population of actual stakeholders to your sample. You need to consider each group, how they relate in size to each other, and ensure that your sample is a credible compliment. In other words, if the population affected is all women within a certain age group but your methodology is to interview 20 of them, then you might not want to claim a population size of, say, a large city. One reason would be that if the population of women in your city were in the thousands, then interviewing only 20 makes it unlikely that you would capture the essence of the full picture of responses needed. A second consideration is that if your population is all the women in a large area, you probably will need to employ a quantitative methodology with a random sampling procedure in order to gain credibility

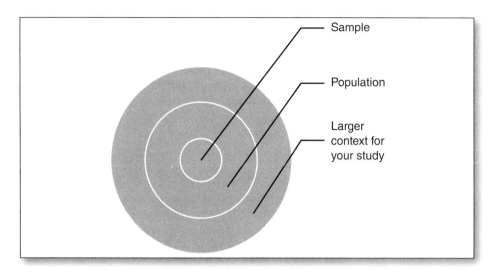

Figure 5.8   Relationship of Context, Population, and Sample Size

in your answers. If you need to reach a large population but equally want to capture a rich personal experience, you may want to consider mixed methods.

Figure 5.9 demonstrates a sample (the innermost dark area) for a study focusing on multiple variables. An easy example might be a population for whom you were measuring education (variable A) and how that overlapped with role in employment (variable B) and race (variable C). An author for a study like this one needs to convince readers that his or her sample is indicative of or contains each

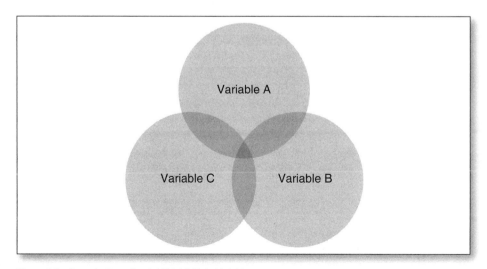

Figure 5.9   Sample From Study With Multiple Variables

of the three variables. If this were your study, your words would need to demonstrate these relationships and the logic through which you would find your sample.

In Figure 5.10 (below), we see a similar instance, also with three variables but with one that actually contains both of the other two. An easy example of this might be a racial subset of the population we discussed above. Again as author, your words need to demonstrate the relationships between the variables you study in the populations from which you will find your samples. The size and relationships between the subpopulations that demonstrate the variables will, in some instances, be critical to the credibility of your sampling procedure.

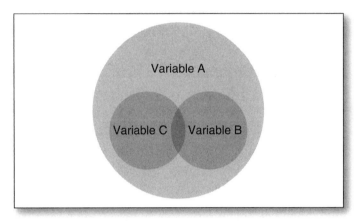

Figure 5.10   Sample Population Created by Two Variables Within a Larger Group Displaying the Third Variable

There are many means by which researchers gain access to their sample populations. We will discuss two in general: convenience samples (basically you get a hold of people you know or those you have easy access to through a group membership, etc.) or a random sample (appropriate when you have access to a large group and can pick a certain number of them using a randomization technique). There are pros and cons to each sampling method.

Random samples are, by definition, statistically likely to be representative of the larger group. This is because in order to be random every person in the group had an equal likelihood to participate. Credibility in a random sample depends on your random controls and the means of obtaining access to the sample population (Garson, 2002). An example of an easy random sampling method is to draw the sample from a hat, as long as a slip of paper includes everyone in the larger population then all have an equal chance of being drawn or not. There are tables of random numbers that can also help you set up a true random selection technique.

Convenience samples are easy to obtain as you are drawing on relationships or networks to which you have easy access. Credibility of your results will depend on convincing your reader that your sample equates to a large degree with the population from which they are drawn. As an example, if your population is all women then your sample might need to mirror the same percentages of racial characteristics as found in the larger population. Whether or not this would be a concern would depend on to what extent your topic was one that might create variation across cultural boundaries. The closer the match, the more likely a convenience study will be seen as credible, depending on sample size (Brause, 2000; Rudestam & Newton, 2007).

 Tracesea asks: *Is it possible to use more than one sampling method in my study? For example, what if I start with random sampling but don't get a big enough sample size, can I use convenience sampling to fill in the gaps?*

Answer: The two types of samples that we see together, which are frequently used in the award-winning dissertation samples we have collected, are *purposeful* and *convenience.* There are a range of ways to encourage people to participate that could cluster close enough as to be used together; this would be a question for your supervisor/advisor or mentor. However, you can never fill in a random study with people you found out of convenience because, by definition, random requires an equal chance to participate or not and your choice would negate that. If you don't get enough people in your sample, you have to go back to the ethical review board and ask permission to recruit from an alternative population. Your options should, again, be discussed with your supervisor.

Activity 5.4 Developing the Size and Scope of Your Study

This activity may be best started at the individual level but completed as part of a group exercise where all participants discuss the pros and cons of each size and scope decision.
Procedure

- Draw out each relationship and describe them as with the figures above. You might have a circle for your entire population. Within it would be the group or groups you are studying and then a sub-circle for the one or more variables you hope to measure. Your drawing should demonstrate their relationships.
- Can you easily convince someone looking at your diagram that the people or groups you will invite to your study would be able to provide valid evidence considering the relationships you have drawn out?
- How large is the full population as compared to the sample you can easily question?
- Is it convincing to believe that answers from your small group will represent the larger group as well?
- What are some criticisms or concerns that you imagine might come up when readers are asked to believe that your small group is representative and contains adequate experience of the variables or experiences you are studying?

- How can the size and scope of your study be altered to answer some of these criticisms and concerns in order to increase the credibility of your findings?
- Is your methodology appropriate to the size of your population?
- What kind of sampling procedure are you going to use?
- How will you ensure you have access to a population the size you need to build credible results?

Local Context

There are several considerations you need to tease out about your local context. Which ones will be important in your study may be largely because of unique factors dependent upon your university requirements and your research design. For each of the following points, you will need to decide which, if any, have enough bearing on your topic, your ability to gather data, or the credibility of your study as to be worthy of consideration and discussion.

Figure 5.11 Find out who is in charge, meet with them to discuss your study, and get them on board. Having the support of stakeholders and others who hold power is often essential for gathering the data you will need.

Source: Comstock Images/Comstock/Thinkstock

Stakeholder Buy-In

Who are the people who "own" the data you need for your study? What do they care about and how must you craft your work to satisfy their needs? Many doctoral studies fail because data became impossible to get and the work required to redo the study to match the data that were available seemed daunting. It is naïve to think that people from any particular group or organization will be allowed to answer your questions without you also having obtained permission from the organizational powers that be. Why not find out now what rules exist and begin to at least send out preliminary requests to see what barriers may exist.

It is postpositivistic to say that no knowledge is neutral, but likely you will find that to be the case when you begin to ask for permission to collect data. Scrupulous attention to your study or, more importantly, to the *intent of your design,* is the norm. Research is political, and to the extent that your findings have the potential to uncover negative aspects of a group, you can be relatively sure your request will be denied. For these reasons, you may wish to interview your primary stakeholders. What are the issues they care about that, at least tangentially, touch on your concerns. A research design that would address both concerns may be your best political move (Krathwohl & Smith, 2005).

Archival Evidence

Stakeholder buy-in is also critical with a design that relies upon archival evidence (data previously collected and on file). Some data, however, may be a matter of public record, as it was partially funded through federal money and is not part of your country's laws on the security of data. Student data in particular are covered and require, in most instances, parental consent before you can obtain permission to access them.

Nevertheless, there remain large and frequently easily available amounts of data that are available for use in your research. Census data, local government-funded data studying particular populations by your local government, or data at large from government agencies are all likely to be available. Your librarian should be a great help in assessing which of these are available in your area.

Your Context's Relationship to the Significance of Your Study

Finally, as you consider your context, you need to keep in mind how it bears on any claim to significance you might make. It may nullify your study if it is found not to meet the requirements of doctoral work because of a small or completely local sample. This decision is largely dependent on the standards of your university and decisions by your committee. Your field of study may also have an impact on how big is big enough. As an example, a business major might not be able to make a claim for a strategic implementation in his/her field with a sample as small as 50 or 60. A schoolteacher, on the other hand, might claim significance of the same size sample, dependent on the relationship of that sample to the size of the school or district. We refer you back to the discussion on size and scope earlier in this chapter.

Figure 5.12 Your sample size in relation to the larger group is just one of the considerations to make when determining if your study will be deemed significant.

Source: ©iStockphoto.com/mikdam

Validity and Reliability

We have found that students may either stress about validity and reliability or not consider them at all. Both are unfortunate. To be valid, your research design—or the way in which your instruments measure your concept—needs to be logical so that the findings that develop from your data build credible results. Consider a target. If your research design is a valid measure of your situation, you have hit the center of the target. As Sapsford and Jupp (1996) point out, every study ends with a conclusion where the author(s) develop an argument on the basis of their evidence. No matter what else may be true about their methodology, data collection, or analytical design, their arguments must be built upon a logical structure from which the credibility of this argument develops.

While this text is not comprehensive enough to delve deeply into all the kinds of internal and external validity that may bear on your topic and design, there are two we wish you to take into account from the beginning. Why is it credible that your sample population has the same level of diverse experience as the wider population so that, at the end, you will be able to argue that your data speaks for this wider population, who you will argue should pay attention to your findings? Second, how well can you justify that the instruments you are using or the way you are asking questions will actually lead to the results you hope for? In other words are your measurements valid and on what basis can you make that claim (Pease, 2009; Sapsford & Jupp, 1996)

A reliable design is one where the majority of your data cluster around the center, or in other words, data from a majority of people, over a varied set of instances, still produce that cluster in the center (Bataille & Clanet, 1981; Thomas, 2003). A study will be reliable whenever your data cluster well, as this shows that your questions or measures produce consistent results but, like a cluster of arrows that only hit the outer rim of the target, you might not be asking the right questions, and therefore your data are not valid. On the other hand, you may end with data all over the entire range of possible answers with few, if any, clustered in the center, which would be indicative of a study that asks valid questions but for which there is little reliability. These issues are mentioned here as an introduction to the goal of your data collection and analysis and will be discussed again in Part Two, as we discuss how you write up validity and reliability, and in Part Three, when we discuss how you test for them (Bataille & Clanet, 1981; Garson, 2002; Krathwohl & Smith, 2005).

Chapter 5 Checklist

- ☐ I have done significant work to fine tune my design.
- ☐ I understand how to track the logic in a research design.
- ☐ I understand the theoretical issues involved in methodology.
- ☐ I have an idea of the methods I would like to use in my research.
- ☐ I understand issues of size, scope, local context, validity, and reliability.

Where Should I Go to Dig Deeper? Suggested Resources to Consider

Creswell, J. W. (2009). *Research design: Qualitative, quantitative, and mixed methods approaches* (3rd ed.). Thousand Oaks, CA: Sage. On pages 5 through 11, this book has a particularly clear discussion of the philosophical worldviews that underpin most theoretical approaches to research.

Garson, G. D. (2002). *Guide to writing empirical papers, theses, and dissertations*. New York: Marcel Dekker. Section IV, "Presenting Your Case: Telling a Story," pages 177 through 221, gives you a great picture of the endgame you are striving for. To the extent that you can begin with the end in mind, your path may suffer fewer detours along the way. Also, pages 190 through 197 give an excellent overview of the different types of validity and reliability you will want to consider as claims in your methodological design.

Hawking, S., & Mlodinow, L. (2010). *The grand design*. New York: Bantam Dell. This is an excellent, readable book by notable authors about the way theory plays out in the complex quantum scientific worldview. Model-dependent realism allows the student to build a model that fits his or her context and circumstance.

James, W., & Gunn, G. (2000). *Pragmatism and other writings*. New York: Penguin Group. A revision of the seminal work on pragmatism by William James. A must read for anyone following this theoretical path.

Mauch, J. E., & Park, N. (2003). *Guide to the successful thesis and dissertation: A handbook for students and faculty*. New York: Marcel Dekker. Pages 97 through 143 and 167 through 199 cover the characteristics of a sound overview or proposal as conducted as per the U.K. model of dissertation and thesis development.

Robson, C. (2002). *Real world research: A resource for social scientists and practitioner-researchers* (2nd ed.). Oxford, UK: Blackwell Publishers. This book has a very good section on validity, types to consider, and threats that may need to be taken into account.

Group Exercises

Playing "devil's advocate" may allow every member of your dissertation study group to dig deeper into any flaws that may still occur in the logic of their study.

Procedure

1. Every member of the group draws out his or her dissertation logic using the models in Figures 5.1 and 5.2. (Note: A student example is included as Appendix C.)

2. Passing the drawings around the group, each member writes questions about the logic on self-adhesive notes and attaches them to the drawings.

3. Members discuss the questions related to their design and update as appropriate.

Figure 5.13   Playing "devil's advocate" with other students can help improve everyone's work.

Source: Digital Vision/Digital Vision/Thinkstock

Conclusion to Part I

You have now traveled through the basic linkages and considerations appropriate for any doctoral-level research design. Many specifics will need to be considered in tandem with your advisor and as appropriate to the system and theoretical research stance of your university. Few students will make just one pass through this material; rather it is, as stated in the introduction and Chapter 1, a spiral path of development. Nevertheless, Part I has given you a solid understanding of what is involved in a dissertation, your first exploration of finding a topic, the basics of methodology, a discussion of how theory influences your design, and an overview of the parts of a research design and their logical relationships.

Hopefully you have built a good relationship with your advisor, and that person has signed off on your work so far. If not, that will be your next step, as we cannot know the strength of your design as it now stands. Even with a solid base you may find that you feel unsure of one or more sections and will wish to explore the resources we have included in the digging deeper sections in each chapter.

At the point when you and your university feel your design is strong enough to support writing it up in a formal pattern, you will progress to Part II, which focuses on the specifics to be included in each section common to a doctoral research proposal. As stated in the introduction, you and your advisor may cut back on some aspects of this design, when and if they are not required in your research setting. Now it is time to remember our quote from J.L. Newcom, who stated that he spent three years only to realize that the dissertation was not only about the work he would do but also largely a lesson in how to discuss that work with other professionals (DoctoralNet, 2012). This is the topic of Part II.

PART II

WRITING AND DEFENDING YOUR PROPOSAL

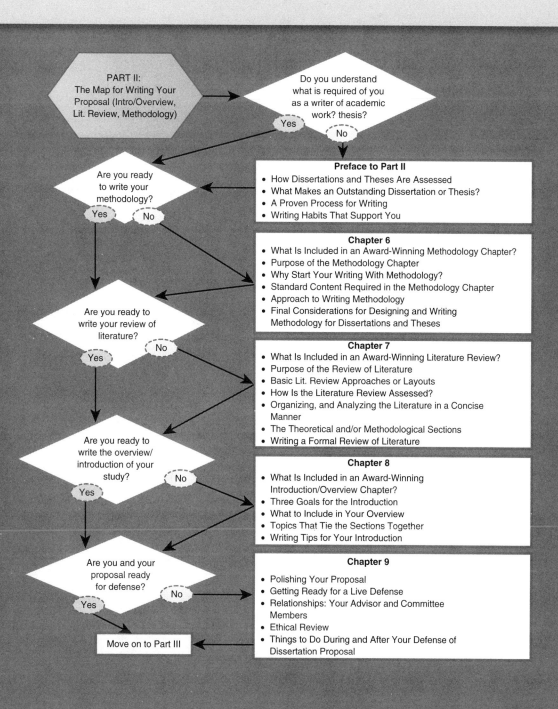

PART II:
The Map for Writing Your Proposal (Intro/Overview, Lit. Review, Methodology)

Do you understand what is required of you as a writer of academic work? thesis?

Yes

No

Preface to Part II
- How Dissertations and Theses Are Assessed
- What Makes an Outstanding Dissertation or Thesis?
- A Proven Process for Writing
- Writing Habits That Support You

Are you ready to write your methodology?

Yes   No

Chapter 6
- What Is Included in an Award-Winning Methodology Chapter?
- Purpose of the Methodology Chapter
- Why Start Your Writing With Methodology?
- Standard Content Required in the Methodology Chapter
- Approach to Writing Methodology
- Final Considerations for Designing and Writing Methodology for Dissertations and Theses

Are you ready to write your review of literature?

Yes   No

Chapter 7
- What Is Included in an Award-Winning Literature Review?
- Purpose of the Review of Literature
- Basic Lit. Review Approaches or Layouts
- How Is the Literature Review Assessed?
- Organizing, and Analyzing the Literature in a Concise Manner
- The Theoretical and/or Methodological Sections
- Writing a Formal Review of Literature

Are you ready to write the overview/introduction of your study?

Yes   No

Chapter 8
- What Is Included in an Award-Winning Introduction/Overview Chapter?
- Three Goals for the Introduction
- What to Include in Your Overview
- Topics That Tie the Sections Together
- Writing Tips for Your Introduction

Are you and your proposal ready for defense?

Yes   No

Chapter 9
- Polishing Your Proposal
- Getting Ready for a Live Defense
- Relationships: Your Advisor and Committee Members
- Ethical Review
- Things to Do During and After Your Defense of Dissertation Proposal

Move on to Part III

Preface to Part II: Assessments, Headings, Layout, and Writing Tips

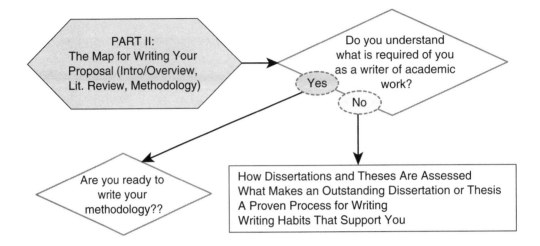

During Part I, we introduced you to the series of thoughts and processes that should have led you to an inclusive view of the ideas needed in your dissertation. Still, you may find there is a long distance between having firmed up your ideas and being able to write them into the rigorous structure of a dissertation or thesis. One of our current students told us, "*I don't know why they call it writing, it is more like engineering. We all think we can write, but only after we are involved in the process do we realize how complex it is and how many pieces there are to try to make it work*" (Hamilton, 2012). Since that is true, Part II and Part III are the specific structures and linkages that you, as the engineer of your dissertation or thesis, need to employ in order to make your ideas go forward and be respected as research.

This is a preface, with tips and tricks for easier procedures that you may wish to revisit as you begin to write each chapter or section. Few doctoral candidates have approached any work previously in their careers that will rival the complexities that you face as you write. Whenever possible, it is best to use all the organizational tools at your disposal, reach towards and engage outside help, join groups and forums, and so forth, not to heedlessly follow all the advice you are given but rather to keep a perspective on your work, the academic world, and what this all means to your career path.

The Questions Answered in This Chapter:

1. By what standards are dissertations assessed?

2. How do different universities approach the process of writing a dissertation or thesis?

3. How do I keep track of my ideas?

4. What structures need to be in place as I write in order to save me time later?

5. What habits can I develop that will help me throughout my writing?

6. What organizational help is there for me to keep all my ideas together?

How Dissertations and Theses Are Assessed

Assessment of dissertations or theses is the topic of much literature in higher education. Many layers of complexity come into play. First, different professors on your committee will each have different backgrounds. Second, universities also have a wide continuum of what they see as important: practice, theory, or research design. Third, within protocols adopted for research across disciplines you may find some research structured in a linear fashion or postmodern ideas that develop a wider network of influence.

Advisors also vary widely, especially in how much they are willing or think it's appropriate to help or offer guidance, leading to a great range within the work of doctoral candidates. Researchers and academics may not use the same language to refer to the same or similar components or characteristics of research design. Universities also vary widely as to how many guidelines they place on committee work or how wide a range of final dissertations or theses they will accept. All of these factors lead to variation within assessment practices (Albertyn, Kapp, & Frick, 2007; Brause, 2000; de-Miguel, 2010; Finch, 2010; Wise et al., 2009).

Assessment Rubrics

Two formats for assessment are widely discussed in the literature. The first are used by professors who are primarily concerned with the dissertation or thesis document being well engineered while demonstrating mastery over the logical flow of writing to a linear research standard. The second type of format is primarily focused on assessment of the quality of ideas without concentrating overmuch on the science. Two authors inform the joint and somewhat restructured rubric to be found in Appendix D (Albertyn et al., 2007; de-Miguel, 2010). We recommend that you utilize this rubric with your advisor and committee as a point of discussion in order to uncover more information about the particular standards to which your work will be held.

Internal Consistency and the Idea of the "Golden Thread"

Albertyn et al. (2007) introduces the provocative idea of a "golden thread" that ties the readability, the research undertaken, and the overall quality of a dissertation together for the reader. When analyzing the difference between award-winning dissertations and others that earned graduation, this idea of a golden thread becomes more obvious. Award-winning dissertations float above the more mundane peers because the authors develop a unique voice that is specific to the person writing and make it obvious how every section relates to the topic of their research without falling into redundancy, all while maintaining a level of readability and pace that keeps the reader moving through what are sometimes long and arduous documents. We will try to demonstrate these golden threads with examples as we discuss the structure of putting together the various chapters in Part II and Part III.

What Makes an Outstanding Dissertation or Thesis?

Throughout Part II and Part III, we will use examples from a small meta-analysis that we did on what makes for outstanding work. Included were 24 award-winning dissertations and theses from 18 universities around the world. Some were written using the model of development common in the United States, others the European model. They were analyzed across a number of variables and will be used as examples to illustrate writing, format, and structural issues.

A Proven Process for Writing

Prepare for Publication Right From the Start

We find that it is time-efficient to set up your document from the very first day as though it will become your final draft. Therefore, before you begin to work with your ideas, you need to fully understand the guidelines developed by your university for final publication.

Step 1: Find out what style manual or publication guidelines are in place. Look for templates and use them if they are available. If they are not available, build your own and base them on a mixture of the style manual and documents from recently graduated students, preferably from your advisor. Make sure templates include differences between style manuals being used and graduate school or university guides. For example, levels of headings for the chapters are sometimes dictated by the university and are not the same as in the reference manual. This is also often true for figures/tables, pagination, running headers, and so forth.

Step 2: Set your bibliographic reference software to correctly cite and reference all literature according to above guidelines. Test out your software's equivalent of "cite while you write," for the insertion of citations and the development of references automatically by your software while you are writing.

Writing Effectively and Efficiently

As you start writing or every time you pick it up again you will be faced with "an abundance of riches." In other words and from a more frustrated position you'll have just too much "stuff" to deal with. Are you challenged by too many PDFs and/or previous versions of your ideas? Do you have an assortment of documents that may have some good things in them but also include many ideas that are out of date? This is likely the case, as you have spent a considerable amount of time reading important literature, engaged in new thoughts and conversations about your topic, and so forth. You have pondered your topic from many different angles, each probably resulting in some level of archival documentation, every step obtained and developed from a different point of view. This next activity helps you organize, efficiently begin, and continue your writing process under these circumstances. It is the same process that we use to write all our books.

Activity: Setting Your Writing Up for Publication From the Beginning

Procedure

1. Locate which documents, PDFs, videos, and so forth pertain to your dissertation research and put them in one place.

2. Complete a final edit of your headings and subheadings on the word processing document that you intend to become your final draft document as well.

3. Double check that all headings and subheadings are correctly organized on a "document map," "navigation pane," or whatever language your word processing software uses to indicate a sidebar with organization of your headings (as referenced in Chapter 3).

4. Create folders within a master dissertation folder on your computer, each titled the same as your first level headings.

5. Sort and move copies of all your documents into your folders. Note—some documents may be copied into more than one place.

6. Build an organized rough draft of your entire document by opening and skimming every document you have placed under every heading. Cut and paste entire sections into place. Do not worry at this stage about issues such as appropriate voice and so forth. Your goal is to see what goes where.

7. If, when cutting and pasting, you are concerned your words that are too close to the original authors', simply make a comment to yourself off to the side to reword when you come back as you rewrite.

Figure Preface Part 2.1 Set up a series of folders on your computer to keep all of your documents organized.

Source: ©iStockphoto.com/alexsl

8. Do not stop to think too much about the final stages of your writing. Your goal is to keep the organization moving quickly.

9. Notice any sections or subheadings that are lacking material and make a note about them in your research journal.

10. Highlight everything in the document and change the text to the correct font. This will begin to help the document have the final look and feel required.

11. Turn on dictation software, if you are using it, and proceed to read and rewrite your chapters or sections one at a time. Remember to go back to your dissertation/thesis sample models as appropriate to remind yourself use of correct research language, topics to be included under each section, and so forth.

12. Develop a system of saving your documents with the date included in the subject line. This will allow you to come back to earlier writing and will prevent anguish should you decide that an earlier version had strengths that later versions lost.

13. Save your documents to a server to prevent loss. Use services such as Dropbox or iCloud and ensure everything that has to do with your dissertation, your data collection and analysis, and all drafts are saved there.

Quick Writing Notes to Keep in Mind

Headings and *subheadings* function as the skeleton to your larger document. To your reader, however, the purpose of headings and subheadings becomes critical. As people who read dissertations all the time, it is likely that your committee will first seriously consider your table of contents. They may carefully analyze how the headings flow from one to another. It is easy to quickly understand the logic behind the work through the headings and subheadings the author choses to use. Areas where your logic wobbles or your ideas are not honed to a point of crispness will show up quickly. As your ideas mature, so will your headings and subheadings. We will discuss what headings and the tables of contents from award-winning dissertations show us over the next few chapters.

Your word processing software should develop your *table of contents* easily. It is useful to check it early in the writing process and to keep it up to date as you write. Follow your software instructions to insert a table of contents, and then carefully check it for accuracy. As long as you have created your headings and subheadings correctly, as shown by your document map or navigation pane, then the table of contents should reflect this same structure.

References should develop at the end of your document as you write, if you are using your bibliographic software correctly. Again, check this as you begin to write, and make sure that this list is up-to-date before you shut down for each day.

Special terms develop and change, as do your ideas during the writing process. When you complete each chapter, it is a good idea to go back to that section just to ensure that you have noted all special use of language.

 Tracesea asks: *This is the first time you've mentioned special terms. What does it mean to "note all use of special language?" Can you give me an example of special language and its notation within a dissertation?*

Answer: Every field of study has language, such as "at risk" children for educators, "risk management" for business, "human or cultural capital" for many issues that deal with people. Often called operational definitions, each of these will have a specific meaning, and will have been written about by experts in your field. Keep track of anything that might be considered "lingo" along with references and page numbers of where other authors explain them. Then attach your list somewhere or embed it in the language of your first chapter, depending on what is seen as appropriate to your university, in your final document. By defining your terms, you save yourself grief caused by misunderstanding during final review, defense, or Vita.

Respect the process of writing. Whether you consider yourself a researcher or a student, you are, from the start until at least the time you finish, also a writer. There is an ebb and flow of writing process that will go more easily for you if you respect it. Because writing requires whole brain synapses to fire in logical progressive order, it is best not to look at it like a wall or barrier to finishing, which you are trying to climb over. That approach will limit you to asking, "So I should just do . . . here—right?" It is never a knee-jerk reaction with only one outcome being the "right" one. Writing well requires an understanding of the flux of ideas as well as personal body energy and focus. We would recommend that you choose to write for as long as the ideas flow and you find it interesting and that you don't push so hard you become exhausted.

Tracesea asks: *So, what if the ideas are not flowing, and I am having trouble writing anything at all?*

Answer: Nothing stops us short like confusion. We have found that writers block generally stems from one of two underlying problems: either you don't understand enough about the logic of what is required to know what to put in that section OR you don't understand the problem you are facing with your own research enough to address that section yet. Either way, back up, find what you are missing that is blocking your ideas, and then move forward later.

Momentum over comes inertia. Even if just checking a reference, try to do something each day.

You may find that the development of your final thesis is spiral in its growth pattern, much as if you followed the curve below from the outside inward. In other words, as shown in Figure Preface Part 2.2 (below), as your ability with language and your critical analysis of your ideas increase, you continue to

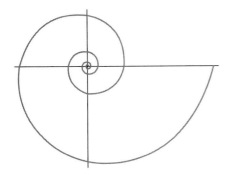

Figure Preface Part 2.2   Inward Spiral of Writing Process

come back to each section over and over, tightening the structure until it matures sufficiently to be given over to your committee or editors. Imagine that the lines crossing the spiral represent any one idea. As you can see, there may be a longer distance between considering each idea over time, but in the end the circumference of what you write develops.

Different Approaches to This Material: Per University and Part of the World

Because we are writing for an international audience, it is wise to note certain variations on the documents that will be required at different stages during your dissertation or thesis journey. To the extent your university uses a typically European model, you will likely be required to write a prospectus or other document for a proposal meeting or progress review panel at the end of your first year. This document will focus on the literature review, which is covered in Chapter 7 of this book. You may or may not have to write much about your methodology at this time, but we have been told by students using this model that they believe it is useful to at least acquaint yourself with these ideas early in the process. This book is laid out in the system of considering the ideas with the methodology placed first and foremost, because it has been our experience that when those decisions are considered early in the process, then finishing the final work is much easier. In the United States, you are frequently required to defend a proposal that is in essence the first three chapters of your final work but written in the future tense. It is on that model which this book is written, because we believe it to be the most universally useful for students no matter what system they are in (Garson, 2002; Mauch & Park, 2003).

This book is also written as though you will write five chapters. First will be your introduction—an overview of your work—next will be your review of literature, then your methodology, finally your findings, and then your discussion of your study in the context of your field, still referred to in some parts of the world as conclusion. Dissertations and theses, however, do not necessarily have five chapters, yet they all have those components. You as a writer might choose to divide any one of these standard chapters into two parts in order to make the logic of the flow of your work easier for the somewhat uninformed reader. As an example, in one of the award-winning dissertations we will discuss, a marine biologist studying digital photography decided to divide his literature into two chapters. His second chapter reviewed all the theoretical components that created the structure upon which his process was based. His third chapter was a review of digital photography especially focused on its use in different systems of analysis, such as photojournalism, scientific photography, photography, the legal system, and so forth.

Different disciplines also are inclined to use different stylistic components in order to enhance the clarity for their particular readership. An example of this is to use a progression of numbers as well as words to illuminate headings, such as: chapter 3, 3.1; heading 1, 3.1.1; a subheading for heading 1, 3.1.2; a second subheading, 3.2; a second heading; and so forth. This style is widely adopted in sciences, engineering, and mathematics.

To some extent, all writers of a final dissertation document retrofit what happened into the final dissertation or thesis they write. If you are a student from the university using the model of thesis work more common in the United Kingdom, you may feel this is especially true, because it is unlikely you have written much of your methodology (unless you followed this book) before you implemented your ideas. You may not have considered all the subtle ins and outs of your theoretical design prior to data collection. Having worked with students from all over the world, we now understand that, no matter what system guides them, all students work towards the same goal: a final document whose architecture matches the constraints of scientific research throughout the world, while coherently using their own voice and perspective to discuss their work.

The Relationship Between Ideas and Structure

We find it helpful to spend a small period of time discussing the relationship between ideas and structure as it pertains to writing your dissertation or thesis. As a rule of thumb, every idea has one place that it is discussed in depth and may have one or more places where it is included as part of the flow of your writing and in which you may choose to refer the reader to the larger discussion should that be necessary to add clarity. As an example, the use of document maps and bibliographic software is one that we have found runs as a thread through our discussion of writing a dissertation as part of this book. We discussed it in detail in Chapter 3 but have mentioned it and referenced that detail at other times.

You will find that your research questions, purpose of your work, and methodology are necessary threads to tie throughout your thesis. As you plot your headings, you should be able to decide which place will include the major discussion of any one topic. Then, as you are writing and you want to note that topic again, as an example—the purpose of your work—you can easily look up where the main discussion is and refer your reader there.

The components that drive the relationships between ideas and structure, around and within your research framework, may be difficult for you, as a novice researcher, to put together in a coherent fashion. When that is the case, you may find that diagramming your work first can be quite helpful. We have found that if you can diagram it you can write about the relationships that you see much more easily than if you are trying to imagine them all in your head.

Writing Habits That Support You

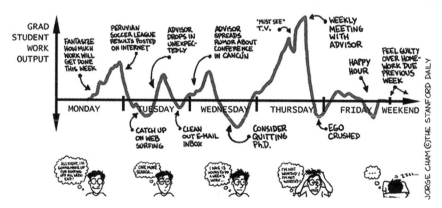

Figure Preface Part 2.3   PhD Comics on Graduate Workflow

Source: From Jorge Cham's *Graduate Workflow,* PhD Comic. Originally published by Stanford Daily.

Alana says: *While the "15-minutes-a-day" plan was the way I got through my own dissertation, it no longer works for me when writing big documents, such as this book. There are too many complexities in my life for me to take off a few minutes all the time to do anything, and so now I prefer to map out the entire structure in my head and on paper first, then set aside a day or two every week to work on the document. I write it and then the next week edit it and then send it off to Tracesea, who tears it apart, and together we rework it. The activity above about setting up your writing for publication supports the pattern of writing that works for me now. The result follows the spiral growth previously mentioned.*

Critical Analysis and Structures to Help You Develop It

What is critical analysis? Some authors describe it as thinking about thinking or why and how you are thinking what you are thinking (Herr & Anderson, 2005, Loseke, 2013). In its essence, it is the ability to look at any one thing from multiple points of view in order to tease out the fullest possible explanation or discussion of whatever it is you are writing about. Some people are very good at critical analysis on their own, but many others find it very useful to work in a group and discuss various aspects of writing as they move through the dissertation or thesis process. Tools that may help with critical analysis include the following: listing advantages/disadvantages, SWOT analysis, force field analysis, and so forth (King, 2002).

Group discussion, while not always focused on your work, may encourage new ideas, which will ultimately play out in your own analysis. To that end, there are many local and virtual groups you might investigate. Some will have more structure than others, and you will know for yourself if you would benefit most from a group that employed outside facilitation.

What to Avoid

Bias

What Constitutes Bias?

You may have come to your research (and especially if you're going for an applied doctorate) because you had a feeling something was "wrong." In a recent group we facilitated, two students had chosen topics addressing issues of leadership because they had personally been insulted and disrespected by an autocratic boss. Two other students were studying the impact of cultural experience on our world. One was looking at the leadership across multinational, virtual environments, and one educator was studying standards in education as they are impacted by teaching young people about their culture. A principal of an elementary school in the group was studying formative assessment, because it was something she was sure was going to work in her school—but she had, as of yet, been unsuccessful in getting it implemented. Can you see in these examples how the students' ideas for their research work were consistently driven from their own personal experience? Would you say the same is true of your topic?

Being involved in a personal level with ideas about your topic does not, in and of itself, constitute bias. Rather, bias is when you, as a writer, are not able to adopt a neutral stance as you discuss your topic and in the way you set up your methodology. Let's take the above examples one by one.

If the people studying leadership can discuss both ends of the leadership spectrum from autocratic to collaborative, in neutral terms that are backed up by research (discussing both the pros and the cons), then they have won half the battle. The other half is determined by the extent that they are able to ask questions of their participants, without in some way setting up a hierarchy between one side of the leadership continuum and the other.

The two people in the group who were studying the impact of culture, on the other hand, need to deeply explore literature about culture and its effects on the context of their studies. They both come to the topic influenced by their own experiences. The educator needs to have literature based on research that discusses both cultural education and its effect on academics. Both of these people may find that a quantitative study (to the extent they have a large enough population to justify it) might suit their needs, because with quantitative work they form a hypothesis of cause and effect and then test it.

Finally, the principal needed not only to understand the blockages that resulted in her staff improperly considering formative assessment and its potential, but she also wanted to engage them in the answers. If she asked, "What gets in the way of your implementation?" her readers might conclude she had displayed bias. If, on the other hand, she asked two questions, "What do you see as the pros and cons of formative assessment?" and, "What challenges exist for student implementation?" then her questions would likely be received as those without bias. If she had the time to implement it, an action research study would work well to engage her staff in uncovering the answers.

Another type of bias revolves around assumptions your writing might point out about racial or gender differences. Avoid all but neutral tones and ensure that, unless gender is specifically part of your topic, your pronouns are nonspecific and assumptions are not being made (Roberts, 2004; Rudestam & Newton, 2007).

How Can You Avoid Bias?

The examples above discuss three ways in which bias may be avoided in your writing. The first is to discuss the spectrum of your topic in terms of a continuum, with each point critically analyzed in terms of its pros and cons. The second is to consider whether and to what extent you can employ quantitative research methods, thereby using your data to prove your hypothesis about the cause and effect you have experienced. The third most common way to avoid challenges of bias is to develop your qualitative data collection and analysis in such a way that it nests the potential for the challenges you see within neutral grounds. In this way, your human subjects respond to your topic/questions from their point of view, without ever sensing your underlying suspicions or premises (Rowlands, 2002).

What Are the Standards of Neutrality Against Which Your Work Will Be Judged?

Your reader should not in any way be able to surmise your feelings on the subject you're studying. Your use of academic language should remain neutral at all times. Your questions can in no way be seen to lead your human subjects in one direction versus another. The voice of your writing must be that of the neutral observer, written in the way that any outside, unbiased, scientific laboratory would discuss your topic (Bryant, 2004; Rubin & Rubin, 2012). There may be exceptions to this rule if you are following an emancipatory or critical theory path. As with anything in the realm of the art of research, if you are going to break a rule, be ready to defend how your tact fits your philosophical and theoretical stance.

Other indications of bias are ambiguity (avoid generalizations) or several challenges that are specific to survey instruments. These include the way in which answers are ranked, using loaded language, or asking leading questions in interviews (Garson, 2002).

The Two Rs: Redundancy and Rambling

Poor writing can destroy even the best research possibility, so it may be wise to consider why it occurs in the first place. Rambling and redundancy are the most common errors. They read to your committee as a sign of not understanding either your material or the framework of the dissertation itself. Both of these things can be helped. To have a better handle on the material that you are learning, it is useful to discuss it with others. You'll find that as you explain something to someone else, it becomes more concrete in your own mind, thus leading to clarity of writing as well. As has been recommended in Chapter 1, the secret to understanding the framework for the dissertation is to have several models to which you refer constantly. Use them as guidelines, choosing a number of varied dissertations so that you can see the range your work needs to fall within.

Figure Preface Part 2.4 One way to get a fresh perspective on your work is to read it out loud to yourself.

Source: ©iStockphoto.com/qingwa

Another factor that could contribute to rambling is that you have worked too hard on one section for too long and have lost the ability to overview what you write. As one student said, "I find that is the problem I have with reading and writing my own work. I read and write and read and write again. I find that I get dead eye quickly. I need to learn how to be a better refiner" (McNeal, 2011). There are three concrete hints for getting past what this student calls the "dead eye." First, take a break. Second, read your work out loud. Third, use your word processing software to highlight the path of your work as well as the work itself (Bryant, 2004; Wyse, 2012).

You may find your words ramble for similar reasons as those discussed above for redundancy. You may not have discussed this topic enough for your thoughts to be precise, or you are just too tired to be writing. Both will produce weak sentence structure, run-on paragraphs, and other writing errors that will either put your reader to sleep or confuse them. The same three hints for getting past "dead eye" also help to prevent rambling: Take a break, read your work out loud to yourself, and use the structuring within your word processing software to help keep your thoughts in line.

The Dos and Don'ts of Writing

It is outside the scope of this work to do more than highlight the most common writing issues. It is incumbent upon you to find the writing help you need in order to reach the academic standards of your university. Nevertheless, there are a few common issues we will mention here to get you started.

Keep in mind that tense can be a confusing issue. If you are writing the proposal prior to being given permission to do your research, all comments about that research must be in future tense, because you have not done the work yet. Should you use the same words on your final dissertation or thesis, you will need to rewrite every section in order to make the tense in the past. When you write about other authors and what they have done, this is always in the past. Yet if their findings are still true, then these are present tense.

"Data" are plural. Therefore it is appropriate to say data were, these data, and so forth. It is a mistake to write "data is" or "was." It is also incorrect to use "the data" if you are speaking of your data—which should be referred to as, "these data," "these" being the demonstrative determiner to indicate data in your study. Other specific writing errors to watch out for include writing in a passive voice, which has to do with a verb structure that is not active. As an example, it is much stronger to say, "develop writing habits" rather than "writing will develop."

Your dissertation should be written from your professional voice. Occasional use of the first person instead of the more formal third person may be seen as preferable when discussing special considerations or to build a personal emphasis on your ideas in that section. Still, these should be limited and, for some universities, are not seen as ever being appropriate. All issues of form and style should be discussed with your advisor as needed, and we always recommend you make use of whatever editing options your university provides. Some universities may allow you the latitude (and we like this) of you "coming clean" in a subheading, "the researcher." This is often in the introduction or methodology chapters, and it allows an honest reflection of your context, beliefs, and so forth.

Do

- Rely upon only *acceptable academic sources* for your citations, references, and discussion of literature. If you think about it, would you accept the word of a doctor who only used web-based discussions of the quality of the drug in the prescription he was giving you? No, you would want him to be familiar with the latest random controlled trials and to understand both the positive qualities and the risks in the drug. Likewise, your committee expects you to understand the research behind every idea you put forth in your dissertation.

- *Deliver your work to a peer review expecting to receive blunt and honest criticism,* with suggestions of how to make it better. Submitting your dissertation work for review is not much different from what will happen later in your career should you decide to write a book or be published in a journal. All of us, students and professors alike, must submit our written material expecting it to come back severely criticized. I recommend you consider doing what we do—read the reviewers' comments once, put your work away for a few days, and then come back to it when enough time has elapsed that you can dispassionately review it piece by piece and make the changes suggested. Reworking the document after peer review requires a distance from any emotional attachment to what you have written previously. Putting the work aside for a couple of days

Figure Preface Part 2.5 Make sure you understand what acceptable academic sources are and don't rely too heavily on web-based sources to support your work.

Source: Photos.com/liquidlibrary/Thinkstock

will ensure you can look at the ideas with a cool mind. A good reword after a review always makes your work better.

- *Attribute every strong statement you make in your dissertation to whomever has come before you that agreed with it.* None of us are naive enough to think that you, as a doctoral student, will not have strong opinions about your topic—of course you will. The rub is that until you receive your degree, the academy will not value or acknowledge your opinion on its own. Like a child learning to walk, our first opinions must be supported by others. This is part of the rite of passage, and we all have faced it. You may have to write several books before your opinion will be widely valued and then only when it is regularly cited by others. Therefore, read through your dissertation and look for any and all strong statements. Then go find authors who agree with the statement, cite, and reference them. This will do two things: It will broaden your awareness of your ideas and where they fit in with the literature of your topic, and it will make your dissertation academically defensible.

Don't

- Procrastinate.

Figure Preface Part 2.6   Social networking is just one of the many distractions we can use when we want to procrastinate.

Source: From Jorge Cham's *Procrastination,* PhD Comic. Originally published by www.phdcomics.com.

- *Cut and paste source material.* Don't cut and paste from electronic resources directly into your document without making a note to rewrite and revamp that section in your own voice.
- *Fall into negative self-talk and stop working.* Remember, at the beginning we pointed out that a dissertation or thesis was an endurance test? This will be even truer when you face whatever demons you may have collected in your head regarding your ability to write. We recommend you look at them objectively and tell them to shut up!

Prewriting Checklist

❒ I understand the standards to which dissertations and theses are assessed.

❒ I understand the purpose of the methodology chapter.

❒ I understand how my university approaches the process of writing up a dissertation or thesis and, therefore, how to approach the work in this book.

❒ I am able to set up a solid structure and keep track of my ideas.

❒ I understand what habits I can develop that will help me throughout my writing.

Where Should I Go to Dig Deeper? Suggested Resources to Consider

Beins, B. (2012). *APA style simplified: Writing in psychology, education, nursing, and sociology* (1st ed.). Malden, MA: Wiley-Blackwell. Sometimes it is easier to learn the basics of a complex style such as APA by reading a book designed to help you navigate. Always be sure though that the book matched the edition that you are required to use.

Goodson, P. (2013). *Becoming an academic writer: 50 exercises for paced, productive, and powerful writing.* Thousand Oaks, CA: Sage. "This book describes a model for taking control of the academic writing process: the POWER model (promoting, outstanding writing for excellence in research) and provides weekly exercises to improve your writing control" (p. 3). In two weeks you will see improvement in your academic writing.

Wheeldon, J., & Åhlberg, M. (2012). *Visualizing social science research: Maps, methods, & meaning.* Thousand Oaks, CA: Sage. This is a wonderful and thorough book on using graphic organizers to illuminate research design, data collection, and data analysis. This is a good resource to help your writing, especially of complex situations or structures.

Wyse, D. (2012). *The good writing guide for education students* (3rd ed.). Thousand Oaks, CA: Sage. This book is excellent as a catch-up for doctoral students who may not have been involved in academic writing recently. Good examples lead the reader through first draft, comments, and how upgrades were made. Topics covered range from research, avoiding plagiarism, to referencing and all the bits in between.

6

Are You Ready to
Write Your Methodology?

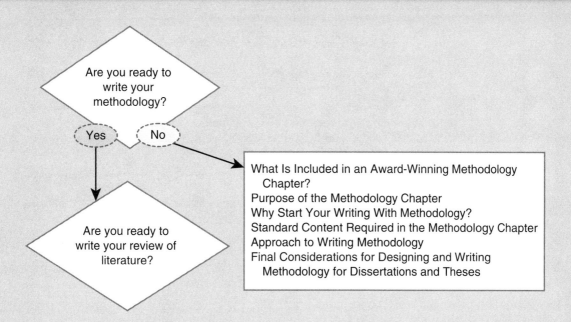

Are you ready to write your methodology?

Yes　No

Are you ready to write your review of literature?

What Is Included in an Award-Winning Methodology Chapter?
Purpose of the Methodology Chapter
Why Start Your Writing With Methodology?
Standard Content Required in the Methodology Chapter
Approach to Writing Methodology
Final Considerations for Designing and Writing Methodology for Dissertations and Theses

S TOP! If you have not already read your literature, designed your ideas, and put together a defensible plan, as outlined in Part I of this text, the answer to the question above is NO—you are not ready to write your methodology section(s). However, if those things are in place you may be ready and this is the chapter to help you decide if now is the time to delve in and write about the research you are proposing to undertake. We are suggesting that you write only after you have analyzed your literature, determined the gaps that support the need for your research, and uncovered the key issues you wish your work to clarify and build upon.

The purpose of this chapter is to build upon the outline of headings and model dissertations you already have in place. The goal is for you to be able to address the concerns of your committee as they assess this section of your dissertation or thesis. In order to do that, we discuss the topics related to methodology and how they thread throughout these documents. In addition to methodology writing dos and don'ts, we give you checklists for conceptual and theoretical frameworks and problem statements. The chapter ends with a checklist for ethical review, data collection, and data analysis.

Both the introductory and methodological chapters contain a portion of your methodological logic. As universities differ in approach and guidelines, we leave it up to you how much of your methodology you will later unfold in your introduction to your study and how much or which parts you will hold back to the finale of your proposal in your chapter on methodology. We offer what basics may be considered in each and leave it to you, your university, and your advisor to decide the specifics.

The Questions Answered in This Chapter:

1. What is included in an award-winning example of a methodology section?

2. Why do you suggest I start writing methodology first?

3. What is the purpose of the methodology sections?

4. What is the basic layout of the methodology chapter?

5. What portions of methodology may be included in your first chapter?

6. What is the best writing approach to ensure that it makes sense and flows?

7. What is the collection and analysis of qualitative and quantitative data really like?

8. What do I need to keep in mind for mixed or iterative methods?

9. What do I need to keep in mind about writing the different sections in this chapter?

What Is Included in an Award-Winning Methodology Chapter?

Methodology chapters vary in structure according to the methods they need to discuss. While all include an overview, the purpose and questions, the population and sample, how the data will be collected and analyzed, and a discussion of how ethical issues will be overcome, it may be said that those dissertations or theses which rise above the norm will use the methodology chapter as a means to tie together the threads laid out in the review of literature.

Reviewing Wakefield (2012) as an example, this author discussed complexity and cybernetics, laying out orders of thought as the main balance of her review of literature. Her research was to apply narrative inquiry to human systems of people working in nonprofit organizations so as to evaluate whether and to what extent they displayed modes of interaction that could be said to be fractals. She was looking for third order cybernetic constructs. To this end, her methodological chapter followed a fairly straightforward pattern, while also tying in the fractal as an outcome searched for through the discovery process.

We can see through her headings how she accomplished this:

Chapter 3: Methodology

Introduction

Methodology

Research Question

Operational Definition of a Fractal

Choice of Method

Conceptual Design

    Subjects

    Research Context

Qualitative Data Collection

Transcript Analysis

Validity

Ethical Considerations

Timeline

Limitations

Significance

Conclusion (Wakefield, 2012, p. 5)

Figure 6.1   How stable is your methodology?

Source: Chad Baker/Digital Vision/Thinkstock

Purpose of the Methodology Chapter

It may seem odd to both suggest that your methodology is the heart of the document that supports your study and then to ask what is its purpose, but we think it is worth considering because, unless you have a clear idea as to why you are writing this section, you may miss the point and produce, instead of a convincing argument for how you will answer important questions, a rather pedantic discussion of the pieces. In a recent slide show, we used the graphic of a hand pulling out a single block at the bottom of a stack—just the picture created the tension of "would the whole thing tumble with this block removed?" Methodology is similar to a stack of building blocks, and your reader, who most of the time has vastly more research experience than you do, will be asking if each and every block you give them adds sufficiently to the stability of the whole. It is your purpose with this writing to set up the building blocks of your research study in such a way as to convince your reader that your methodology is strong and will resist the tensions created by data collection and analysis in the real world (Booth, Colomb, & Williams, 2008; Garson, 2002; Hoyle, Harris, & Judd, 2002; Leedy & Ormrod, 2005).

There are two basic types of structures upon which your methodology will lay: fixed and flexible. The gold standard of the fixed design is the random control trial in which all your ideas, in fact every particle of your methodology, is fully planned and laid out prior to asking for ethical approval to proceed. Usually empirical, there will be less tolerance for changing procedure, questions, and so forth, or for error, as most analysis will be statistical. A flexible design, on the other hand, will usually make use of qualitative, mixed methods, or iterative methodologies. These designs are interactive with the environment, allowing researchers the advantage of being able to capitalize on early findings and to probe more deeply. Ideally suited for studies about the human condition, there would be debate in some parts of the world as to whether a flexible design is "scientific." Most agree today that if systematic and principled, based on academically approved frameworks, all commonly accepted methodologies can be considered "scientific" in nature (Pease, 2009).

Why Start Your Writing With Methodology?

"Working on Section III first allowed me to get to the crux of the dissertation first so that the literature review flows seamlessly into the methodology. Thank You so much!!! I wish they had taught us this in the class modules when we were beginning the drafting process!" (Jodi Leffingwell, DoctoralNet, 2012)

Where do you start writing? Many resources suggest that you first develop the review of literature, others have you starting with the introduction, but we take the stance that you will more effectively move through your dissertation writing process when you start with your methodology. Those who believe the former point out that because we are held to a high ethical standard in scientific methodology to be neutral, it is important that students have read and discussed all possible literature on the topic (Glatthorn & Joyner, 2005; Hart, 1998). Others will point out that the literature review uncovers gaps that methodology might then fill. Just to be clear, we do expect *that prior to writing anything, you have completed a comprehensive reading of what literature pertains to the topic of your study*, across fields, and so forth, yet believe that if you write methodology first, you will have less redundant writing than with any other path.

This does not mean that you do not need to delve deeply into the stream of academic ideas embedded in your topic. Your review of literature still must be detailed, and if you are partially replicating another study, you will need to know what discussions are needed to back up your methodology.

We have seen many doctoral students get to defense of proposal and their literature review lets them down. Why? Because they started the literature search when their methodology was not yet formed—and in the end they do not have literature on the variables they chose to study (when quantitative comparisons are being done) or on key background topics and considerations (when qualitative or mixed methods work is proposed). This leads to a lot of discussion at defense as to how/why they chose those particulars for their study and sometimes results in a significant rewrite. Starting with your methodology allows for you to avoid this scenario.

This chapter will build upon the work you will later do in your introduction to set up the context and purpose of your problem. Leave those notes aside for a moment, as your methodology builds on that foundation and starts with the problem statement and goes on to address how you will study those concerns or ideas. Examples from award-winning dissertations and theses illuminate these ideas and should propel a deeper conversation between you and your advisor/committee as to best or appropriate flow of that "golden thread" discussed earlier (Albertyn et al., 2007).

How the Methodology Chapter Fits in the Logic of the Proposal

As pointed out in Chapter 5, the basics of the logic of a proposal are that it starts with a problem, one that has wider significance and is also measureable in your local setting. From that you develop the purpose of your study and the questions you want to ask. Then you move on to develop your methodology— qualitative, if you need to understand the human elements and motivations from a few people, and quantitative, if you want to draw comparisons from one attribute (or variable) to another and have a large population/sample to survey. Mixed methods will be helpful if you want a little of both or to explore a situation over time or explain a situation from multiple points of view (Creswell, 2009; Pease, 2009; Piantanida & Garman, 1999).

Have you ever watched the construction of a skyscraper? If you have, you will notice that first they dig a very deep hole and pour in all the foundational elements below ground. The next step, though, is surprising, as they then build the elevator shaft, which is in the center of the building and reaches from the base of the foundation all the way up to what will be the roof of the structure. Each floor is raised and tied in to the support of that elevator shaft. For dissertations, the analogy is apt. First you begin to read everything you can about your subject and somewhere along 50 or more articles, you begin to have solid ideas about the particular problem in the particular local context that you will study and the way in which you will address your research. This is the foundation. If you feel you have gotten that far, then it may be time to build your elevator, which is your methodology. It will support every section in the rest of your proposal, in fact in the rest of your dissertation document. Do you think you might be ready to begin building the elevator shaft? If so, read on.

Figure 6.2 Your methodology is like an elevator shaft, it connects all the other sections of your dissertation.

Source: Jupiterimages/Photos.com/ Thinkstock

Standard Content Required in the Methodology Chapter

Your methodology sets the eventual height to which you aspire, in research terms, and should be broken into the following sections:

- Your introduction to the chapter reminds your reader of the <u>importance of your study.</u>
- Your background and purpose take your reader from why you are doing your study through what <u>questions you are asking or what hypothesis you are testing.</u>

- You then introduce any <u>conceptual or theoretical issues</u> that impinge upon the ideas you are researching or the way in which you are asking your questions.
- Your methodological design includes a discussion of the <u>participants, population, and /or sample</u> from which you will be gathering data, how you are contacting them, what data you are gathering, in what fashion, and how you will analyze it (<u>data collection and analysis</u>).
- You then discuss the <u>ethical issues</u> of consent and confidentiality.
- You acknowledge your conscious boundaries to this study (<u>delimiters</u>), the <u>assumptions</u> you're making, as well as the <u>limitations</u> you are forced to work under. In other words, a student who is evaluating at-risk populations in schools may set a delimiter that sets up a boundary to include lower socioeconomic status (or not). He or she may be forced to work under certain natural limitations because of the context of their study, such as a poverty level that is slightly above the state average, which may or may not affect the study's replicability. Both are mentioned in this chapter.

You close your chapter with the conclusion that reiterates the basic elements of the design leading your reader to naturally understand how it addresses your problem. At this point you have essentially come full circle (Creswell, 2009; Glatthorn & Joyner, 2005; Rudestam & Newton, 2007).

Remember that the full template of potential or proposed headings for this chapter can be found as part of Appendix A and that the rubric in Appendix D also applies.

Setting Up Internal Consistency: Linkages From Methodological Design to Other Parts of Your Proposal

Each of the underlined phrases above indicates an area of discussion within your methodology chapter that will have direct linkages within your document to other sections. These linkages are explained below:

- The <u>importance of your study</u> will likely also be discussed in your introduction/overview.
- The <u>questions you are asking or what hypotheses you are testing</u> are threads that run throughout your document: introduced in the overview, led up to by the literature, used as a sorting mechanism for discussion of the findings, and drawn to the conclusion in your last chapter.
- <u>Conceptual or theoretical issues</u> are generally discussed in more length in the review of literature—unless they are methodological issues, in which case they are often detailed in chapter 3.
- Your methodological or research design, including <u>participants, sample,</u> and <u>population</u> and <u>data collection and analysis,</u> is introduced in your introduction chapter and then discussed in detail in your findings and conclusion.
- <u>Ethical issues</u> may be brought up in your overview but they are discussed in detail with your methodology and then alluded to as necessary in your findings or conclusion.
- <u>Delimiters (the parameters you the researcher place on the study)</u> are the boundaries through which you tighten your design.
- <u>Assumptions</u> and <u>limitations</u> (potential weaknesses in the study) are the constraints you or your circumstances impose. They may also come up as you discuss your context in your introduction/overview and again during your explanation of the findings and conclusion.

You can see that your dissertation or thesis is not constructed like a train with one chapter covering a topic and then leaving it, but, as we said in Figure Preface Part 2.2, is a spiral with the key topics, almost all of which tie to how your study is run.

Figure 6.3   It may seem like each chapter is a separate car, linked together to make a train, but in actuality your dissertation is more like a spiral. You will revisit topics over and over again as you progress.

Source: Comstock Images/Comstock/Thinkstock

What Portions of Methodology Should Be Included in Which Chapters?

The constraint in writing for an international audience across disciplines is that there is no one "right" place for a discussion of the various portions of this logic.

Your introduction to the study provides background to the methodology while also including contextual background for the study. Portions of your methodological logic to consider to be placed in this chapter include the following: a clear statement of the problem, research questions/hypotheses, limitations of the study, clear statement of purpose, and so forth. The introduction chapter is fundamental to understanding the nature of a study; its importance to setting up your study cannot be overrated—in fact, this is why we recommend you write it or at least revise it last, when you have the rest of the components you are working with in place. You may choose to repeat some of these (certainly your research questions) in later sections. Be sure to copy and paste these verbatim—any variance creates unnecessary questions. You may also redirect your reader back to earlier sections as necessary.

The literature review can be tailored to the issue (problem statement) and proceed from a methodological point of view as well as from a topical one. What is important is that the variables, conditions, or ideas that you are measuring in your study are discussed in your literature.

The chapter that focuses on methodology expands on all these ideas to include participants, instruments, conditions, ethics, and so forth. A basic list of headings for this chapter includes the following: Introduction, Purpose and Problem Statement, Research Design, Population and Sample, Data Collection Procedures, Data Analysis Procedures, Instruments, Credibility, Validity and Reliability, Limitations, Assumptions and Delimiters, Researcher's Role, Human Subjects Protections, and Summary.

Approach to Writing the Methodology Chapter

As discussed in Chapter 1, we assume that you have at your disposal several model dissertations and that you have pulled together a final document and headings as indicated by Activity 1.2 and further discussed in the Preface to Part II. You are then ready to proceed with each section; reading others' work, deciding what information you will include, and structuring then restructuring every segment so that it flows together logically.

There are several indications in your writing when you are up against a topic that you don't fully understand. Take these as warning signs: One of the most common is when you want to start a sub-heading by directly quoting some famous authors' methodological material. Quotes are often areas that indicate you are less than 100% sure of your own voice or substance, and if this is the case, keep reading until you have found that security (Goodson, 2013).

Methodology Writing Dos and Don'ts

Do

- *Write with your own voice* and ideas, citing others who agree with you rather than quoting them. Nothing displays early stage or immature thought processes in dissertation writing more than an overbearing amount of sentences telling the reader what other writers have said. This is an indication of your own insecurity about your topic. It shows up most commonly in the methodology section where doctoral students frequently write sentences such as, "Creswell (2009) points out that qualitative research . . . " My suggestion is that you write all those sentences, and then, when you go back and edit, you highlight them and ask yourself what it is *you* wanted to say? Then rewrite something as, "This study makes use of qualitative evidence to . . . " and cite Creswell.
- Remember that your reader understands research methods better than you do. Therefore, you do not need to spend a lot of writing space telling them about the basics of research or defining common terms. Nothing displays lack of mastery like starting a section by explaining through citations and references what types of discussion that section must hold.
- *Refer to other sections where an aspect is discussed in length rather than be redundant.* Since the methodological topics will be discussed from different angles throughout your dissertation, it may seem difficult to avoid redundancy—work with your award winners or models and see how they solved this problem.

Don't

- *Use words for which you are not completely sure of the meaning* or process involved. As an example, if you are inclined to do a qualitative study because you want to interview people, do not call that study phenomenology until you are completely sure what phenomenological data collection and analysis procedures would entail. The same goes for every methodological word that you use.
- Describe your methodology differently in each section. As an example, if your data collection procedures include five different methods, be consistent in how they are mentioned.
- *Change the way in which you describe your problem or purpose from section to section.* Remember that even small changes in language can imply large changes in methodology. As an example, one student's words kept wandering from whether the purpose of her work was to study cultural curriculum in her school or to study the effects of that curriculum. The purpose as it is first stated would lead her to

Figure 6.4 Using too many quotes in your writing can indicate a lack of mastery over the material.

Source: ©iStockphoto.com/ anna_elsewhere

do an evaluation study of the curriculum, the second would require a much wider range of mixed methodological input and a specific definition of which "effects" she was looking for.

- *Use textbook explanations in the methods sections.* Your reader understands what the terms mean. Should you be using a variant on the normal use of the term for theoretical, philosophical, or methodological issues, these are discussed in your terms of use section and referred to again as needed. Such variations must be built upon the work of a well-known expert.

Final Considerations for Designing and Writing Methodology for Dissertations and Theses

Conceptual and Theoretical Frameworks: Final Considerations

Do you understand the difference between theoretical and conceptual design? Ravitch and Riggan (2012) discovered that the term *conceptual framework* was used in at least three different ways: as a representation of the major theoretical tenets, to mean the same thing as theoretical frameworks, and (as it is used here) as a way of linking all the elements of the research process together. They go on to define conceptual framework as "an argument about why the topic matters and why the means proposed to study it are appropriate and rigorous" (p. 7). It is this definition that in our mind sets the doctoral student up properly for defense and therefore expedites the writing process.

In Chapter 5, we discussed the purpose of deciding for yourself what your underlying theoretical stance would be and how it would support your work. Conceptual frameworks take that foundation further by building most of the components into the required content listed above and linking them in such a way as the reader can move easily from section to section. None of these thoughts or ideas exists independently of each other in a research design. The *importance of your study* leads to the *questions you are asking or what hypothesis you are testing*, which must rest on the foundation of how you interpret the *conceptual or theoretical issues* that you discuss. Your local context decides *the population/sample/participants* and your access to those people determine the *data collection and analysis* procedures you design. *Ethical issues* temper your work, as do *delimiters, assumptions,* and *limitations* (Creswell, 2009; Krathwohl & Smith, 2005; Mauch & Park, 2003).

The following excerpts from award-winning dissertations will give you an idea of how it might work together in your thesis.

In the dissertation, "The process of choosing science, technology, engineering, and mathematics careers by undergraduate women: A narrative life history analysis," Hughes (2010) chose to devote an entire short methodology chapter to her conceptual framework. While only six pages long, it serves as an excellent transition between her literature review on gender roles and her methodology. In this chapter, she first discusses gender roles, and when, during the development of a female child, she is likely to move away from science and engineering career choices. Hughes's choice to set this content completely apart ends up making it easy for her readers to understand how her ideas on gender roles both develop from her literature and underpin her methodology. While Ravitch and Riggan (2012) might prefer all of these components in the same section, in this example the components function very well when they are separate.

Ravitch and Riggan (2012) conclude that conceptual frameworks "inform a researcher's process of choice making and framing" (p. 82). Especially if you are a student whose university works on the model more prevalent in the United Kingdom, you will find that the time it takes to build a solid conceptual framework for your study will be worth it tenfold because of how much time it saves you during the write-up of the data analysis, findings, and conclusions section. In this sense, the conceptual framework is a map that helps you not only understand where to go next but that also functions to remind you where you have been as you retrofit a large document into what is usually two or three years of process.

Keep in mind, the conceptual framework may or may not be laid out in the research methodology, even though that is the most frequent place for it. As an example, in the award-winning dissertation, "Racism readiness as an educational outcome for graduates of historically black colleges and universities: a multi-campus grounded theory study," McMickens (2011) chose to include his conceptual framework at the end of his literature review. There he discusses critical race theory, perspectives on racial socialization, and sense making. While his definition of conceptual framework is closer to being equivalent to theoretical foundations, it is not uncommon to see methodological literature discussed in the same location. This example is given just to remind you that it is your choice as to what and where are the best places to include information so that your reader tracks it easily and at a comfortable pace.

Problem Statement Final Checklist

Problem statements were discussed in Chapter 4. Since the standard of doctoral work is that it contributes meaningfully to your field, your problem statement sets your methodology up for success, and as you write your methodology chapter it is a good time to double-check that you can say yes to the following questions:

- Have you justified the importance of the problem using relevant statistics or other documentation of discrepancy through which your reader will conclude that this issue is authentic and needs solving?
- Have you grounded or framed the problem in such a way that it is clear how it builds upon previously published findings or research on this topic?
- Is the research topic meaningful or does it fill a gap in either research or practice?
- Is it obvious that it can be studied? In other words, are there multiple solutions or conclusions that could present themselves and therefore the issue needs to be teased out more to be understood (Krathwohl & Smith, 2005)?

The following is an exemplar problem statement from one of the award-winning dissertations we studied. In his study, evaluating the influence of stakeholder relationships on corporate performance, Finch (2010) takes care of all of these issues directly and concisely.

Researchers have argued that relationship capital is intrinsically linked to shareholder value (Bontis & Serenko, 2009; Daum, 2002; Kaplan & Norton, 2004; Lacey, 2007; see also Ledingham,

2003; MacMillan et al., 2004; Porter, 1985, 2008; Prior, 2006, 2007). The problem is how to understand the empirical relationship between the quality of a firm's relationship with its stakeholders and shareholder value. To confront this problem, I designed and tested a statistical model and instrument that enables researchers to empirically link stakeholder generated relationship capital to shareholder value. (p. 6).

It should be noted that Finch chose to include his entire problem statement in the first chapter, referring to it as the foundation of his methodological work found later in the methodology chapter. In fact, it is not a bad idea to repeat it (verbatim) in chapters 3 and 4 near the beginning of each—this helps ground the reader and yourself as you write.

Ethical Review, Data Collection, and Analysis Final Checklist

To what extent do you understand the real work involved once you start to collect and analyze data? We have found that many students run into data collection and analysis having maintained an otherwise mental distance from it, almost as though they were holding the real work at arm's length. In this small section, we want to highlight issues that may stand before you, depending upon the methodological choices you have made. Hopefully you will have something in place and will be able to answer yes to any of the following questions that apply to your study.

Figure 6.5 Oftentimes, people who promised to speak with you or provide data end up not responding. Make sure you have a backup plan.

Source: © Can Stock Photo Inc. / zetwe

- The people you have targeted as your study participants may not want to engage with your data collection efforts. Everywhere in the world we hear the same story, that data are hard to gather, unexpectedly people are not responding, even though they had promised beforehand that they would. Do you have a backup plan should your data collection procedures stall?
- If you are hoping to use people for the study participants rather than make use of archival data for your study, do they belong to the same group or work for the same organization? If so, have you obtained written permission for your study from the managers of the group or business? Many ethical review boards will require it.
- If you are working in your own organization, do you have access to an adequate number of study participants for whom you have no managerial tasks or are in no position that could be construed as powerful? Otherwise you may be up against ethical issues that will stall your study.

Figure 6.6   Consider the time involved in your data collection and analysis. For every hour of recorded data, expect up to 6 hours of transcription and analysis time.

Source: Jack Hollingsworth/Photodisc/Thinkstock

- Quantitative data collection instruments, especially those you design yourself, are becoming increasingly hard to get past ethical review boards. If you wish to do quantitative designs, you should query your advisors as to the current status of ethical review at your university. Many hours are lost in research design only to find out that even an approved proposal will not pass ethical review. If you are hoping to use a personally designed instrument, do you have another option as a backup? Have you been able to find an instrument used in previous studies for which you can obtain approval and from which you can gather evidence that pertains to your problem and purpose? Have you lined up quantitative software and learned how to use it, to make the task easier?

- If you plan to collect qualitative data, have you considered the likelihood that for every hour of data collection, you will have twice as long or more for the transcription, prior to two or three hours of data analysis? A 1:6 ratio of time is not uncommon. Also, have you lined up qualitative data software to make coding, recoding, and sorting easier? Have you gone through the tutorials and learned how it is designed?

- If employing a methodology which requires iterative cycles of data collection and analysis, have you plotted the timeline from approval to finishing? Have you anticipated an extra 25% in the time resource mix to provide adequate flexibility when unexpected developments take your research in a nonlinear path?

- If your analysis is based upon quantitative data, have you familiarized yourself with the style requirements of your university for charts, figures, and other graphic means of representation?

- If doing a mixed methods study, can you answer yes to all of the questions for both qualitative and quantitative work?

Once you have educated yourself as to the requirements included in each of these questions and can honestly answer yes to all which apply to your methodology, you are in a better place to be able to write the appropriate methodology sections of your dissertation or thesis.

Chapter 6 Checklist

☐ I understand features of an award-winning methodology chapter.

☐ I understand the layout of the methodology chapter.

☐ I understand the best approach to writing it so that it makes sense and flows.

☐ I understand what is required as I collect and analyze my data.

☐ I have written a draft of my methodology chapter.

Where Should I Go to Dig Deeper? Suggested Resources to Consider

Creswell, J. W. (2009). *Research design: Qualitative, quantitative, and mixed methods approaches* (3rd ed.). Thousand Oaks, CA: Sage. Creswell remains the easiest to grasp yet is a thorough introduction to research methodology.

Gliner, J. A., Morgan, G. A., & Leech, N. L. (2009). *Research methods in applied settings: An integrated approach to design and analysis* (2nd ed.). New York: Routledge. An excellent text recommended by one of our reviewers as a great basic for quantitative research.

Maxwell, J. A. (2013). *Qualitative research design: An interactive approach* (3rd ed.). Thousand Oaks: Sage. A classic. This book offers a concise yet rigorous and thorough examination of qualitative design.

Morgan, G. A., Leech, N. L., Gloeckner, G. W., & Barrett, K. C. (2011). *IBM SPSS for introductory statistics: Use and interpretation*. New York: Routledge. Chapters 1, 3, and 6 respectively are a must read for quantitative researchers covering variables, research problems, questions, measurement, and descriptive statistics and the selection of and interpretation of inferential statistics. This is written in down-to-earth language and augmented by a thorough example that uses data from the High School and Beyond study.

Ravitch, S. M., & Riggan, M. (2012). *Reason & rigor: How conceptual frameworks guide research*. Thousand Oaks, CA: Sage. This provides an explicit and in-depth discussion of how to employ conceptual frameworks as a means to increase and ensure that the primary to the party will be rigor in your overall research design.

Sapsford, R. (2007). *Survey research* (2nd ed.). Thousand Oaks, CA: Sage. This is an excellent resource for quantitative work.

7

Are You Ready to Write Your Review of Literature?

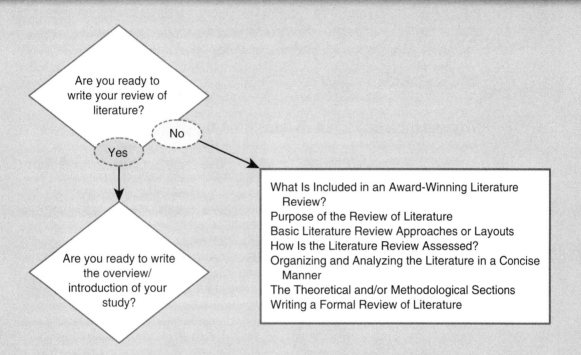

Are you ready to write your review of literature?

Yes

No

What Is Included in an Award-Winning Literature Review?
Purpose of the Review of Literature
Basic Literature Review Approaches or Layouts
How Is the Literature Review Assessed?
Organizing and Analyzing the Literature in a Concise Manner
The Theoretical and/or Methodological Sections
Writing a Formal Review of Literature

Are you ready to write the overview/ introduction of your study?

S TOP! If you have not already collected a wealth (approaching 100) of examples of what you believe to be excellent pieces of literature and research foundational to your study, then the answer to this question is no. Part I of the book might serve you better if you are also just starting to read literature.

The purpose of this chapter is to help you write the perfect review of literature, which will lead your reader to easily understand your topic, the purpose for doing your research, and the methodological or theoretical ideas that impinge upon your decision making. In order to do that, you will need to understand first the basic approach and layout of the chapter, including the standards for assessment by which it is usually judged. We will then cover how theoretical and methodological literature might be addressed. The chapter ends with hints and suggestions for a successful literature review chapter.

The Questions Answered in This Chapter:

1. What is included in an award-winning example of a literature review?

2. What is the purpose of the review of literature?

3. How do I incorporate theory in my review of literature?

4. What do others look for in the literature review?

5. What is the basic layout of a literature review?

6. How do I incorporate theory or methodology into my literature review?

7. What is the relationship between my review of the literature and my methodology?

What Is Included in an Award-Winning Literature Review?

For this discussion we overviewed three award-winning dissertations, one each using qualitative, quantitative, and mixed methodologies (Paige, 2007; Pershing, 2003; Scharff, 2005). While this is certainly a convenience sample, several aspects were consistent between them: (1) length, (2) organization, and (3) scope. All three contained a review of literature that was over 60 pages in length, and while length is never an absolute measure of quality, given this chapter's inclusion in an award-winning document, we may conclude that their conversance with the literature in their field was both comprehensive and convincing. Second, they were organized into a discussion of their topic/subtopics that lead the readers to easily understand how the author determined what concerns to focus on and how to pursue their own study. Finally, their literature review drilled down from a very wide scope through the ideas and research to the specific. As you will see from the example below, Pershing (2003) goes so far as to exactly outline the expected correlations she will search for in her study.

Chapter 2: Review of the Literature

Introduction

Convergence Versus Nonconvergence

Development of the Directiveness Continuum

    Autocratic and Democratic Approaches to Management

    Communication

    Organizational Cultures

    National Value Differences

    The Directiveness Continuum

How Subgroup Membership Affects Beliefs About Management

Models Linking Values and Beliefs With Workplace Behavior

Socialization Process

Core and Periphery Values — Resolving the Conflicts

The Value of Studying Subgroups

Subgroup Characteristics

Age

Theoretical Relevance

Expected Correlations

Gender

Theoretical Relevance

Expected Correlations

Nationality

Theoretical Relevance

Expected Correlations

Education Field

Theoretical Relevance

Expected Correlations

Level of Education

Theoretical Relevance

Expected Correlations

Functional Area

Theoretical Relevance

Expected Correlations

Hierarchy

Theoretical Relevance

Expected Correlations

Subgroups Lacking Theoretical or Practical Relevance

Strength of Subgroup Influences

A Taxonomy of Subgroup Influences

Elements of the Taxonomy

Implications of the Taxonomy

Ethical Issues

Summary (Pershing, 2003, p. iv)

Purpose of the Review of Literature

At the basic level, your review of literature informs your reader of the main ideas, topics, arguments, or disagreements upon which your study rests. Therefore, at that level, the purpose of your literature review is to set up the topics of your study. It is for this reason that we point out the necessity for a one-to-one correspondence between ideas and the topics you investigate in your study. We have seen many dissertations or theses wobble during defense because topics covered in the research were not discussed in the literature or vice versa.

Taking it to a higher level, Patton (2008) points out that the purpose of a review of the literature is not exactly to "review" but really to place your work within the greater academic traditions of your field of study in order to better understand the contribution of your work to the field. It is a means to the end of understanding our "intellectual heritage." Therefore, you are "after" those authors who formulated the basic ideas upon which your field of study rests. You are also pursuing your current place in the developing stream of ideas. And as with moving down any stream, we need to make peace with where we are—others may be ahead of you and considered more provocative or leading edge. All research is needed, and it is just as valid to restudy an older position in a new way or in a new context as it is to develop new ideas. However, you need to know where you are in that stream, to discuss it and to differentiate your voice from those of your colleagues.

Once you have gathered the literature/ideas that inform and support the reasons and purposes of your research, you will also need to consider where your study rests theoretically and methodologically within your field. To the extent that your study will push the norm of either theory or practice you will want to discuss those ideas as separate topics.

Therefore, taking together all of these considerations, you may have developed and collected literature that could be discussed under the following headings: history, theoretical issues, issues of practice, issues of policy, methodological considerations, and subtopics that will lead directly to the variables or discussion points relevant to your research.

Figure 7.1 The purpose of a literature review is to place your work within the larger context of work that had been done in your field of study.

Source: Goodshoot/Goodshoot/Thinkstock

Basic Literature Review Approaches or Layouts

There are three basic approaches or layouts to your review of literature. Rudestam and Newton (2007), in *Surviving Your Dissertation,* remind us that many movies start with a panorama shot of the countryside, quickly panning in closer and closer until the viewer is all consumed by the major action of the drama. A literature review often develops in much the same way. You may choose to include the historical development of your topic, its impact on a wide range of issues, the development of the legal aspects of the issue, and so forth. Keep this section short (a few paragraphs), as these points seldom lead directly to the ways and means in which your study questions or methodology develop. This broad to narrow approach leads you to discuss how your literature answers very specific questions and ultimately very specific discussions about the authors you have read and their work. You might diagram this approach as a triangle with the broad section on the top, leading your reader down to the specific section at the bottom (Bloomberg & Volpe, 2012; Hart, 1998; Patton, 2008).

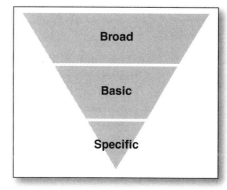

Figure 7.2 Common Approach to Writing a Review of Literature

Figure 7.2, right, illustrates this approach from the broad topic, through the basics of the specific areas you need the reader to understand in your research study, through to the specific discussions that lead to the variables you will measure.

One of our reviewers points out that this diagram is best conceived in tandem with the reverse, as shown in Figure 7.3, explaining that detail increases with critical analysis as your topic gets more specific (Gloeckner, 2013).

But what if you are pulling from diverse fields of study? Researchers pushing the edges of knowledge in their field, along with policy analysts, social scientists, and so forth in disciplines that require a broad-based background might instead find themselves constructing a literature review that is more like a Venn diagram of three overlapping circles. In this case, you would first discuss the broader areas

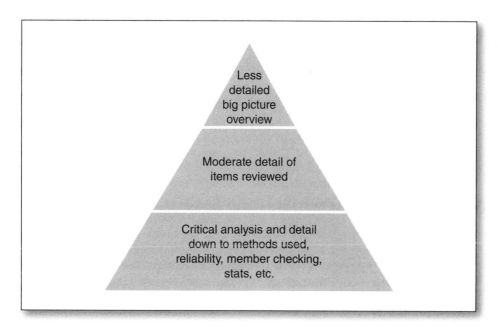

Figure 7.3 Level of Detail in Sections and Analysis

and then the places each pair overlapped. Finally, you would move to discuss the central portion that incorporated all the literature you had discussed as it related to your study.

The third and last approach and layout of your literature review might be a case where your topics, although diverse, fit together without overlap, much like a jigsaw puzzle. As an example, this might happen if there was a historical evolution that developed four distinct variables of measurement, all of which had bearing on the topic you were studying. You would then describe each part of the puzzle and how they related to each other through their edges and to your topic (Libberton, 2011).

Figure 7.4 illustrates, should you take this approach, building a literature review so that your reader understands the diverse topics that led to the logical evolution of your study. Quantitative researchers may choose to organize around sample groupings or divisions, independent or dependent variables, geographic categories, or how a theme plays out internationally, nationally, regionally, and then to the problem area. Historical categories in literature may also help organize your thoughts as in the example of a student studying how to improve calculus. Evidently this was a topic of concern for 30 to 50 years over the last century (Gloeckner, 2013).

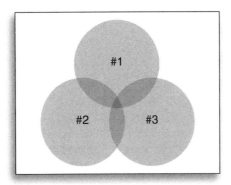

Figure 7.4 A literature review that pulls form diverse fields of study but where topics overlap can resemble a Venn diagram.

Figure 7.5 Finishing a literature review built on individual pieces of information.

Source: Ryan McVay/Photodisc/Thinkstock

How Is the Literature Review Assessed?

As you see in the assessment rubric in Appendix D, the literature review is held to a minimum standard of being well researched, well presented, and your discussion judged as adequately assessing or interpreting the work of previous authors on your topic. What you want, however, is for your literature review to be elegantly written, presenting ideas and drawing out their importance in such a way as to draw your reader into your work. You want your reader to see the significance of your work as it plays off of the ideas of others. You do this both in who you discuss and in your conceptual understanding of the theoretical, methodological, and research literature on which you are basing your ideas.

In the Preface to Part II, we discussed that critical analysis is the writer's ability to look at something from all angles. This is especially true during your review of literature, and the degree of sophistication to which you bring your best thoughts in this section will do much to convince your defense committee of the worthiness of your project and ideas. Since academic analysis is seldom a standard skill for new researchers, you might consider reading award-winning dissertations in both your field and those that match your methodology.

In order to fully consider an important aspect of your topic, you may decide to break the review of literature into more than one chapter. Reasons for doing this might include the following: a variety of theoretical ideas that need to be discussed at length, a desire on your part to separate a methodological discussion from that surrounding your topic, or perhaps the technological breakthroughs that illuminate the reason your topic is critical.

Your ability to discuss each topic from multiple angles will also do much to convince your committee of the neutrality of your stance in the research. It is especially important that your reader finishes your dissertation completely convinced that you have discussed literature that agrees and disagrees within itself. It needs to be clear that your review of literature is not so narrow as to support just one particular outcome to the questions you are asking. Slanted views of the literature lead the committee to ask questions, such as (a) if all the literature has answered the questions already, then why are you asking them again? or (b) have you not dug deep enough yet to uncover areas of disagreement within the topics you are discussing? Academia being what it is, there are always disagreements or subtle areas where previous researchers have differed one from another. It is a requirement of depth that you have read enough to have uncovered such areas and are prepared to discuss them.

Organizing and Analyzing the Literature in a Concise Manner

In Chapter 3, as we discussed your beginning investigation of your literature, we suggested that you begin to take notes in bibliographic software and that you record specific ideas of interest in everything you read. Those notes will become critically important now. First decide upon the headings you wish to discuss, then consider which one of the three types of layouts discussed at the beginning of this chapter (upside down triangle, Venn diagram, or jigsaw puzzle) best suits your needs in order to lead your reader carefully through your topic (Libberton, 2011). Finally, open up all your bibliographic references that have been sorted into topics and subtopics and begin to arrange in your mind what the most important ideas are for your reader to understand. Remember, you have read hundreds of articles or books on this topic and every other consideration that goes with it. Your task now is to condense the substance of that into a coherent discussion that can be easily followed (Figure 7.6). Consider researching mind mapping or other forms of graphic organization to help put your thoughts together.

Figure 7.6 Your task is to condense the hundreds of articles you have read into a coherent discussion that is easy to follow.

Source: ©iStockphoto.com/higyou

Organizing Authors and Ideas

Organization will make a great deal of difference as to how easily your reader follows your discussion. Your job is to carefully guide your reader to what you consider the most important aspects, while still giving an unbiased discussion of the work that pertains to your subject and your research design. What does not work is throwing in everything you have read and letting your reader sort out the meaning.

Figure 7.7 (below) demonstrates the way you read, one author at a time with each author donating an idea or two to the topic of your study. You can see that some overlap and others don't. The headings will vary as they might be dependent or independent variables, findings, and so forth; the point being that you read and develop the ideas appropriate to your methodology one author at a time, but as you will see this is not the way to discuss them.

Author	Concept A	Concept or Idea B	Idea C	Problem D	Solution E
Heifetz	X		X	X	
Benden	X	X		X	X
Klaus			X		
Hotz			X	X	X

Figure 7.7   How We Pick Up Ideas as We Read

If, in our writing, we follow the horizontal arrows in Figure 7.7 (which represent the way we acquired the information), we would say: Heifetz talks about Concept A, Idea C, and Problem D. Benden talks about Concept A, Concept or Idea B, Problem D, and Solution E. Klause talks about Idea C. Hotz talks about Idea C, Problem D, and Solution E. If you write in the same chronological fashion that you acquired the information, you will quickly put your readers to sleep.

Therefore, as shown in Figure 7.8 (below), an adept writer discusses things in terms of concepts or ideas, teasing out variations among authors or research studies. In this way, we would say: Concept A (Heifetz, Benden), Concept or Idea B (Benden), Idea C (Heifetz, Klaus, Hotz), Problem D (Heifetz, Benden, Hotz) and Solution E (Benden, Hotz). This organizational structure is a better format for clearly presenting the important topics discussed in your literature.

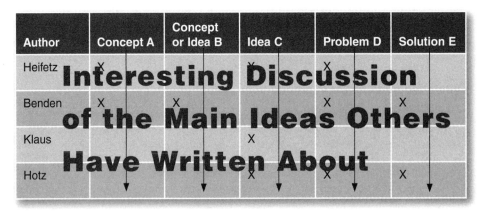

Figure 7.8   The Development of an Interesting Discussion or Critical Analysis of an Idea

Analyzing Gaps

Many authors, indeed some universities, suggest or require you to include a discussion of your analysis of gaps that may exist within the scope of literature of your topic. In an ideal world, your topic fits within one of those gaps, and therefore you highlight it in that discussion. A gap may show up if you organize your ideas in a similar fashion to the graphic organizers above. It may be that while the topic has been researched under many conditions, none of them exactly match those of your local context. Or you may see that a variable within your local context has not been sufficiently studied. You may even have a unique perspective so that your discussion of the literature uncovers which of your unique ideas would add to the overall study (Bryant, 2004; Glatthorn & Joyner, 2005; Hart, 1998; Roberts, 2004).

Figure 7.9 Remember to go back to the roots of the tree to quote and cite primary authors rather than staying out on the branches.

Source: ©iStockphoto.com/Orla

To help uncover gaps, you might also think about which of your sources would be considered primary or secondary. A primary source is an author who has a unique idea and may have researched aspects of it for a number of years, becoming an expert as she used her work to develop distinctive ideas. Primary sources use data they have collected upon which to build their ideas. A secondary source is someone who uses those ideas, references and cites them, building nuances as they go. Secondary data sources include archives of data collected, often by government agencies and for which special permissions may be needed to work with the raw data. As you read, you should be able to determine which authors fall under which category. *If you were to draw a tree with the primary authors at the roots [and trunk], multiple secondary authors' ideas branch out from this well-developed trunk into many directions* (Figure 7.9). A common mistake for doctoral candidates is to quote from secondary materials without justifying why they did not revert to primary sources instead.

A gaps analysis is an important procedure to undertake to see what the roots of the primary sources may allude to, but which so far secondary work has not confirmed or denied. You have uncovered a problem or situation worthy of greater study—what makes it worthy is that some gap in what is known still exists and your study will help fill that hole. Where the linkages between primary and secondary resources are weak or missing, it becomes graphically apparent where gaps still exist. In other words, your work might answer a question that could fill one of those gaps. For quantitative work you may find it useful in identifying gaps to include differences in findings and effect sizes.

Activity 7.1 Exercise to Create a Better Review of Literature

Earlier, we suggested that you ask your university for guidelines on what they consider to be a rigorous review of literature. If you found no clear guidelines available, it is reasonable to assume that 75 to 100 pieces of peer-reviewed literature might be a minimum number to be used in your writing. This is perhaps about average for the review of literature for a dissertation or thesis. It is likely therefore that you have read approximately 150 to 200 articles, which, at an average of three read and notated per week, equates to approximately a year of reading (Walden University, 2010).

Which articles, of all those you have read, are worthy to be included in your final writing? Those which contained information that led to the terms that define your final research questions will easily make this list. Still, you may have difficulty deciding on some of the others. Those about which you can answer the following questions with a yes! meet the highest criteria for inclusion.

The following are criteria for analysis of rigorous and relevant articles within a review of literature:

- Was this article published within the last three to five years? While this may not matter for some topics, most new research needs to be based or at least obviously aware of the latest in your field. Will this article demonstrate that you understand what is current?
- Have you read the articles to which this modern work refers? Do you know which are the seminal pieces of literature that should be mentioned in your study?
- Does the author draw out a complete explanation? After you read an article, you are left with a sense that they either explained something very well and/or that you understand what they were discussing better or more fully than before.
- Have you seen these ideas before? If so, is there any indication that this author is an original source (i.e., this is someone that others cite and reference)? If no and these ideas seem to be important to your argument, go through this author's references and keep tracking back until you find the original source. You should strive to always include original sources in your literature review.
- Rate the author's quality in building a logical argument. Do they seem to think critically and deeply about their (and your) topic? Generally, if you have found the article provocative in some way, there is a spark there—now ask yourself about whether their scholarship goes deep enough so that it can be a foundation for your work? This may be demonstrated through an analysis of the interrelationships within your topic area. Another clue would be an author who discusses procedures or assumptions, is transparent in his reasoning, and demonstrates an expertise on which he bases his ideas. If the ideas are good but the scholarship is weak, see if you can find other articles that back it up, or, better yet, improve upon it.
- Is this article quotable? Does the author write particularly well, put things in an engaging way, or say something startling?
- Have you found other articles that take a differing point of view from this one? If so, make note of the comparison. If you have not yet found opposing points of view, make a note to look for them, as a truly great and neutral review of literature, like a debater, knows the substance of all sides of an argument and then writes what is acceptable from various points of view, leading the reader to why the particular approach was chosen.
- Finally, if this article is research, can you find the purpose, scope, methodology, findings, conclusions, limitations, and contributions of it to the field? If so, then these can be noted in the abstract section of EndNote or whatever database you are using to categorize your literature (Hart, 1998; Walden University, 2010). Other types of studies will be well served by taking great notes on the methods section in the writing: who were the participants, what are the variables studied, which were dependent or independent, how do these authors discuss reliability and validity of their instruments (Gloeckner, 2013)?

Some students have told me they keep this list on the computer and then have a code for their overall impression against these ideas—ranking 1 to 5. The rank is then added to a field in their bibliographic software, allowing them to sort by topics and then rank by rigor prior to writing. Realize that when articles meet few of these criteria they have little to contribute to your scholarly work and are not worth the time it takes to notate them for your references.

The Theoretical and/or Methodological Sections

We said earlier that some authors choose to separate the discussion of theoretical or methodological issues involved in the study into completely separate chapters. This is appropriate when you wish your reader to give some separate consideration to one or both of these. In order to illustrate our point, let's look at the table of contents for a couple of studies where theoretical and/or methodological considerations were very important.

Starting with Espino (2008) we see in the layout of her chapter II that first she reports on research about the Mexican American experience in various levels of school. Because the theoretical concepts of social construction of education, various forms of capital, and most importantly, critical race theory, are central to her methodology and final arguments, she spends the majority of this chapter focused on these ideas. Even a casual reader, when looking at this chapter layout, would expect a detailed and critical analysis of how these theoretical concepts play into her research design because of the clarity in the layout of ideas through the headings and subheadings.

CHAPTER II: LITERATURE REVIEW

Mexican American Educational Attainment

    Mexican American Experiences in Secondary Education

    Mexican American Experiences in College

    Mexican American Experiences in Graduate School

Summary of Mexican American Educational Attainment

    Theoretical Concepts that Frame the Study

        Social Construction of Education

        Forms of Capital

            Cultural Capital

            Community Cultural Wealth

    Theoretical Framework

        Critiques of Critical Race Theory and Latina/o Critical Race

            Theory

        Summary

    Challenges to the Dominant Ideology: Master Narratives and Counter

Narratives

Master Narratives

Counter-Narratives

Dialectic Relationships and the Decolonial Imaginary

Summary (Espino, 2008, p. 6)

In contrast but for similar reasons, Meyer (2007) separates relative conceptual and theoretical frames and designates an entire chapter to their discussion. The next chapter (not shown here) discusses the literature as it relates to the development of digital photograph techniques (his topic). Notice, being a biologically oriented scientific study, he uses the numerical notation of "Chapter.Topic. Subtopic" prior to each heading. Also note that, again just by looking at the table of contents, the reader is prepared for critical analysis of these discussions when they see that a topic is broken down into its methods, weaknesses, or limitations as is the case with his discussion of Socio-Technical Interaction Networks (STINs) or his critique of Actor-Network Theory (ANT).

CHAPTER 2: THEORY REVIEW

2.1 Communication Regimes

2.2 Social Construction of Technology (SCOT)

    2.2.1 Social construction

    2.2.2 Relevant social group

    2.2.3 Interpretive flexibility

    2.2.4 Technological frames

    2.2.5 Closure and stabilization

    2.2.6 Mutual shaping

    2.2.7 Case studies

    2.2.8 Critiques of SCOT

2.3 Actor-Network Theory (ANT)

    2.3.1 Actants

    2.3.2 Black-boxing

    2.3.3 Translation and enrollment

    2.3.4 ANT methods

    2.3.5 Critiques of ANT

2.4 Socio-Technical Interaction Networks (STINs)

    2.4.1 Similarities and differences between Bijker, Latour and Kling

    2.4.2 Socio-Technical Interaction Networks (STINs)

    2.4.3 STIN studies

    2.4.4 STIN methods

2.4.5 STIN weaknesses and limitations

2.4.6 Future of STIN studies

2.5 Conclusion (Meyer, 2007, p. viii)

For comparison and contrast, this section from the table of contents of the thesis of Apori-Nkansah (2008), who won an award from her university for her work titled "Transitional justice in post-conflict contexts: The case of Sierra Leone's dual accountability mechanisms," illustrates how you might choose to set aside the literature pertaining to your methodology as a part of your literature review.

CHAPTER 2: LITERATURE REVIEW

Introduction

Defining and Conceptualizing Transitional Justice

The Basis of Transitional Justice

Tools for Transitional Justice

    Criminal Prosecutions

        Functions of Criminal Trials

        Criticisms against Prosecutions

    Restorative Justice

        Truth Commissions

        Functions of Truth Commissions

        Why Truth Commissions

        Criticisms of Truth Commissions

    Engaging Restorative and Punitive Approaches

    Choosing to Leave the Past Alone

Transitional Context and Dilemma of Accountability Choices

Criticisms of Transitional Justice

Review of Conceptual Framework and Methods

    Conceptual Framework

    Review of Methods

Discussions Analysis and Conclusions (Apori-Nkansah, 2008, p. iv)

This author chose to discuss the literature on which she based her conceptual framework and methodology separate from the methodological chapter itself. This has the advantage of allowing her to discuss the theoretical and conceptual components of methodology without having her readers bogged down in these details and losing sight of the actual process she is proposing, which should be the focus of the methodology section.

As we have seen, there are many places where you may choose to separate, either through head-ing or section, a group of ideas to make it easier for your reader to absorb their importance within the context of the review of literature. There are several other important reasons an author may set aside certain topics. These include (a) the need to stress certain issues, (b) to carefully examine concepts, (c) to describe complexities, (d) to unpack methodological assumptions, and (e) to analyze issues of argumentation or limitations of what they have read.

Stressing Certain Issues

It is important that you map out the issues in such a way that your reader understands the components of each one as they add to the whole. Whether you might choose to map the issues in chronological, methodological, or political contexts, your intent would be to describe the similarities or tensions inherent within your study. As an example, if you were studying efficacy within an organization, your reader would need to understand the issues/constraints of each of the subsets involved.

Examining Concepts

While your reader usually knows the ins and outs of methodology, they seldom understand your topic area as much as you will after having completed your review. Also, you will want your thesis to live on and inform readers in the future. Therefore be sure to include the basic building blocks of your ideas to ensure all readers can follow your logic. This is perhaps even more necessary if your topic is one in which most people will have some idea or opinion. As an example, students writing about politically charged issues or those involving racial or ethnic inequality may need to examine foundational ideas and concepts upon which public opinions are likely to be based.

Alana says: *As an example, when I first started to work in education I focused on those students who were considered "at risk." An important concept for these students is one of resiliency, which forms the base of an entire set of programs considered to be "strengths based." Prior to any reader understanding the nuances of this work, they would need the foundation of the duality set up by "strengths-based" as opposed to "deficit" models.*

Describing Complexity

Many times authors are studying complex adaptive issues or emerging topics that interact with several systems upon which impinge the behavior or resources being studied. As an example, most business issues fit this model, as they are constantly evolving within and constrained by what has gone before. By definition, the complexity of these problems dismays us because they put us in the center of the tension between the ideal (what we want) and reality (the confusion we are studying). For instance, in perfection we might desire businesses that do everything right or schools that run perfectly. We would wish that all of the staff were happy in their work and had abundant resources at their disposal. The realities in many schools or businesses are that none of these ideals exist.

Whatever the key tensions that surround your topic, you will need to have explored them as part of your review of the literature (Figure 7.10). This discussion is another means of ensuring your reader has adequate contextual understanding of your topic to make judgments on the efficacy of your study. The tensions you uncover may be theoretical, factual, ideological, philosophical, or pragmatic. Your discussion of them will heighten both your critical analysis of the work in your field as well as aid in uncovering gaps that might be filled by your research design.

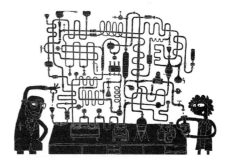

Figure 7.10 Exploring the complexities of your topic can be challenging, but is essential for a good literature review.

Source: © Can Stock Photo Inc. / vook

Unpacking Methodological Assumptions in Previous Studies

As you have researched your issue, you have been exposed to how a variety of others have examined topics similar and tangential to yours. They have based their research methods on their own assumptions or understanding about how best to measure the answers to their questions. It is an appropriate discussion within a review of literature to unpack for your reader these past studies and the assumptions on which they were based. In this way, your writing will naturally flow towards your discussion of your own methodological choices.

Quantitative studies assume that enough is known about the topic and the human relationships that determine its complexities that these can be questioned across large numbers of people using a similar instrument. For years, proponents of diversity have challenged this assumption, playing on cultural differences to argue that use of language may differ among communities to the degree that they make survey results meaningless.

Qualitative studies, on the other hand, assume that data gathered from a few people, albeit data that create depth in understanding of personal relationships to a topic, will have significance to the others in that field. Qualitative studies assume that it is important to understand the personal mechanisms within the relationships between a few and that these can be extrapolated to the groups you represent. The challenge to researchers is to convince their reader that the few represented in the study do have significant background so that their stories inform the larger issue.

Quantitative and qualitative studies read very differently and come to separate types of conclusions. This is a challenge for the mixed methods researcher who wants to play their strengths off of each other in order to build a more complete picture through their data. In order for your reader to understand your topic and the others who have studied it, you need to help them understand these subtleties and how they relate to your study.

Argumentation

Part of your requirement as a reader of literature is to be able to understand and analyze the arguments of the authors you read. To the extent that you do this well, you can also write about it, and your reader will enjoy this as a deeper level of critical analysis found in your final review of the literature. It is also important that you as researcher understand the way in which the main types of argument can be discussed accurately.

What is an argument? How do we analyze it? The principles of argumentation have not changed much since the Greeks and Romans. Stephen Toulmin (1958, later cited and redefined by Hart, 1998) laid out a simple structure that breaks an argument into four types of information:

1. A claim is an arguable statement. It is not, in and of itself, proven to be true.

2. Evidence is the word used to connote data that are being employed to backup the claim.

3. A warrant is the link between the evidence and the claim (since A is true, then B must be true also).

4. Backing includes the context and the assumptions that support the validity of the warrant and the evidence.

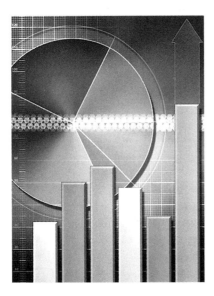

Let's say one of your authors made the claim that their training increased the motivation of staff. You would then look for the evidence with which they backed up that claim. Whether or not you believe their claim will hinge on the degree to which these authors (a) link the staff motivation to evidence that their training is what made the difference, and are able to (b) back up those assumptions. Likewise, your report of their writing needs to include all portions of the arguments they made in order for their points to be completely understood by your readers.

Finally, figures, tables, illustrations, and examples are used to back up arguments (Figure 7.11). Specific instances, like irrefutable data, do much to convince an audience of the validity of a claim. As Hart (1998) points out, "Concrete illustrations are usually much more convincing than hypothetical or generalized scenarios. However, the main and most common form of backing (in a review of the literature) is the legitimacy conferred on an argument through the use of academic style" (p. 182).

Figure 7.11   Figures and tables are excellent ways to provide concrete illustrations, increasing the legitimacy of your arguments.

Source: Photos.com/liquidlibrary/Thinkstock

Limitations to What You Are Reading

Everything you read and especially research will have limitations, and these may be worthy of discussion in your review of literature. This is especially true if your design is aimed at testing an idea in a new way in order to put a previous design limitation to rest. Limitations to the argument may be stated clearly as, "A limitation to this study was. . . ." Qualifiers may point to limitation without the same amount of clarity. Therefore, hopefully, you were on the lookout for words such as probably, some, many, too, or generally as you were reading. It is not wise to base your review on any literature, even if it agrees with your general arguments, when it relies on claims that are easily refuted or it qualifies its claims; it is best to keep searching (Hart, 1998).

Writing a Formal Review of Literature

Preliminary Activities

During your reading, you will have seen how other researchers approached their work, and you will have learned more about the variables you found interesting to study. Along those same lines, you have seen how others write up their work. Hopefully, you made special note of dissertations that you find easy to read or which discuss their methodology in a way that makes sense. It's always best and easiest to write when you have other good examples in front of you.

You will have read enough to prove, at least in your own mind, that your ideas are needed in your field. As previously mentioned, your research might be needed because it fills a gap in the current literature or it relates to other research or puts some new wrinkle of understanding on your field of study.

You have collected enough references that many overlap with each other. As you write on the basic tenets of your topic, you should have multiple references relating to these basic ideas. Does it seem like all your sources are saying approximately the same thing? Searching out nuances is the standard of the expert, and your review of literature is aimed to help your reader understand your topic and set you up as someone who has researched the ideas deeply enough to uncover subtlety.

Figure 7.12 You will need to collect enough references so that you start to find a good deal of overlap between them.

Source: Thinkstock/Comstock/Thinkstock

Procedures

The stated purpose of the literature review is to, "clarify the relationship between the proposed study and previous work conducted on the topic" (Rudestam & Newton, 2007, p. 62). Other authors mention, "Obtaining detailed, cutting-edge knowledge of your topic" (Roberts, 2004, p. 73). Therefore, once you feel you have truly captured the literature in your field of study, internationally as well as nationally and locally (thus displaying the level of influence your final study is likely to have), it is your job to convince your reader of the uniqueness and importance of your study.

Decide what three or four things your reader must understand about your topic in order to hold your research in a favorable light. For some, this will include why your topic is important, the challenges faced within your field, the need for the innovation or strategy about which your study revolves, or perhaps the theoretical discussions that form the foundation for why your study is important.

Then, sort the ideas from the authors you have read, under each topic heading. There are generally four types of discussion your writing might take in each section. Decide which is most appropriate as the purpose of your discussion:

1. Is this an *analysis*, which requires you to differentiate or separate resources and the ideas contained within them, one from another?

2. Perhaps you need to write a *synthesis* of these ideas, integrating or combining separate sections of different resources together. The purpose here would usually be to reorganize what you have read in order to demonstrate principles that you believe to be significant in your study.

3. *Interpretation* would be used to distinguish the relationships between different types of data, theory, and arguments and helps your reader sort them out.

4. On the other hand, you may be discussing the *knowledge* about what you have learned regarding situations, methods, rules, classifications, and so forth of the topics inherent in your study (Hart, 1998).

5. Don't just report the findings; write a critical analysis of what the findings mean within the bigger context of your review of literature.

Look at headings from masterfully written doctoral dissertations or theses and use them as a guideline to lay out what will at first look like an outline of your ideas. Keep maneuvering the headings until the logic of the ideas syncs into place and make sense.

Be sure to make special note of disagreements within the literature you will discuss and/or areas for which you have found no literature. Add gaps or disagreements to your subheadings to hold that space.

Begin to write one section at a time.

Helpful Hints

We've talked about using reference software several times already, but these ideas are so important we think they deserve another mention here.

Capturing and Organizing Notes

Beginning doctoral students rarely understand the importance of capturing every little part of their thoughts in a database from the time they begin. The notes you take now on the ideas you have as you read will become invaluable later. If you don't start a reference library at the beginning of your process, at some point you will have to retrace your steps and capture ideas you have lost. You are doing more than capturing that reference and what you read, you are capturing your ideas about it.

Because you're using a database you will have fields, some of which you may need and some of which you may not need, for each particular type of reference. Be sure to fill in each necessary field every time you pick up and read an article you find worthy of note. This can be done by electronic transfer, depending upon your library, from your library database directly to your bibliographic software file. You also might consider simply typing in the information needed, as oftentimes that is faster than electronic transfer. Never leave a reference without capturing notes about your ideas on the article in the lower database fields. Why did you read this article? What did you find important about it? What ideas do you not want to forget? Make sure that all of these questions are answered before you close out of any documentation on your reading. Most important, transfer that reference to the group or folder that tells you under which headings or subheadings you intend to use it.

Citing and Referencing While You Write

Academic work requires that we acknowledge the other authors whose work we have read and who influenced the ideas about which we are writing. This is not the same as quoting them verbatim. I suggest that you start a habit of writing what you think from your own point of view, and then, at the end of each paragraph, going back to your reference list and acknowledging whose work added to what you have just written. If you are using bibliographic software, you will be able to highlight the references of the authors you want to cite and easily bring that group citation into your writing. The reference software should also simultaneously start a reference list and keep it alphabetized for you. This step alone saves you hours and hours of work. When you have one author who wrote several things in the same year, the software will even go back and add the requisite *a* or *b* after those citations.

There are times your references may change a little. For instance you might discover that you had spelled an author's name wrong or you somehow needed to update some of the fields in the reference. Rather than having to go back through each document in which you have ever used that citation, you can know that by simply refreshing the reference list when you open the document again the updates will occur. As your academic writing goes on for years, this will save you more time than you can now imagine.

As you begin to write, open up your reference software and review ONLY those articles collected under the subheading you are writing to. Write to one subtopic at a time, merging what all the authors said into one coherent whole as per the four types of discussion outlined above. Then going back and cite the specific thoughts that came from one author. The rest of the merged ideas you should attribute to a group citation that includes authors that contributed to the ideas within this section.

Dos and Don'ts

Do

- *Engage in your mind (and maybe in real life) with the authors you are reading.* What questions you would ask of them? How does their thinking enliven yours? Is there a way you can have a conversation with these authors over the Internet, phone, or in person?
- *Read the classics and consider how the thoughts are put together.* Consider the research on which their work was based: the scope of it, the methodology, the implications of the time and context on what was considered the "norm." Part of the task you are on is learning how to think in new ways.
- Write notes about what ideas interest you and *consider how your study will* (a) build on those, (b) move in a different direction, or (c) hone those ideas to your location or context.

Alana says: *As an example, within the realm of action research, my particular expertise, there is a sometimes subtle disagreement about the role of our methodology. Some of us focus on its use in personal transformation as a professional development tool and to enhance our practice. Others find its importance in its potential when used as a tool in organizational development to shift the norms within the context being studied. The two are not mutually exclusive, but they do determine a lot about our focus when we write and ultimately about the literature we produce.*

- *Notice and analyze the linkage between different authors and their ideas and methods.* Be able to discuss the theoretical underpinnings of those who have written work on which yours stands.
- *Keep searching the literature surrounding your topic* until you understand where the disagreements within it occur. This is easier said than done, and everyone realizes that, even as we set it as an academic standard. Should you be reading academic, peer-reviewed literature on your topic and not find disagreements or gaps, you may consider writing privately to some of the authors you are reading and asking them for their opinion as to what gaps exist or what disagreements underlie their field of study.
- *Write in a voice similar to the language and cadence of your speech.* We do not mean use casual voice, but then neither use long words because you think they sound more official. You want your reader to understand the points you are making. As an example, a student wrote, "which originate in the household, among their proximate determinants group . . ." rather than write, "people at home or in the surrounding neighborhoods generally . . ."
- *Use your personal research journal to keep a list of the key words and phrases from your reading that will need to be discussed in your "terms section."* Usually in either your introduction or literature review, assessment of this section requires a substantive, expert definition of every term with which your reader may not be acquainted or upon which your research design rests. These will be cited and referenced, so keep track of both the terms you come across and the authors who define them most efficiently.
- *Frequently double-check to ensure that all topics covered in your instruments or interviews are discussed.* Ensure that there is a one-to-one correspondence between topics that you have included in the research and those which you discuss in the chapter.

Don't

- *Stop searching as soon as you have enough to build the argument you want to make.* It is frequently true that after you have found all that you think you need from your literature, you find either a new innovative idea or authors who disagree with your basic premise or logic, both of which add greatly to your study. The guideline is to keep searching until everything you read mirrors what you have read earlier. Another rule is to keep searching back (reading the references quoted in the articles you are reading) until you find the source material for the bigger ideas that you are working with. Looked at in a practical light, both of these help you and your work seem mature. Have you ever had a conversation with an adolescent where, excited because they had just learned something new, they told you many things that were obvious? If you have chosen your committee well, they will be like the adult in that example and will know a great deal about the topic you are discussing. Therefore, in order to have your document read like that of an adult, you need to cite and reference the most important material and make sure your arguments are well founded.

- *Mistake the number of citations for quality of the research.* It might be true that you or the article you are reading have a large number of references, but they do not reach to the beginning of the understanding of the work, nor are they inclusive of all the main ideas in the field.
- *Assume that because no one has done your exact study that there is no literature on it* (Patton, 2008). Rather, look for the topics that impinge on yours. As an example, a student we worked with was studying why people trained in science do not stay in the field, which, at the time, was a new topic. She needed to study all the human resource literature on retention in jobs of all kinds and then question the specifics of her field. She also needed to look into what psychologists knew about job satisfaction, making career choices early rather than later in life, and so forth. To be well grounded she needed to look into philosophical writings on happiness and satisfaction.

Chapter 7 Checklist

- ❏ I understand features of an award-winning literature review.
- ❏ I understand the basic layout of a literature review.
- ❏ I know how to incorporate theory into my literature review.
- ❏ I understand the role of methodological literature in a literature review.
- ❏ I have written a draft of my literature review.
- ❏ My literature review draft is sophisticated and includes critical analysis.
- ❏ My literature review points out gaps in the literature.
- ❏ I have done a critical analysis, not just reported about the literature I referenced.

Where Should I Go to Dig Deeper? Suggested Resources to Consider

Hart, C. (1998). *Doing a literature review: Releasing social science research imagination.* Thousand Oaks, CA: Sage. This entire book is excellent, but we believe every student should be familiar with pages 143 through 195 for his or her discussion of analysis of literature and how to write it up.

Group Exercises

Figure 7.13 Agree to meet with your group once a week for 10 weeks; this can be in person or online.

Source: Brand X Pictures/ Brand X Pictures/Thinkstock

A Ten-Week Timeline to Full Draft of Review of Literature

Many doctoral students would love to wave a magic wand, get all the dissertation help they need, and have their review of the literature done for them. While it takes a considerable amount of time to locate, read, and notate in a reference software more than 75 peer-reviewed articles (the standard in most universities as a minimum for a review of literature) there are steps that will make this section go faster. This article discusses those steps as part of measurable action. In other words, by applying the second step of action research, the measurable action step, students can have their ideas tested and verified as they go along.

For this you will need a group of other students who will work with you. Work together as a writing/study group and hold each other to the following standards of action. Agree to meet face-to-face or online once every week for ten weeks and discuss the following topics. When necessary read each other's' work and give feedback.

You will notice that about half way through these ten weeks there are several tasks that focus as much on the methodology of your research as the review of the literature. This is because it is important that your literature leads to the questions you ask, to your methods, for your research.

Measurable Actions

Week 1: (And each of the 10 weeks of this exercise) agree to find three to four new articles, books, or content for your review of literature. The key element that needs to be discussed every two weeks or five times by your support team is how the new material adds to your research methodology. For instance, if you find an article discussing one of the major subtopics that add to your general dissertation topic, your group should ask you (and you should ask yourself) how it might enhance the ideas or variables you will test through your methodology.

Agree to check in and hold each other to this standard in this first meeting. You may also want to discuss how you are keeping notes, which software packages you are using, and so forth. Finally, spend some time reading and analyzing a few examples of reviews of literature to see what you like or don't like in others' work.

Week 2: Chart your ideas to make it easier for your team to give feedback on your logic. List the citations of each article on the left side of a graphic organizer, spreadsheet, or table. The second column will be the first main topic, the next column the second topic, and so forth. Thus if an article or book is important to more than one topic in your dissertation, you make note of it in more than one column. Go further than just checking that Author A goes here. Instead, include the basic ideas that Author A has that support the topic in that column. Share your chart with your colleagues and give each other feedback as to whether the development of the topic is interesting and what questions may need answering.

Week 3: Go through a selection of the best of the research articles that you have in your library. Start a spreadsheet with the seven concepts of research along the top: purpose, scope (size of the study), methodology, data collection and findings, data analysis and conclusions, limitations, and contributions and lay out which studies used what types of methods to study topics similar or tangential to yours. Discuss your findings with your colleagues and ask for their help as you discuss your methodological ideas.

Week 4: Map out your research questions and the methods in which you will ask questions of your participants as you gather data. For instance, if you are going to interview people, write out the questions then go back to your chart of authors and citations and make note of which ones have information that support your asking that question. Highlight those questions that you instinctively want to ask for which you have no literature. This becomes a list of what you need to search for next. Share this with your group and check in to ensure that everyone is progressing and adding the requisite number of authors and articles each week.

Week 5: Since this is a halfway point, it is a good time to catch up on any tasks that were not completely done to your satisfaction. These four tasks have given you a solid background in the logic of what to include in your final literature review. In your weekly meetings with your colleagues, be sure to check in to see if you each have added at least 15 studies to your library of literature.

Week 6: This week's exercise has you looking deeply into your favorite piece of literature. Discuss it with your colleagues, going over the seven concepts of research if it is research or if it is a book. Discuss its main points and how it relates to both your literature and your methodology. Help each other analyze their favorite pieces of literature by discussing the logic these authors use, how they substantiate their main points, and what you like best/least about the article or book.

Week 7: This week begins the first of three weeks where you work on writing your chapter as well as finding more literature for it. The basic headings for a review of the literature are as follows:

Introduction to Chapter (describes content and organization of chapter),

Key Words and Phrases Defined

Overview or Panorama of Your Topic

The Debates Inherent in a Discussion of Your Topic

Overview Discussion of the Headings of Content Important to Your Study

    Topics 1, 2, 3, and so forth

Specific Discussions That Lead Your Reader to the Ideology/Ideas/Research Questions or Probes Behind Your Study

    Topics 1, 2, 3, and so forth

Overview Discussion of the Literature Pertaining to Your Choice in Methodology

Gaps in the Literature

Conclusion

Cut and paste in a general outline of your content and of how you see the chapter developing and discuss it with your writing/study group. Be critical friends for each other asking, Does it make sense? Does it naturally lead to the methodology?

Week 8: Spend time this week drafting the material that will go into each section. Write as though you are the expert and are discussing the topics, then back up what you say with citations. Use multiple citations when many authors have agreed with a specific sentiment. Check each other's work by reading for strong sentiments that are not adequately backed up by literature, as these all will need citations. Help each other work on developing a natural voice when discussing your topics. Move away from sounding like a book report and into sounding like an expert.

Figure 7.14   Week 10 is a time to celebrate all the progress you have made.

Source: ©iStockphoto.com/koya79

Week 9: Take the critical ideas expressed in last week's meeting and refine your writing. Write your new or rewritten sections in red so that your writing/study group can easily see what is new. Once again support each other as critical friends.

Week 10: This is your final week. Look over how much you have done, how much more secure your ideas are, and make a list of what else you still need to do. Celebrate with your writing/study group the progress that you have made. Discuss whether you want to continue for another ten weeks after taking a week off for rest.

Most reviews of literature can be written in a ten-week period, once the literature itself has been found and cataloged. If you had a good percentage of your literature before your writer/study group formed and started this ten-week process, then you may be very close to finished and ready to disband. If not, you may want to repeat the effort, next time interspersing your writing with the preliminary work of the first four weeks.

8

Are You Ready to Write the Overview for Your Study?

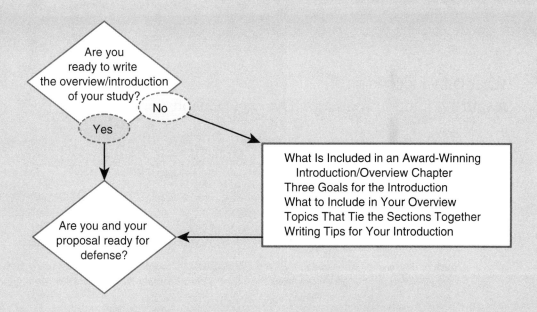

Are you
ready to write
the overview/introduction
of your study?

No

Yes

Are you and your
proposal ready for
defense?

What Is Included in an Award-Winning
Introduction/Overview Chapter
Three Goals for the Introduction
What to Include in Your Overview
Topics That Tie the Sections Together
Writing Tips for Your Introduction

S TOP! If you have not considered what materials belong in the literature review and methodology chapters, we do not believe you should start to write your introduction or overview (usually your first chapter). This is the most important chapter of your study, as many readers will not make it past your introduction if it is not clear and concise.

The purpose of this chapter is to help you write an outstanding introduction to your doctoral thesis or dissertation. To do that, we will cover the three purposes of your introductory section, what to include in the most common content headings, the range of topics seen in award-winning dissertations and theses, as well as some writing tips.

A traditional orientation has this chapter being written first, and if that is the requirement of your professors or university, then you should clarify in outline form what topics overlap with later chapters. This chapter discusses the local context of your study but only outlines the topic that is discussed in depth in your review of literature. Likewise, this chapter touches upon and sets up the logic from the topic to your methodology, but the specifics are left to later chapter(s).

The Questions Answered in This Chapter:

1. What is included in an award-winning example of an introduction/overview chapter?

2. What are the goals and purpose of the introductory chapter?

3. What do I include in the overview chapter?

4. What are the common headings for this chapter and what should I discuss under each?

5. What writing tips should I keep in mind?

What Is Included Is an Award-Winning Introduction/Overview Chapter

Having gone over the general topics that you might consider for inclusion in your introduction, we now will look more closely at two particular award-winning theses. There is a range of choices as to the basic underlying logic you will use in your introductory chapter. Each of the two dissertations we discuss here is indicative of one side of that range.

Introduction of the Topic

Hughes, (2010) in her discussion of the process of choosing science, technology, engineering, and mathematics careers by undergraduate women, chose to focus her introductory chapter on the issues involved in her topic. This is evident through analysis of her topic headings:

- Evidence of Underrepresentation
- Reasons for Underrepresentation: A Brief Summary
- Alleviating the Problem: Current Policy Context
- Gender
- Conclusion
- Chapters in the Dissertation

This author's first paragraph jumped into the heart of the discussion through a short history of the length of time in which a disproportionate number of women in science, math, and engineering has been noted. She goes on to discuss major federal policies aimed at impacting those ratios and ends with a question as to whether and how much those policies have been effective. She continues to lead her audience through a quick synopsis of previous studies and into the research questions that define her work. Through each topic heading listed above, she builds a case, step by step, that persuades her audience of the worthiness of her topic and her consideration of it as a narrative life history, rather than a straight qualitative or quantitative research design. While not discussing methodology directly, she sets her case through consideration of the human, woman-oriented, life choices that would lead to career decisions.

Introduction of the Topic and the Methodology

At the other end of the spectrum, we see Pershing (2003) clearly was writing with a strict scientific orientation with an introductory chapter that might very well stand in as a synopsis of the entire work. As you will see from her headings and subheadings excerpted below, almost every topic in the first three chapters was covered in brief in her introduction chapter.

CHAPTER 1: INTRODUCTION TO THE STUDY

Introduction

Statement of the Problem

Purpose of the Study

Theoretical Basis of the Study

     The Utility of Seeking Management Improvements

     Subgroups Membership and Management Beliefs

     The Directiveness Continuum

     A Conceptual Model

The Theory in Brief

Research Questions

Research Hypotheses

Research Design

Significance and Social Impact of the Study

Definition of Terms

Assumptions and Limitations

Summary

Organization of the Paper

Three Goals for the Introduction

Let's start by considering the purpose of the introduction section. In general, there are three things you want this chapter to do. First, you want to greet your reader by making them feel comfortable with your topic in the context of your study. Second, you want to discuss the logic of your research methodology.

Figure 8.1 Your introduction is like conducting a job interview. You will want to make the reader feel comfortable, understand the context, and convince her that she wants to continue on with you.

Source: Creatas Images/Creatas/Thinkstock

Finally, you want to persuade the reader that your study is important and the questions you will answer have significance through the way in which you discuss your topic and your methodology. It is important that you do all three things well. The introduction of each chapter is analogous to being an employer who is hiring someone. You want to make them feel comfortable and understand the context of the work, while making sure they are convinced that their time is well spent working with you (going deeper with you into your research).

Others consider the introduction a narrative hook (Creswell, 2009). How can you convince the readers (your committee first and foremost) of why this is important work? This is often accomplished using statistics that show that the need for the study is glaring—for example, a 50% failure rate in university engineering calculus classes for more than 50 years or the homeless rate in large cities or the teenage homeless rate—something that grabs the reader and makes it clear that there is a problem that needs to be addressed and you have a way of addressing it (Gloeckner, 2013).

What to Include in Your Overview

Your first chapter of your thesis or dissertation is meant to be an overview, for both your proposal and for your final defense of the entire document. This means that you will likely write this chapter three times. First, as you begin, you will write it in order to help you sort out the logic of the proposal without having to write about the literature or methodology with the depth required in chapters 2 and 3. Second, prior to defense of proposal, the chapter is rewritten to include the subtleties that have developed and to ensure accuracy. Third and finally, after data collection and analysis are complete and chapters 4 and 5 are in at least a solid draft form, you will rewrite your introduction, literature review, and methodology chapters to reflect the past tense and to update your introduction chapter with findings and conclusions.

The way in which you organize your first chapter is largely dependent upon the guidelines for dissertation or thesis as presented by your university and the degree to which they adhere to the principles of linear Newtonian research, which is seldom wrong, even if it is not always adhered to today. If your university has no particular guidelines for this chapter, your final goal is to present a short paragraph or two about every logical point needed for your reader. You have two goals: to both intrigue your reader and to establish their understanding of the literature and your methodology.

As we have said throughout this book, prior to writing it is strongly suggested that you read the introductory sections of two or three final dissertations in your topic of interest and/or those that use your methodology. As you pull together those headings and compare them to the ones presented here, feel free to build your own unique logic.

Whether or not this chapter is defensible depends upon two things: whether or not you have all the parts and pieces that your readers require and whether or not you have established a clear logic for your proposal. This logic will link the problems in your local context through the literature on your topic and on to the methodology through which you will study your issue.

The following headings and content guidelines can be taken as a solid rough outline for what is needed in your introduction and how to put it together.

Headings and Content for Your Introduction to the Study

Introduction to Chapter

The introduction is usually two to four paragraphs that discuss the significance of the study in your field and/or to your specific local or national issue. This section quickly demonstrates, in a couple of paragraphs, that this topic is worthy of study, with citations that tie your topic to other authors in your field. It concludes as you discuss the organization of the chapter.

Context for the Study

The contextual background to your study is its base foundation and is only covered in length in this chapter. Therefore, it is incumbent on the success of your proposal that your reader understand the specifics that are often known only to insiders. While this section may or may not have its own heading, here you develop the general topic that your research studies in depth. You need to establish the importance of your topic in that context. While concise, and not overlapping the later literature review, this section should make liberal use of citations and references to which you will also refer in your more detailed review of literature.

When we teach the transition from the topic or ideas around which your study evolves to your problem situation, we suggest you uncover the situation locally. What we call the problem situation, including any local perceptions or data that bear on your topic is included in this section. From this foundation, your purpose and problem statement naturally evolve.

Problem or Purpose Statement (or Both)

The problem statement is the logical foundation for your research and sets up the logic from which your methodology develops. It also introduces your topic in such a way as to convince your audience it is worthy of research. We discussed it in length in Chapter 6 as a component of your methodology. It should include specific data about the problem in the context that you are studying it. Problem or purpose statements conclude with what will be studied. For quantitative work, the variables to be studied and the proposed relationship between them are discussed.

Logically, quantitative studies often progress from a problem, while qualitative studies give a summary of the purpose of the study and the local problem it investigates. Mixed methods studies need them both. These logics are set up from the beginning as you quickly discuss the following subtopics (Creswell, 2009). Consider which of the following purposes may be the foundation of your study: understand, evaluate, investigate, design, explain, influence, develop, deepen understanding, investigate processes involved in, or complete an impact analysis of. These are not inclusive of all that are possible but should help you see the verbs that relate to the purpose of your study.

Nature of the Study

Your discussion of the work entailed in your research establishes what is to be studied and where. The subtopics below are usually discussed in a paragraph or two each and will scaffold your ideas to lay the foundation for a solid research framework (methodology). These come in no particular order as each author may order in a number of ways. Just ensure each logically builds upon the last.

Theoretical Context

Your theoretical context includes the theories, epistemological, and/or ontological considerations as applied to your general topic. Since this section often describes the way you think about the issues you study, it is most often placed at either the beginning or the end of the logic that develops the nature of your study. Much of this work may have developed in previous centuries. To balance your philosophical ideas we recommend you peruse such authors as Richard Feynman, William James, and Steven Hawking in order to ensure your thoughts include current scientific understanding and context.

Local and Societal Context and Significance

This section explains your methodological choices in context. As an example, a qualitative study develops out of a human issue in an environment where people are willing to share their lived experience with a researcher. Quantitative studies develop external validity and significance easily when a larger group is available for study and the subject has been at least partially studied before and the researcher can use or manipulate previously validated instruments. In medical studies, internal validity (as shown by the efficacy of the treatment) holds the significance of the study. In social sciences and evaluation research, the outcome of the intervention holds the greatest significance.

Figure 8.2 Provide clarity for your reader by defining key terms and jargon.

Source: Hemera Technologies/AbleStock.com/ Thinkstock

Hypothesis (for Quantitative Studies) and Research Questions (for Qualitative Studies) and Both (for Mixed Methods)

This section concludes the introduction to your study but is not the end of your chapter. Consider it the finale of your logic, which might be stated . . . *"Because I think like this and live in this place, my study will use this methodology and address these questions or prove/disprove these hypotheses or null hypotheses."*

Operational Definitions (Explanation of Jargon if Necessary)

Where authors include their definition of terms is a matter of either personal or university choice. Check with the guidelines of your university and then, if it is not specified, make your choice dependent on where you think the reader needs it the most. As an example, if your terms impinge on your methodology, then you may choose to place them following that discussion as part of your introduction.

If your terms will illuminate the literature/readings you discuss in your literature review, then that may be the better placement. The goal is to provide clarity from your readers' point of view, so that they don't have to look far for the definition of terms they are reading.

This section is usually either indented or has hanging indents with two to three line definitions as derived from experts. Each must have an expert citation and reference. Be sure to include any and all terms that would be considered jargon to anyone outside of your professional niche.

 Alana says: *My advisor at Columbia referred to limitations as a way of taking things "off the table" so they couldn't be discussed by the stricter members of the T. C. staff. While seldom so contentious, they do allow a candidate a certain amount of power to say, "Yes, I considered that, and decided it was one of the limitations of the study."*

Limitations of the Study

Every proposal contains several types of limitations: (a) assumptions or facts upon which the ideas or logic are based that have not been validated in this context, (b) issues with scope or size of the study where the researcher may not be able to have access to a population large enough to test the whole premise upon which it is based, and/or (c) potential areas of weakness in the design of the study itself.

You should note that it is worthy of your attention to carefully define your limitations from the very beginning, as they cycle back to you at the end of your research. As an example, not infrequently, a limitation to a study will be the size to which it is confined, because of time and finance issues. Also frequently, the recommendations of the author at the end of his study will be for further investigations over a broader scope or with fewer limitations as to funding. Limitations also keep you "safe" from certain topics being brought up or discussed during your committee hearings. As an example, should there be finite reasons within the context of your location from which you chose the methodology of your study, a discussion of those in the limitations section will prohibit your committee from requiring a change in methodology.

In examples from the award-winning dissertations at the beginning of the chapter, Pershing (2003) listed seven limitations. They were (a) single location, (b) an unusual type of organization used for the study, making replication an issue, (c) correlation shown but not causality, (d) use of self-report data, (e) not including issues pertaining to personality, (f) only one aspect of the topic studied, (g) some possible bias that may have leaked into the research design even though every effort was made to keep it out.

Delimiters

Since a delimiter is not always a concern, it should be noted that these segment the participants for your study from the full range of population of which they are a part. For example, a delimiter might be studying only the at-risk students as opposed to the wider population within a school. While sometimes in the same section as limitations, they are very different. You may choose to discuss them under their own heading as well. Delimiters make your study stronger because they set clear intentions.

Examples from the award-winning dissertation by Paige (2007) use delimiters in the context of discussing limitations when he says, "Due to the demographics of the rural/small city population of the research area, all participants were Caucasian and middle class, a condition Livingstone (2001) identifies as 'dominant class bias'" (p. 23). Purposeful sample selection using criteria preestablished by prior major studies went a long way in helping to mitigate this limitation. Additionally, although gender and ethnicity are not significant factors delimiting the current study (Livingstone, as cited by Paige), equality in participant gender was observed in the current study.

Significance

Your significance section explains why your study should be considered important: first to your context, then to your field of study. You might look at it as your least subtle bid at being persuasive. It will include a statement of any gaps in the literature that this study should begin to fill. If you expect this study to lead to positive social, political, organizational, or educational change, then the logic of that outcome is discussed in this section. The significance of your study will be addressed again after you have gathered and analyzed your data. You will have to discuss whether and how much your actual findings lived up to these expectations. Believable but persuasive are good guidelines to keep in mind.

Summary

Your summary or conclusion is a transition statement that quickly reminds your reader of the topics that were covered in this chapter and leads to a logical statement of the importance of your study. The section closes with statements of what to expect in the review of literature and the methodology. Some authors choose to have another paragraph or section that outlines for the reader the logic of the rest of the dissertation or thesis.

Topics That Tie the Sections Together

Three elements or discussions tie the introduction chapter together because they weave throughout many of the sections. These include your discussion of your topic, context, and literature. While we have mentioned particular locations where each is likely to be most evident, they really are so intertwined as to be impossible to separate easily. Therefore, we suggest a bit of caution to you as a writer: Remember that all these things will be discussed at length in chapters 2 and three, therefore anything you write about your topic, context, or literature in your introduction can be later be perceived as redundant should you go into too much detail here. What follows is a brief discussion of the kinds of things readers need to understand in your introduction chapter.

Discussion of Your Topic

Your reader needs to have a short synopsis of the general details that anyone well conversant with your topic would know. Consider this helpful to him as you "level set" the topical environment of your study. As an example, if you are discussing a leadership issue specific to study participants within an organization, you might discuss an overview of the topic in terms of the last few decades of change and how they have impacted leadership. Consider your discussion of your topic in the introduction chapter to be of similar length and breadth as you might discuss in verbal communication with someone with whom you are acquainted but not best friends. A general overview will get your reader off to a good start, and your review of literature will inform them with the depth needed to properly analyze your study.

Figure 8.3 The discussion of your topic, context, and literature are three elements that should be tied together in your introduction, because they weave throughout many sections of your dissertation.

Source: Phil Ashley/Lifesize/Thinkstock

Discussing Your Context

Your context may include a number of topics: your industry; your location; the race, gender, immigration status of your study participants; the age or socioeconomic status of your population, and so forth. These specifics interact in unique ways that should be introduced and discussed in enough detail as to carry your reader throughout the rest of your document. As an example, if you are studying at-risk populations of youth, you cannot assume that your reader understands what might be considered normal outcomes of the life circumstances that have put these youth at risk. On the other hand, you do not need to discuss outcomes of research about these populations, because likely they will be discussed in depth in your review of literature. Since one of your primary purposes in the introduction section is to persuade your reader that your study is worthy of attention, you need to discuss your context in enough detail as to be compelling but not in such a lengthy discussion as to make your review of literature redundant.

Discussing the Literature in Brief

Literature will be cited and referenced throughout your introduction section. Be aware, that as a doctoral candidate, without a previous academic research history, you cannot make strong statements on any topic without proper citations and references. That being said, your introduction is not the place to discuss these previous authors work in any detail. Nor is it necessary to "preload" discussions of research literature with an author's name and year of publication. A good rule would be to write as though you are speaking professionally on the topic and then go back and fill in the citations of all of the work that led up to your ability to hold that discussion.

Methodological Design

The extent to which your methodological design is appropriate for inclusion in your introductory section is almost entirely dependent upon your placement in the world and the degree to which your university subscribes to linear, scientific research standards. A methodological design section gives your reader a brief overview of the specific material in the methodology chapter. Think in terms of each topic required in your methodology chapter being covered in the introduction in a sentence or two, at most a brief paragraph each.

Writing Tips for Your Introduction

What goes wrong when people fail defense of proposal? In my experience, if things are going to go I changes, it is because your first chapter is not coherent enough. In other words, your writing was not adequate in helping your reader feel comfortable with your subject, discussing the logic of your study, or persuading them that the topic was worthy of interest and that your design would uncover the new knowledge you were aspiring to.

Alana says: *As a reader, I sit down with a new dissertation. I read the abstract—OK, I think I understand where this is going (if I don't understand the abstract already this writer is in big trouble). Then I start to read the first chapter, and what I expect to see there is a cogent discussion of this person's study. There are several things that may get in the way of that goal:*

- *Too much writing about the topic. I don't have to be completely convinced, I just need to get a solid glimpse of the problem being faced and to understand why it is important.*
- *A methodological structure that wobbles. A student will fail if I can't see how the questions being asked of the participants will answer the purpose of the research as stated.*
- *Things being said in too many different ways—some of which seem to contradict each other. This happens a lot with purpose statements—make it one statement and then repeat it, but don't have the purpose statement four times in the same chapter.*

I suggest you leave your work for a week or more and then overview it, by reading it out loud, to see where your first chapter may lose your audiences' attention or where it may contradict itself. Remember your first chapter is your ambassador—you don't want it to be confusing or your committee may never read further.

Dos and Don'ts

Do

- Read and reread, edit out all unnecessary words or redundant phrases. *Make your writing as concise as possible.*
- Consider the pace of each section in relation to the one before and after. As an example, do you have an overabundance of detail in one section followed by a concise paragraph or two in the next? *Balance the pace and the amount of detail throughout.*
- *Have people who are not engaged in an academic setting read your introduction* and tell you where they get confused or have questions. Rewrite those sections so that they are clearer.
- *Wait a week* after you think it is perfect and then go back to *reread it out loud again.* Continually ask yourself, "Is this persuasive?"

Don't

- *Make sweeping or grandiose claims or write about how things "should" be.* This is one of the most common mistakes for new academic writers, driven by passion. The world is a complex place, and as you progress in research you will find that many of your original assumptions don't hold up in other circumstances or contexts. It is also true that no human being has the right to tell others how things should be. Even if you are writing about some perceived wrong in society and the world, even one that may be illegal, it is wise for you to move past a sense of indignation and into calm logic. Rewrite until you display unbiased and calm perspectives on the pros and cons of each situation you describe. This will also keep your writing from seeming immature and therefore increase the possibility that your ideas will reach the stakeholders who are in a position to make a difference.
- *Use the words many, most, some, and so forth.* These are considered vague attributions and force the reader to ask who is involved in the many, the most, or some of the people about whom you refer? Your reader will also want to know how many are involved in those words and to whose work you can attribute these ideas? Each and every vague attribution needs to be rewritten in clear and explicit explanations. You might consider quantifying a percentage out of a total population or referring explicitly to the scope of a particular research study that you are discussing. Remember that the purpose of your peer review and defense is that your readers will force you to quantify all elements that seem vague. Save yourself grief and use an editor's help to catch problems prior to turning your work over to your committee.

Figure 8.4   Make your introduction clear enough so that people who are not engaged in an academic setting can understand it.

Source: Photodisc/Photodisc/Thinkstock

Chapter 8 Checklist

❒ I understand features of an award-winning literature introduction/overview.

❒ I understand the three goals of the introductory chapter.

❒ I understand the basic layout of the overview chapter.

❒ I know how to discuss my context in the overview chapter.

❒ I understand the role of limitations and significance in the overview chapter.

❒ I have written a draft of my overview chapter.

Where Should I Go to Dig Deeper? Suggested Resources to Consider

Bloomberg, L. D., & Volpe, M. (2012). *Completing your qualitative dissertation: A road map from beginning to end* (2nd ed.). Thousand Oaks, CA: Sage. These authors do a great job of discussing the perfect introduction for a qualitatively based research thesis.

Sapsford, R., & Jupp, V. (1996). Counting cases: Measurement and case selections. In R. Sapsford & V. Jupp (Eds.), *Data collection and analysis* (pp. xxi, 360). London: Sage in association with Open University. Since the purpose of the introduction is to persuade your reader that your study is valid and credible, this book's focus on data collection and analysis within quantitative work offers guidelines that will be helpful.

Wallen, N. E., & Fraenkel, J. R. (2001). *Educational research: A guide to the process* (2nd ed.). Mahwah, NJ: Lawrence Erlbaum. This is a classic for educational research and should be seen as a total examination of the decisions and challenges of scientific research within an educational setting. An introduction that adopts this model would be convincing.

9

Are You and Your Proposal Prepared for Defense?

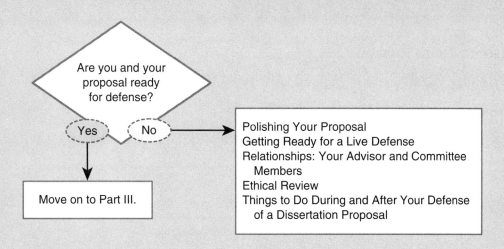

Are you and your proposal ready for defense?

Yes → Move on to Part III.

No → Polishing Your Proposal
Getting Ready for a Live Defense
Relationships: Your Advisor and Committee Members
Ethical Review
Things to Do During and After Your Defense of a Dissertation Proposal

STOP! If you have not obtained preliminary agreement about your proposal and your writing, and have not yet produced a clean copy—relatively free from errors—then you are not yet ready to proceed to this phase. You need to have sorted out your table of contents, collated the agreement between your citations and your references, and ensured all is in agreement with the style manual of your university.

The purpose of this chapter is to help you easily finish the last few items that wrap up a dissertation proposal and help you move it on to your advisor and committee with a solid sense of what you might expect. Included as topics are (a) what's needed in an abstract, (b) setting yourself up for success with your committee, (c) moving past difficult criticism, (d) ethical review, and (e) what questions you might want to ask at the end of your defense of proposal. While this chapter is in many ways more directly applicable for students who are working through their doctoral degrees in the United States, those of you who are working from universities based more on the European model will find the discussion on abstracts and working with your committee appropriate to your experience as well.

The Questions Answered in This Chapter:

1. What can I do to ensure my proposal is ready for defense?

2. What is required in an abstract?

3. What can I expect from my committee and their review?

4. How can I make the most of criticism?

5. What do I need to know about ethical review boards?

Polishing Your Proposal

As you polish your proposal, you will be upgrading the scholarly language and level of critical analysis involved in the entire document. As you improve the level of your writing, you also should look for the most significant point, upon which the logic of your entire document hinges. It is useful to track back the internal cohesiveness of your entire document, double-check correct use of tense in your verbs, and perhaps consider a mock defense, utilizing the help of others to prepare you for tough questions that you may face.

Prepare your very clean, relatively error-free iteration for committee review in plenty of time for them to read it prior to your final defense or vita. Then prepare your slides and practice both your presentation and your answers to possible questions that may come up on your topic and choice of methodology.

Abstracts

What exactly you include in your abstract and the word limits, writing guidelines, and so forth is set by the style manual from your university. While we will discuss guidelines and templates based upon those common in scientific research, there are generally two basic forms of abstracts: descriptive and argument based (Goodson, 2013). Based upon research of journal abstracts, "descriptive abstracts" are those that overview the objectives, methods, and results of a study. Using that analysis, the abstract sequence we describe below would be descriptive. Goodson also discusses "argument based" abstracts that would include a logical progression of ideas aimed at influencing the reader to agree with the basic premises of the article or theoretical study. This form of abstract would be more appropriate for theoretical theses then research-based studies.

We recommend that you know ahead of time what is considered an acceptable abstract length according to the standards of your university. Many journals limit words to a maximum of between 350 and 450. Many universities limit an abstract to one page. Whatever length is allowed, your sentence structure must be concise rather than run on. Also, each thought will logically build on the last, much like building blocks, leading your reader through your methodology to the central ideas of your study.

Guidelines/Template From Scientific Research

A common form in scientific research is a seven-sentence abstract. To use it, fill in the following sentence stems with the specifics from your study. The form used below would be appropriate for the final thesis or dissertation, after which we will discuss changes to consider when at the proposal stage.

1. The purpose of this study was . . .

2. The scope (or population) of the study was . . .

3. The methodology used (include data collection and analysis) . . .

4. Findings from the study show . . .

5. Conclusions reached . . .

6. Significance of the study is . . .

7. It contributes to the literature . . .

 Alana says: *I like the use of this seven-sentence abstract and wish more fields/journals would require it. Searching for research becomes very easy when the format for the abstract is similar and illuminates all aspects of the research.*

When at a proposal hearing, the same template for guidelines is appropriate; the author merely expands on data collection and analysis while not including findings or conclusion.

Here are some form and style tips for your abstract:

- The abstract cannot exceed the guidelines of your university.
- Maintain scholarly language, of importance are concise sentence structure and readability.
- Ensure each sentence adds value to the reader's understanding of the research.
- Use the full name of any acronym and include the acronym in parentheses; you can thereafter refer to the acronym. If you do not refer to the acronym again in the abstract, there is no need to identify it.
- Abstracts do not have paragraphs; the text is one long paragraph with no indentation.
- Do not include references or citations in the abstract.
- Maintain the style of your university (Walden University, 2010).

Alana says: *Having been on both sides of the dissertation defense process, as mentor and advisor on the one hand and as a reader on the other hand, it is always amazing to me the things I see as a reader I don't always see as an advisor. I've come to understand that this has to do with the fact that when I am advising I have a deep relationship with a student and so I am blinded by the progress they have made and cannot always see the deficiencies they*

(Continued)

(Continued)

still face. This will likely happen to your mentor and advisor as well. That is why the university requires that your work is overviewed by people who have not read your work up until this time. It is their guarantee that someone will catch areas of your study that are not yet mature. Therefore, the best thing you can do for yourself, as a student, is to expect new and substantive criticism when you pass your work into a defense situation. Few pass without any revisions being suggested or required.

Things to Watch Out for

Remember, your abstract is the first ambassador of your ideas to any reader. Therefore, grammar, punctuation, and spelling errors become a reasonable excuse to criticize or condemn your work prior to even reading it. A common and inexcusable error is not to have your research problem at the forefront of the discussion. Equally important are the purpose for your study and your research questions or hypotheses. Without these basic elements any careful reader will end up merely asking, "So what?"

Preparing Your Slides

Universities vary as to whether and how to use slide presentations during defense. If this is a requirement for you, then prepare to talk no more than 10 minutes. Assume that everyone in the room is familiar with your study and that it is not necessary to go over every point in detail. Rather it is your task to highlight the internal cohesiveness of your document with an overview of the context, literature, and methodology as they pertain to your study. Few words, large font, and a simple slide presentation is the norm rather than colorful, pictorial, or animated presentations. Let your ideas carry the day, not your media ability.

Getting Ready for a Live Defense

Doctoral students frequently feel unhappy or upset after both their defense of proposal and defense of dissertation processes. Maintaining a positive attitude when receiving criticism is part of the task, but it also helps to understand the defense in light of the entire journey. Two things can help: One is to understand the process from your committee's point of view, and the second is to set yourself up for success by developing solid and supportive expectations. Remember the dissertation defense should be a celebration of your work. You should know more about your research than anyone in the room (Gloeckner, 2013).

The Defense From the Professor's Point of View

Professors generally see our work as that of "helpful guidance," and we enjoy encouraging students while supporting them in learning new skills and tackling the more provocative levels of a topic.

During defense and while reading dissertations or theses, our job changes from helper to one of guardian of the systems we represent. Half of our job remains helping the students do the best they can, but we also are aware that it is our task to make sure that all of the work published from our universities passes the scrutiny of the regional certification boards and maintains the university's good reputation.

Set Yourself Up for Success

Expect that you will receive criticism and that it will lead to more work on your dissertation than you or your advisor previously thought you needed. Depending on where you are in the world and your topic, it is reasonable to expect to be closely questioned on your methodology.

Figure 9.1 During defense the professor's role changes from helper to guardian of the university's reputation.

Source: Jupiterimages/BananaStock/Thinkstock

You can prepare for this by double and triple checking for a one-to-one correspondence between your questions, your methodology, and your outcomes. There should also be a connection between your literature review, your questions, and the variables you expect to measure to answer those questions. Remember, you have written chapters and sections as separate pieces. The defense ensures that they have become one integrated whole. You can save yourself some time at the end by doing a lot of upfront work and massaging the correlations between chapters so that they become evident and specific.

Going through defense of proposal and dissertation should leave you with a better understanding of the academic process. It is helpful to look at it as a series of lessons rather than of hurdles you have to get over on the race to the finish. The rigors of peer review don't get easier with time, although they do become familiar. Therefore, especially if you want to publish your work later in different venues, know that you will go through this process over and over for the rest of your life. Get comfortable with how it feels and how you respond to the sticky parts, such as strong criticism. An understanding of academic rigor is also a key lesson. It takes a certain kind of strength and courage to revisit work, throw out entire sections, and redo them in order to meet higher standards than we ever knew existed prior to starting. Doctoral work is not for fools or lazy people. This is where you prove your strength.

Building on a Solid Foundation

You need to have built your proposal on a solid foundation. Your committee and readers must be able to glance at your table of contents and see a solid set of headings that logically add up naturally to a formal research study. Come back one last time and look at your model theses, review their table of contents as compared to yours. If you are missing any of the commonly used sections or subsections, you should add them. Without a solid structure to the logic of your work, as shown through your headings, your dissertation or thesis will collapse under the pressure of your defense of proposal process.

Figure 9.2 If you have built on a solid foundation, your research will go more smoothly.

Source: ©iStockphoto.com/dja65

The doctorate is your degree. It is up to you to know what to do, when to do it, and how it will get done. You must be proactive in your education and not wait for someone to tell you about changes, publication manuals, or APA.

Do not take any corrections, suggestions, or feedback as something negative. It is to make your paper better, not to hurt your feelings. Be mindful that your readers are scientists and researchers, not necessarily educators, and nonacademics.

Remove the superfluous adverbs and adjectives. A writer can write, Alexander and the Terrible, Horrible, No Good, Very Bad Day. A researcher says, "Here are the data which leads us to believe the day was awful."

Dr Elizabeth Johnson,
DoctoralNet, 2012.

The Two Approaches to Reading a Dissertation or Thesis

Most committee members will read a proposal in one of two ways: either from beginning to end, in a linear pattern, or the methodology section first and proceed backwards, reading the literature review second and the introduction last. Likewise, when reading final work, many readers start with the findings and conclusions and then backtrack to see how they are set up and justified in the early sections.

The following section investigates two scenarios, using examples from defense hearings that did not go so well for the student.

Scenario One

If your committee reads your proposal from beginning to end, then the introduction must read well. When you are just becoming familiar with the research at hand, it is important that this chapter is short and informative. If this chapter is overly verbose and is not straight to the point, you may lose your reader right at the very beginning.

Your committee members read the literature review trying to gain more insight into what is being researched as well as for details of your topic and what has been researched prior to your study. Instead, all too often, they may find a long treatise on a subject. Approximately halfway through the chapter, attention may lag and the reader may begin wondering what all this has to do with anything.

Continuing on to your methodology chapter, some, if not all, of those questions may be answered, but there is also a likelihood that the reader instead gets caught up in the methodology issues. Unless the three chapters are very tight, if your committee is reading a proposal from start to finish, there will be places where attention will lag and questions and judgment begin to come in. You want to avoid this to the fullest extent that you can, because at this point your committee members are likely to be filled with ideas for revisions, ready to focus on specific areas of your document in their attempt to help you make it stronger.

Scenario Two

The second way to read a dissertation proposal is to start with the methodology chapter and get a good handle on what the person's methodology is and how she intends to apply it to a certain subject. If this is the case with your committee, your methodological choices need to be airtight. Your writing needs to have avoided the pitfalls of over reliance on quoting various authors. You need to convince your committee that you are ready to collect and analyze data without much further support. This requires your discussion to seem mature and logical.

Your committee members then move on to the review of literature with a critical eye on whether and to what extent it backs up the need for and illuminates the ideas behind the methodology. Hopefully, your discussion of prior research leads to a natural and easy understanding of the methodological choices exhibited in the methodology chapter. Equally important is that your writing demonstrates maturity of ideas and a critical analysis of the work on which your study is based.

Finally, your introduction should back up everything the reader thinks they understand from having perused the other chapters. At this point, your proposal either makes complete sense or it does not. To the extent that your committee members are logically minded individuals, they should be well prepared at this point to offer succinct and targeted comments.

Comments and Revisions

Depending upon the way your university manages its defense process, you will receive comments and requirements for revisions either verbally, in written form, or both. The comic below illustrates the challenges you may face. Be sure to set up, whenever possible, an ongoing pattern for communication should you later realize you did not exactly understand the revisions required.

Relationships: Your Advisor and Committee Members

Moving Past Issues to Greater Support

Figure 9.3 Set up an ongoing pattern for communication in case you realize that you didn't really understand the revisions that are required.

Source: From Jorge Cham's *Aura of Logical Distortion,* PhD Comic. Originally published by www.phdcomics.com.

Doctoral mentors or advisors are meant to aid a doctoral student in efficiently finishing their degree. To some extent, you choose them. Unfortunately, there are a few things you and/or your professors may do to inhibit the process. There are generally three types of problems that may exist: (a) The advisor or committee member is not considered supportive, (b) they do not give timely or helpful feedback, or (c) the student consistently does not understand their instructions.

Not Supportive?

Students, advisors, or committee members might consider starting their relationship by coming to an agreement about what types of support will be given, under what conditions, and what is considered a reasonable timetable for response. It is never too late for these agreements to be reached, so if you are disgruntled because you feel as though your advisor is not supportive enough, have a frank conversation with that person. Advising doctoral students is an interesting journey, because on the one hand students are on a rite of passage that requires proving they have reached a certain level of

Choose your committee wisely and treat it as a hiring process. Be clear about the role and purpose you expect them to perform for you. I recommend you include a combination of process and content experts to ensure that both elements are addressed early and often in your work. The process expert can ensure that your methodology is appropriate and properly conducted and that the limits of the method are addressed as well as the strengths. The content expert will help you ensure that you have adequate coverage of the literature and that the conclusions you are drawing are supported by other scholarship as well as your research. They will be a rich source of pointed questions and critical thinking. Remember that you're not asking them to do your work but rather to certify what you have done, so be prepared and don't waste their time. Your mentor is your most important hiring. You need someone who is prepared to endure your moments of despair and elation and keep you grounded in on the past and making progress. They have to have the moral courage to kick you when you need it and coax you when you need it (Dr. Ken Long, DoctoralNet, 2012).

Figure 9.4 Sometimes it can seem that a professor's feedback is always critical, but don't take it personally.

Source: Creatas Images/Creatas/Thinkstock

mastery on their own. On the other hand, leaving doctoral students to flounder around for years, as was the old-style of working, did not lead to positive educational outcomes.

A doctoral student's work needs to be 100% their own responsibility. It is never your committee's responsibility to check in on how you are doing, although some may do so. Are you feeling your advisor is not supportive? Ask yourself whether and to what extent you have been unwilling to manage your own doctoral process. If the answer is that you have been waiting for them to help motivate you further, then take self-responsibility to figure out the process and come to them to gather their agreement to your ideas.

Another way that an advisor/mentee relationship may seem to lack support is if the professor's feedback is consistently critical. Some students seem to expect that their work on a dissertation will proceed much as all the work they have ever done on class projects proceeds, without many challenges. It is not uncommon for the first efforts at dissertation writing to be far off the mark, and therefore feedback may seem for awhile overly negative. Again, this is a matter to discuss one-on-one with your mentor/advisor and use their comments to make your work better. Take personality disputes out of the equation and know that criticism is not meant to be personal.

Lack of Timely Feedback

Students also complain that they don't get timely feedback from their mentors and advisors. Different universities have different standards, so the first step for you when disappointed in the amount or timeliness of the feedback you receive is to check with the university as to whether there are discrete standards to which they hold professors. Remember, while your work is your entire focus, your professors juggle many requirements, of which your dissertation is only one. They likely have several students and classes on their workload and so have to manage each. Generally, it is considered timely to get back to a student with dissertation writing within two weeks. This allows for the substantial amount of time they take to read, mark, and give feedback. Some advisors and students like to set up regularly scheduled meetings, for example, once a month or even once a week in the data analysis stages.

Figure 9.5   Consider setting deadlines with your professor for the return of comments and then sending email reminders as the date approaches.

Source: Hemera Technologies/AbleStock.com/ Thinkstock

Alana says: *I believe in charting a course from the beginning of the dissertation process through the end, helping students develop a timeline that will get them finished in time and then relying on them to come to me when they need specific help.*

Advising and help need not come exclusively through your university, but look into the references/testimonials of any outside resource, such as an editor or coach, which you use carefully. There are, unfortunately, many businesses or websites that prey on students and offer help that would cost you your degree because they introduce plagiarism or dependence on work that is not yours.

If, after considering the full situation, you still feel as though you are not receiving timely feedback, the second step is to begin to manage your communication with your mentor advisor more closely. When you turn in your work, you might consider asking your professor for a particular deadline for when you can expect to receive their comments. Then, as the second step, within a few days of that date you could write a quick email reminding them that the deadline is coming up and asking if it is still feasible. In this way, it becomes unlikely that your work slips out of their attention.

Alana says: *While not allowed by all universities, I requested and was released from working with my first advisor at Columbia. It was a very good decision, and I graduated quickly once I found someone I could work with. That did not make the professor I fired a bad advisor, it just meant that our styles of communication were so different that it rendered me incapable of learning from her. What we see more of now are student going outside of their university for support, then taking more or less finished documentation to their advisors. You have many resources available.*

Does Not Give Instructions

Doctoral students also complain about a professor who seems never to be available to them, rarely, if ever, giving instructions. This again may develop out of an old-fashioned view from the advisor on the mentor/advisor relationship. It used to be understood that students had to manage the whole process, and your mentor/advisor may have gotten their degree with that understanding; therefore, they may expect you to read and explore published dissertations or theses and model them with little or no instruction. No matter how much your university guides the work of your advisors or committee members, it always proves to be true that students who manage their own process rigorously are those who finish first.

Mature doctoral students may be managers or directors in their professional field. It is interesting that in the student role, these same individuals may not manage people on their committee or even their own time. To the extent that you can manage the expectations of your advisor rather than the other way around, you will be able to finish quickly and efficiently. The way to do this is to be crystal clear in your timeline, to meet those deadlines, and to stay in light touch with your mentor/advisor about your process. Having a full dissertation or thesis land on an already bulging work process has been described as "raining anvils." It isn't a pleasant experience for your professors, and they are less likely to give your work the time or attention you desire. The more that you are able to empathize with their point of view and stay close enough that you stay on their mind, the more likely they will respond as you wish.

In summary, much can be done to improve the mentor/advisor relationship with doctoral students by communicating about and setting specific expectations as to support, timing, and feedback. The mentor/advisors probably graduated in a time where students had different expectations than they do now. Discussing this openly on both sides will do much to further your relationship and to build a strong format for communication between you. If, on the other hand, despite all your efforts it is still clear that you and your mentor/advisor do not agree on what constitutes supportive, timely feedback then it is our opinion you should discuss this with your academic advisor or the university faculty administration. You will need to assess your own situation to find out the best way for you to make sure you have a productive advisor/student relationship while completing your doctoral work.

Re-engaging, Especially if You Have Been Away From the Process for a While

A student in a forum wrote, "*I am struggling with communication with my advisor. How do I re-engage? I feel blocked and ashamed that I have not made progress which makes me want to hide until I have a product to deliver.*"

Maybe you have found yourself addressing communication with your advisor or committee, as this student was, from the angle that teachers are somehow bigger and more important. Your advisor and committee are more likely to think in terms of peer review. It is likely that they have more work than they can do and so they do not worry when students drop out of sight. That does not mean that when you come back they will not be pleased for you. No professor wants to see you become part of the 50% who do not finish.

I would just drop this person a line saying, "Time off for . . . (personal issues or whatever) is now over and I am working to deliver . . . for you to read by mid . . . (month)—How will your time be around then?"

Handling Criticism

You may be angry or unhappy when you receive strong critical comments, especially during Defense of Dissertation or Defense of Proposal. Maintaining a positive attitude when receiving criticism is a difficult task, one everyone faces somewhere along the dissertation journey. There are ways of addressing this challenge both before you enter your defense and after you have gotten the criticism and can't get past your reaction.

Figure 9.6 Try to consider criticism as a gift, because it forces you to consider outside opinions, work through them, and ultimately produce better work.

Source: ©iStockphoto.com/kmr-co

Before You Go Into Defense of Proposal

Since difficult or negative feedback on your work is part of the peer review process and will continue throughout your professional academic career, the best thing you can do is to adjust your attitude to expect it. There are rare instances in which a student proposal passes with few comments or revisions required, but this happens less than 5% of the time. The best solution for anyone whose work is being reviewed is to stop any emotional attachments you have to your work and to view it dispassionately. All criticism is a gift of sorts, as it forces us to consider outside opinions, and when we work them through, the effect is increasingly pleasing. This is especially true at proposal defense, because any tangles that are found here only serve to make your data collection and analysis more targeted to your research and make it easier to finish at the end.

After You Have Received Difficult Criticism

Once you have received difficult criticism, you need to gain perspective on it to prevent any possibility that you might overreact. If the review is written, the best thing is to form an agreement with yourself that you will read it all the way through and then put it away for two to four days without reacting. In those days, life will have continued on its own path, you will have been distracted by other situations, and you can come back to the comments with less angst, having put the situation in perspective. These comments are, after all, made in order to benefit the quality of your work overall. While they slow you down right now, they ensure a good ending.

When you revisit the review, first choose three things that you see as being the most legitimate suggestions. Take out your writing and work just on those three things. Each day continue on this path until you have chipped away at all of the easiest and most direct criticism that you received. This will help motivate you to tackle the hard parts.

 Alana says: *My tactic is to read the reviews, forcing myself to be neutral—they are talking about the work from their particular point of view. Then I put the reviews down and don't come back to them for a couple of days—at that time I am ready to dig in and start considering how to make the changes that would hit the mark they have left me. Remember, peer review always makes our work stronger, once we are tough enough to take it. Also you might want to keep in mind that sometimes the person reviewing is not tactful—one of the reviewers on this book said my writing was "almost incoherent." Just take that in stride, look for the sections they might have been referring to, and improve them. At the end, great work is what we all strive for.*

Try to understand the broader issues, reflect on the differences between your work and that of model dissertations, and then make an appointment to discuss what you understand as necessary changes prior to doing much substantive writing. As an example, I'm currently working with a student on her proposal defense. Her committee uncovered some inconsistencies in her logic and the way sections are written. She is facing another couple of weeks of work and of course wishes it were over. If you find yourself in this situation, becoming overwhelmed will not be helpful. Consider your revisions one more task you have to complete prior to being able to collect data and dig into these revisions with the same expertise as you have handled the rest of your doctoral work. It may have been unexpected to you, but it is not an unusual situation.

After you have spent some good reflective time and know that you can tackle this, as you have all the other challenges you faced along your doctoral career, make an appointment to approach the person who made the criticism. Go into that meeting ready to discuss what you understand from their comments, what you have seen by looking at finished dissertations, and what approaches you have already thought of. In this manner, you demonstrate to the professor your own level of professionalism and expertise and move out over the role of student towards the role of peer. This, after all, is the purpose of the dissertation process, and most professors will respond very well.

In summary, there are several things you can do to move the anger and frustration you feel when you hear strong criticism of your doctoral work. As I said, it's part of the academic process and happens to everyone.

Ethical Review

It is outside of the purview of this book to go into much depth about the ethics of research and the ethical review board process. Nevertheless, it is at the time of the defense of proposal that doctoral students are first trained in and then make application to their universities ethical review board.

Many similarities exist from the student experience point of view between defense and review. It is important to note that ethical review boards may require revisions of entire sections of your proposal. Much as you first investigated the guidelines of your university, looking for and finding model dissertations, it is wise and advisable for you to follow a similar pattern as far as documentation required and ethical standards. We suggest you talk to students who may have recently passed defense and have begun collecting data. We also recommend you ask specific questions regarding guidelines of your advising professors. Depending upon where your university lies in its views on the protection of participants during research, an ethical review can be particularly rigorous. It's always wise to know what you're getting into before you have to face it.

Things to Do During and After Your Defense of a Dissertation Proposal

Doctoral students are often surprised to find that they need dissertation help more after they've passed their defense of proposal than before. The proposal is an arduous scholarly task, but after the proposal when you're engaged for the first time in significant personal research, it becomes the true rite of passage. This is when your dissertation methodology is tested and you work to make sure that your dissertation research passes the final defense. In order to most efficiently navigate the waters of data collection and analysis, here are five things you can do during and after your defense of proposal.

Figure 9.7   Get your questions about requirements for the final work answered when you have your full committee together.

Source: ©iStockphoto.com/photosipsak

Step 1: Ask Your Committee What Specific Things They'll Look for in Your Analysis of Data

You can start to understand the expectations of your doctoral committee if you're armed with questions about the endgame of data collection and analysis during the defense. Perhaps your mentor or advisor will ask some of these questions for you, but you can't count on that. Remember, your committee members have experience doing this kind of research, and it's their job, to help you be successful. Therefore, come prepared and make sure that before you leave the defense you understand the answers to the following questions:

- What can they tell you about the pitfalls that you might encounter in completing your data collection and analysis?
- What will they look for in terms of credibility, rigor, and reliability as determined by the specifics of your form of data collection?
- What tools do they recommend you use to make your job more efficient and easy?
- Is there anything else that they can think of that will help you?

These four questions serve a double purpose, not only do they help you move forward efficiently, but later, they allow you to push back a little bit if you find that, after you're done with most of the work, a committee member comes up with entirely new expectations for your work. It may help calm down academic fervor a bit if you say, "These weren't at all the things you told me about when I asked what your expectations were at the time of the defense."

Figure 9.8 Journal about all of your research work as you are doing it.

Source: Stockbyte/Stockbyte/Thinkstock

Step 2: Take Good Notes/Journal Your Data Collection and Analysis Procedure

Starting at the defense, take very good notes, especially as your committee answers the above questions. After that, however, it's very important that you journal what you're doing as you do it. This should include the date, the time you spent, the activity, and the outcome. Why? Because it's part of the rigor of scientific research to be able to show evidence of such a log, and because you'll be required to write up your data collection procedure. Such notes make that task easy. The more specifically you write to your data collection and analysis explanation, the less likely that your committee will question your rigor.

Step 3: Send Preliminary Data Analysis and Findings

Ask permission first, but work to be able to send all your committee members your final outline of your data collection and analysis prior to writing it up. This will save you hours of time because it allows them to ask questions when they follow your logic or they question your analysis. It's much easier to answer the questions: "How did you arrive at that conclusion?" Or, "Can you tell me specifically how many disagree with this finding?" Or, perhaps, "I do not follow you there, could you also see these data as implying . . . ?"

The data collection and analysis section of dissertation work was for me, and I believe it's for everyone, a rite of passage. This is the time when you test your own ideas against academic peer review. It's always easier to test preliminary ideas, get feedback, resync and reimagine your data, enlarge your findings, and test again rather than writing it all up, only to be shot down when you get back the peer review.

Step 4: Keep Asking Questions Until You're Sure You Understand What Others See in Your Data

First-time data collection and analysis is for many people a hard period of time. For one thing, you are anxious to get out and be done with it. On the other hand, it is a rich time, and you may never again get to experience the daily intrigue and enjoyment of analyzing great quantities of data and discerning the outcomes of what you learned.

Just as many people experiencing the same event will have different stories about what happened, so too, many academics looking at the same data will have different analysis of the meaning uncovered. For this reason, data collection and analysis shouldn't be a completely solitary task. Brainstorm what you're doing and what you are finding with this many people as possible. Hopefully one of those will be your mentor or advisor.

When experienced researchers suggest things you do not understand, this is not a time to just shake your head and agree. Rather, keep asking, what do you mean by that? How did you reach that conclusion? Can you help me? I do not understand your logic.

Step 5: Read All the Dissertations You Can That Model Your Methodology

Writing up a defensible analysis of data is not an easy task, especially the first time you do it. Therefore, I highly recommend that you read at least half a dozen dissertations, no matter what the topic area, that use a methodology similar to yours. As you read their chapters 4 and 5 ask yourself, am I convinced? Did they build a solid case for their findings? Do they tie their data collection and analysis back to their research questions? Do I believe they fulfilled the purpose of their research? Make notes of what works for you in each section and then mimic the things that work well when you start to write up your own work.

Figure 9.9   Read at least six dissertations that model your methodology.

Source: Hemera Technologies/AbleStock.com/Thinkstock

Those questions are the same ones that your committee will be asking when they read your write-up of your data collection and analysis during your final defense of your dissertation. If you follow these 5 steps, you'll find that the process is less mysterious and that you pass your final defense with fewer required updates.

Chapter 9 Checklist

❏ I have polished my proposal, and it is ready for defense.

❏ I understand the role of my committee's review.

❏ I am prepared to receive criticism and have a plan for how to productively handle it.

❏ I understand and am prepared for the Institutional Review Board (IRB) process.

❏ I know what I need to do during and after my defense.

❏ I have successfully completed my defense.

Where Should I Go to Dig Deeper? Suggested Resources to Consider

Brause, R. S. (2000). *Writing your doctoral dissertation: Invisible rules for success.* London: Routledge Falmer. Pages 133 through 142 contain a detailed discussion of the defense process, including questions frequently asked during an oral defense.

Garson, G. D. (2002). *Guide to writing empirical papers, theses, and dissertations.* New York: Marcel Dekker. Pages 290 through 307 offer further discussion of choosing a committee, providing a checklist for the proposal hearing, and a discussion of the defense from the perspective of a university built on the European model.

Mauch, J. E., & Park, N. (2003). *Guide to the successful thesis and dissertation: A handbook for students and faculty.* New York: Marcel Dekker. Pages 143 through 198 build on the discussion by Garson, adding functions of the committee and assessment guidelines to which you may be responsible.

Roberts, C. M. (2004). *The dissertation journey.* Thousand Oaks, CA: Corwin Press (pp. 184–191); Glatthorn, A. A., & Joyner, R. L. (2005). *Writing the winning thesis or dissertation: A step-by-step guide* (2nd ed.). Thousand Oaks, CA: Corwin Press (pp. 221_226). Both of these books have scenarios as to what to expect from a defense at a university using the model most common in the United States.

Western, S. (2012). *Coaching and mentoring: A critical text* (1st ed.). Thousand Oaks, CA: Sage. This gives both advisor and student an excellent and academic view of the potential of this relationship.

PART III

FINDINGS/CONCLUSIONS AND WRITING YOUR FINAL DISSERTATION OR THESIS

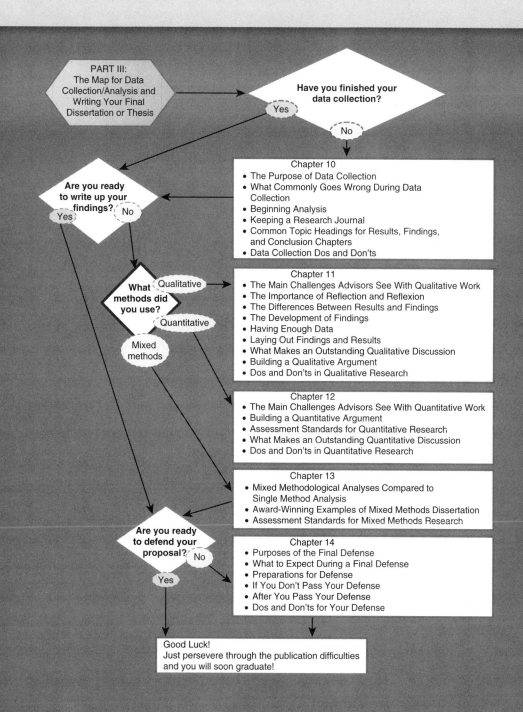

10

Have You Finished
Your Data Collection?

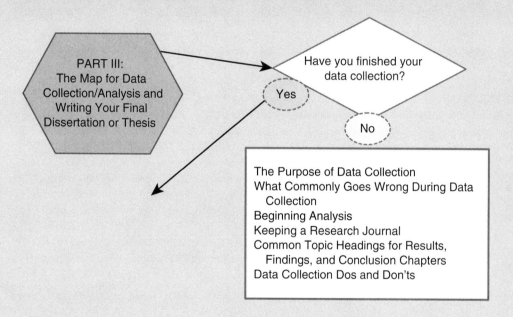

PART III:
The Map for Data
Collection/Analysis and
Writing Your Final
Dissertation or Thesis

Have you finished your
data collection?

Yes

No

The Purpose of Data Collection
What Commonly Goes Wrong During Data
    Collection
Beginning Analysis
Keeping a Research Journal
Common Topic Headings for Results,
    Findings, and Conclusion Chapters
Data Collection Dos and Don'ts

The purpose of this chapter is to go over the challenges that are common among beginning doctoral researchers in the data collection phase of their research. Included is information about common mistakes, a discussion of how you know when you have enough data, and what to do in situations where more are needed.

The Questions Answered in This Chapter:

1. Why should I keep my purpose in mind while collecting data?

2. What are the common problems faced during data collection?

3. What should I do about them?

4. How do I know when I have enough data?

5. What should I do if I need more data?

6. How and when do I begin analysis?

7. Why should I consider keeping a journal during data collection and analysis?

The Purpose of Data Collection

You have a clear purpose for doing this research, something you want to accomplish, and you have spent time analyzing its potential importance to your field. In order to capitalize on that potential significance, you should keep your purpose in mind throughout your data collection and analysis process. Your goal for data collection is to capture quality evidence that then translates to rich data analysis and allows you to build a convincing and credible answer to the questions you have posed.

What Commonly Goes Wrong During Data Collection?

Permissions Are Withheld

After you receive your ethical review but before you are able to engage your study participants, you may face challenges within the organization that will be providing the data. In earlier chapters, we recommended that you insist upon written letters of permission from organizations prior to completing your proposal or applying for ethical review. This does not make your research guaranteed, however, as both personnel and company policies change. Several times we have had to aid doctoral students who were scrambling to revamp already approved methodology in order to satisfy new stakeholders.

> **Aha Moments:**
>
> While your sample may participate in the survey, there is no guarantee they will finish all the questions.
>
> (Jodi Leffingwell, DoctoralNet, 2012).

Where Are All the People Who Said They Would Participate?

It is not at all uncommon for doctoral students to complain that for some reason all the people who said that they would participate in their research have suddenly disappeared. One student realized, well into her research process, that her questions were intimidating to her participants; however, they were afraid to look ignorant. The result was that very few completed surveys came back. As you will see in Jodi's quote above, even if surveys are returned, they may not be complete. Either way, getting enough data to work with has become a greater challenge in modern research settings because people are tired of being asked questions by strangers and they understand how long a survey or interview might take.

Participant selection issues may vary within qualitative versus quantitative studies. Qualitative researchers may have difficulty obtaining people who are willing to take an hour or more as participants, whereas the numbers required for statistically significant results may be difficult to obtain for the quantitative study. After those immediately available for your study have been exhausted, selection of others who meet all the criteria set up by your proposal may be daunting.

Researchers need to remember that providing data can be a time-consuming event on the part of the participants. No matter how much you have worked to make the topic one of interest to them, at the moment you need to collect data, they still need to stop what they are doing in order to give you their time and attention. Of course you were diligent and got verbal permissions from the people of whom you're going to be asking questions. Of course, you even gave them a pretty specific timeline as to when you would be coming back to them. Nevertheless, during the time between that conversation and the day you need to collect data, many things have intervened in their lives. While, of course, you have kept in touch and modified any expectations they might have according when your work would begin, do not be insulted or take it personally when suddenly you find fewer people agreed to your study than you expected. The answer to this problem is to have a backup plan whenever possible. If snowball sampling is appropriate, you can try asking those who are participating if they can introduce you to other people who might be equally appropriate.

How Much Data Do I Need?

If you see your number of participants diminishing, the most natural question is to ask yourself whether and to what extent can you do an adequate study with less? How do you know when you have enough data? This is a hard question to answer, because it is a decision made upon each individual case. Nevertheless, certain standards apply across the board. You need to have enough data to build a convincing case at the end that you in fact know the truth about your situation. It's a question of saturation. In a grounded theory study, as an example, the researcher is held to the standard that repeated data collection

Figure 10.1 Sometimes the number of people who agreed to participate at the beginning of a study can drop significantly as the study progresses.

Source: ©iStockphoto.com/alexsl

added little to the number, quantity, or evolution of their categories or themes within their analysis of the evidence. You need to collect enough data so that much of it is redundant, indicating that you have queried deep enough to find the themes or patterns that exist under the surface of your topic (Pease, 2009).

You might also consider adding a different method, making yours a mixed methods study, to be able to gather more data from the participants you have. Data from a smaller than desired quantitative study can expand exponentially when you add qualitative methods that allow you to dig deeper into the answers to your questions. Researcher using secondary or archival data may also find that the variables in the original study don't quite seem to address their questions. In this case, perhaps initial findings could be investigated further using focus groups and so forth. Should you be considering this, we suggest a long conversation with your supervisor to determine the best path.

The final requirement in all cases is credibility: To what extent do you have enough evidence to claim that credible answers to the questions you asked have developed, and is it believable that a wider or more intense study in the same area would result in the same findings?

Tracesea asks: *You presented examples of quantitative projects adding qualitative methods to gather more data. What if I start with qualitative methods and find I don't have enough data?*

Answer: Although no one answer will fit all scenarios, generally the answer to this is to go back to your original subjects and ask more questions. You have to consider the ethics of your situation. To ask questions using quantitative methods (say through a surveyed or to ask different people requires you to go back to ethical review. If you can probe your same subjects more deeply, you do not require a new review.

What Should I Do if I Need More Data?

If you decide that you need more data and you have completely exhausted the parameters allowed for you by your ethical review, you will need to go back to that ethical review board to obtain permission that allows you to gather more data under different circumstances. This is generally not a difficult task, and ethical review boards typically agree, especially if the rights and privileges of the original participants are in danger because they may have had their time and personal attention taken up by something that proved not to be of value. This is considered a risk benefit issue for researchers.

Beginning Analysis

There is no hard and fast rule about when data collection ends and data analysis begins. It might generally be said that when you are about halfway through your anticipated data collection, you might want to run beginning analytic processes. These will not be accurate but may give you a lot of preliminary information about how difficult your analysis will be, whether you can see your way from these data to the answers to your questions, and this may help guide your final stages.

During preliminary analyses, look for items that are not congruent with the rest. These outliers may be indicators of the arenas in which you need to dig deeper. These data may also provide keys to more valuable insights.

Keeping a Research Journal

It doesn't matter whether you are collecting qualitative or quantitative data; there will be what feels like a lot of moving parts to contend with. A few of the things you will have to deal with are informed consent, the data itself—keeping it adequately locked and under protection—developing qualitative codes and then themes, and running analyses. Many of these activities require completely different organizational patterns and happen all at once. Journals can be very useful tools to help you maintain your sense of positive forward moving, not to mention as a tool to minimize bias through reflexive thinking (Borg, 2001; Ortlipp 2010).

One strategy that works for many is to list ideas as you have them, capturing them on a different page for each type of issue they address. If this becomes too jumbled, develop a different set of icons or stickers, one for each task. Then go back and sort the ideas by adding the icons or stickers. Project management software or cloud-based note keepers, such as Evernote, can also be employed. However you set it up, learn to capture your thoughts even when working with others. Periodically you go through your journals to make sure all those boxes have been checked. There are probably as many ways to organize as there are people.

Figure 10.2 You can use different icons or stickers to categorize and sort out the ideas in your journal.

Source: © Can Stock Photo Inc./Jeremy

As an example of the types of complex thinking you will be engaging in at this point, Ken Long shares his format in this pullout (DoctoralNet, 2012). As you are engrossed in the messages that develop from your data, what you believe at the time to be an "aha moment" or insight, you note it in your journal. Later, you go back and reflect on it, asking questions such as whether it holds up in the greater scope of your work. If it seems worthy of future investigation or writing, then you commit to those actions and later come back to note their results. This generates a clear journal that can be discussed as part of the internal validity of your study as well as keep you on track both in the moment. Immediately the journal helps you avoid becoming distracted, and in the long term it helps you capture what may turn out to be important threads of ideas.

The table below is the basic format I used. I found the landscape paper orientation a better fit for keeping extensive notes. I have shared this simple tool with a number of graduate students whom I am mentoring, and they report similar findings on its usefulness.

The A-Ha! moment or insight	Reflective thinking notes	Commitment to action notes	Results of actions taken

Dr. Ken Long, DoctoralNet, 2012

Common Topic Headings for Results, Findings, and Conclusion Chapters

The process of collecting and then analyzing data comes to completion with the realization that you have the answers to your questions and the necessity to write the results chapter. You may find at this point you're up against all the writing challenges that you faced when working on your proposal. It is wise to think ahead, lay out your chapters and chapter headings for the results, findings, discussion, conclusions, and keep the writing structure in mind as you proceed. For this reason, you may find it useful to look over the following set of basic headings.

You may face the same challenge as in your proposal as to not completely understanding the flow of the final chapters and their relationship to what you wrote in your initial proposal. You have two tasks: (1) to write up your data collection, analysis, and discussion and (2) to tie them back through the whole document with that "golden thread" of internal consistency that is shown throughout all solid pieces of research.

Headings for the Results and Findings Chapter

Note that this section of your writing must maintain complete neutrality. In order to meet that standard, you need to clearly delineate which discussions or variables had the largest frequency of similar responses (majority responses) as opposed to those that garnered some similar responses but are not as important (minority findings). Be sure to discuss all disparate or outlier data fully. Possible headings include the following:

Description of the Participants

Demographics

Research Questions and/or Hypotheses

Description of Data Collection and Treatment

Subtopics as Required by Topic

Description of Analysis

Discussion of Results (not findings)

Discrepant Cases and Nonconforming Data

Credibility, Validity, and Reliability of Findings

Summary

Headings for the Discussion or Conclusion Chapter

In general, your discussion or conclusion chapter ties all the threads of the rest of your document together. Therefore, your literature reappears as in relation to your data and analysis, your proposed significance in the introduction chapter is discussed again as a resulting significance, and so forth. Possible headings include the following:

Overview (includes why, how of study)

Interpretation of Findings (usually listed as per question/hypothesis with reference to discussion of data upon which they are built, Chapter 4)

Significance to the Field (tying the study to the wider literature)

Contributions

Recommendations for Action

Recommendations for Further Study

Summary of Chapter

Data Collection Dos and Don'ts

Keeping an active, neutral research mindset may not always be easy, depending upon your circumstances. The following are good things to keep in mind to help you stay on track.

Do

- *Read and cross-examine your assumptions.* Be on the lookout and cross check with others for where your own worldview is influencing your sense of the reality exposed by your data. If doing interviews, consider giving your participants a synopsis of the meaning you hear and then asking them if you understand their meaning correctly.
- *Discuss your findings and analysis with people whom you consider to have strong intellect and wide or diverse backgrounds.* These discussions are not to take everything they say as the way it should be but rather to open your mind to other options.
- *"Member check,"* go back to your participants and test your themes/theories and ideas about the answers that developed during your study.

Figure 10.3 You can test your theories by returning to study participants and sharing your ideas with them to get feedback on whether you are on the right track.

Source: BananaStock/BananaStock/Thinkstock

Don't

- *Summarize what you hear during your qualitative data collection.* Verbal recordings need to be transcribed verbatim to construct records worthy of analysis. Summaries are not adequate.

- Forget to include a *clear explanation of the demographics* of your final set of participants.
- Forget to include *how often* you met with your participants, *when* and *where* surveys were given, and all other *salient details of how your data were collected.*

Chapter 10 Checklist

☐ I understand the common problems faced during data collection.

☐ I can handle those problems if and when I face them.

☐ I understand how to determine if I have enough data.

☐ I know what to do if or when I need more data.

☐ I am prepared to begin analysis at the right time.

Where Should I Go to Dig Deeper? Suggested Resources to Consider

Guest, G., Namey, E. E., & Mitchell, M. L. (2013). *Collecting qualitative data: A field manual for applied research.* Thousand Oaks, CA: Sage. This is an excellent resource for all types of qualitative data collection and offers you a solid field manual for work with these methods.

Prasad, P. (2005). *Crafting qualitative research: Working in the postpositivist traditions.* Armonk, NY: M.E. Sharpe. This book gives wonderful descriptions of hermeneutics, critical theory, ethnography, and other traditions and how they impact qualitative data collection and analysis.

11

Are You Ready to Write Up Your Qualitative Data?

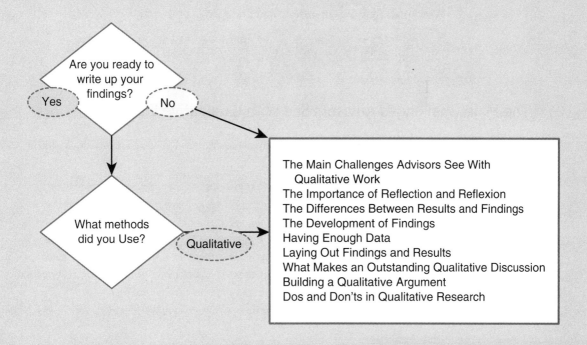

Are you ready to write up your findings?

Yes

No

What methods did you Use?

Qualitative

The Main Challenges Advisors See With Qualitative Work
The Importance of Reflection and Reflexion
The Differences Between Results and Findings
The Development of Findings
Having Enough Data
Laying Out Findings and Results
What Makes an Outstanding Qualitative Discussion
Building a Qualitative Argument
Dos and Don'ts in Qualitative Research

Do you have masses of qualitative data? Are you wondering about the standards you will have to meet as you write it up? The purpose of this chapter is to help answer these questions and to set the doctoral researcher on a clear path towards finishing his or her findings and conclusions in a defensible manner.

The Questions Answered in This Chapter:

1. What are the main challenges advisors see with qualitative work?

2. Why are reflection and reflexion important in the analysis of qualitative data?

3. What are the differences between results and findings?

4. How do findings develop?

5. How will I know when I have done "enough"?

6. How should I lay out my results and findings?

7. What makes the difference between an average and an outstanding qualitative discussion?

The Main Challenges Advisors See With Qualitative Work

What is the difference between reporting out qualitative evidence (dumping it into your document) and analyzing it?

 Alana says: *I can't speak to what other advisors tell their students when they first turn in their qualitative findings, but more often than not, I don't see "findings," I see what I call a data dump. The student merely answers the questions their study asked by pulling together all the quotes that circle around a main position and then dumps them in the document rather than sorting what all the words meant and the complexities of ideas held within them.*

Qualitative Analysis

Once you have collected the full bulk of your qualitative data and hopefully stored it in appropriate qualitative software, you are likely to wonder, what is next? This section discusses both the linear and nonlinear approach to qualitative analysis, each of which has advantages and disadvantages, but neither of which is complete by itself. We are advocates of qualitative research that delves deeply into potential underlying meanings held within the words that were gathered during data collection and which then figures and refigures possible underlying currents or complex meanings. We also believe it is important that researchers (a) know themselves well and reflect upon not only the meaning of their data but also their biases towards it and (b) sort and re-sort data across their research questions looking for new possibilities.

Linear Qualitative Analysis

Most often, doctoral students who are unfamiliar with qualitative data collection and analysis choose to map their interview questions and answers back to their research questions. This may be done in the form of a chart or table, with the research question being in the top left corner and next to it those interview questions that appear to lead back to that question. This is entirely appropriate when laying out your research, because it helps both you and your reader understand the connection between your research questions and your interview questions. It is limiting, however, when you look at your data in that same order as a means of moving towards answering the research questions. Table 11.1 below is an example of such a plan from a doctoral student as she first presented her results and findings.

The positive aspects of this approach are that it lets you go through your data systematically and offers some semblance of comfort that you are proceeding towards the outcomes required. Indeed, as a first step, it is not a bad approach. However, if it leads you to believe this is the way you will receive your ultimate answers, then it is a misleading process and has two problems associated with it that will often cause you more work rather than less.

Linear qualitative analysis is based upon the idea that the person answering your interview questions comes to their experience of the issue you are studying from a similar direction, or that, upon first hearing, you understand what they are saying. Human research subjects are complex individuals, and their understanding of the issues about which you are interviewing are merged into and delineated within their lives in unique ways. They will understand and respond to your questions, each perhaps from a slightly different angle. Therefore, it is likely that upon close examination some aspect

Table 11.1   Linear Outline of Qualitative Data (Williams, 2012)

Research Question	Data Collection Tools	Datapoints Yielded	Data Source	Data Analysis
RQ 1: What are kindergarten and first grade teachers' perceptions of dyslexia's causes and symptoms?	Interviews	Interview questions 1 and 2 1. Describe a child who you've thought might have dyslexia. *If no child comes to mind for question 1, ask the following question:* What symptoms would you expect a dyslexic child to show? 2. Based on your experience and professional learning, what do you believe is cause of dyslexia?	Interviews from selected kindergarten and first grade teachers, with reflective and descriptive notes	Interviews: Transcriptions will be combined with reflective and descriptive interview notes and will be reduced to meaningful segments. Two coders will use open coding, with inter-coder reliability checks.

of the way they answer a later query may have bearing on an earlier research question. The doctoral candidate who only completes the linear analysis will miss these subtleties.

This leads us to the second problem with linear qualitative analysis: the data dump. All too often, doctoral candidates assume that they (a) cannot say something better than their subjects said it and (b) are required to demonstrate how data lead to findings. While either one of these may not be incorrect, taken together they often lead to dissertation disaster. The reader is subjected to pages and pages of quotations from human subjects, and the dissertation does not meet the standard of critical analysis.

Nonlinear Qualitative Analysis

Corbin and Strauss (2008), in their discussion of grounded theory, describe two basic types of qualitative data analysis coding: open or selective. Open coding is when researchers read the entire body of data without preconceived ideas as to what they will find, coding items of interest as they go. These items of interest may include but are not limited to

- full or partial answers to the research questions,
- interesting or provocative ideas,
- agreement or disagreement with previous research literature, and
- discussions that lead to a deeper understanding of the interrelatedness among the variables associated with this issue.

Figure 11.1 Open coding is when researchers look over their data to find themes. Selective coding is when the researcher goes back over the data multiple times to find items that fit in each of those themes.

Source: ©iStockphoto.com/DrAfter123

Selective coding is when researchers go back over their data multiple times to review whether and to what extent previously read items correspond with or disagree with any of the aforementioned items of interest. An example from the Williams study in the last section would be that she would code selectively for all conversation relating to issues that had come up in her review of literature: automatic letter naming, phonological awareness, overuse of certain words, and so forth. Selective coding may include looking for and highlighting particular word usage, the relationship between variables, linkages to literature, or the linear relationship that was discussed in the previous section.

The doctoral candidate may find the idea of nonlinear qualitative coding to be overwhelming. We have heard many students say, I don't know what to look for. This will likely dismay your reader, advisor, or committee, as it implies that you are not the expert on the subject that you need to be in order to graduate. After all, you have spent two or more years of your life looking into what is known on this particular topic. Take heart and have confidence. Read your data as though it is an adventure, one that is taking you into the real world of whether or not your subjects agree or disagree with the other experts of whose work you are familiar. There is no harm in merely reading your data as an outside neutral observer, asking yourself, what is interesting here? Themes will emerge and over time you will begin to feel you understand your topic from a new perspective.

You may start by coding by topic. As an example, we recently started qualitative work looking into doctoral students' use of Twitter. We originally thought that we would be able to identify at what stage in writing a dissertation students were most likely to tweet, and so we entered the selective codes corresponding to the three main stages: designing your topic, writing your proposal, and finishing. What became clear rather quickly was that open codes began to develop: motivation/lack of it, procrastination, requests for help from others, and so forth. Open codes rapidly led us to consider personal motivations for doctoral students to use Twitter. As this book goes to press we are uncovering other ideas from our research on the challenges faced in writing, and so forth. If we had only selectively coded or followed a strict linear path we would have missed many interesting and unexpected outcomes.

We believe you're looking for the "aha" discovery, one which surprises you. Qualitative research would be very dull and boring rather than the adventure it is meant to be, if in-depth conversations with other people did not display ideas that we had previously never considered. Nor would your dissertation study offer much to your field. One technique that allows your conscious mind to go beyond its normal constraints is to read your data prior to going to bed. Then ask yourself, before sleep, what are the issues in your data that need to be resolved or highlighted? Leave some time when you first get up in the morning to write. You will be surprised at the answers your subconscious will bring to your nonlinear qualitative analysis. Be sure to follow, tear apart, and analyze any thought that has a sense of discovery. These unique ideas are the gems you are looking for as you proceed with your analysis. Be sure to discuss them with your advisor or colleagues to tease out their relative importance to your study.

The Importance of Reflection and Reflexion

In one of our other books (James, Slater, & Bucknam, 2012), we point out that there is a need within qualitative research to engage in both reflection and reflexion. Reflection we defined as the internal process whereby researchers make meaning of what they have discovered or done and then come to a conscious conclusion about what they want to do next.

Reflexion on the other hand is a more complex construct revolving around the idea that researchers are never completely neutral when they interact with another person. Who you are, and what you believe, has influenced your research study, its methodology, and the questions you have asked, and ultimately will influence at least your first impression of what you hear from your subjects. Reflexion holds us to the standard of picking apart our own culpability in all of those things and engaging in what Argyris (2002) called "double-loop learning" (p. 5). Essentially this technique means that you first reflect upon what your

Figure 11.2 Reflexion involves looking carefully at ourselves to see how our background, experiences, and beliefs might affect our research.

Source: Medioimages/Photodisc/Photodisc/Thinkstock

qualitative data tell you and then you reflect upon how your background or personal life influences how you look at—and the meaning that you make from—the data you have collected. In this way, the qualitative researchers learn more about themselves at the same time they learn about the subjects which they study. Ultimately, this makes us expert researchers, creating wisdom in our ideas and our work from which others will take new meaning and with which we will influence our fields.

Both reflection and reflexion are necessary. Reflexion by itself can lead a researcher down a rabbit hole of questioning their culpability so much that it ultimately stalls their work. Reflection on the other hand, while it allows us to move forward, make decisions, and come to an efficient ending, does not take our own personhood and its influence on our research into account. Together they are a powerful mix and one that elevates qualitative research as well as the researchers who engage in it (Argyris, 2002; Cunliffe, 2004, 2005; James et al., 2012).

The Difference Between Results and Findings

We have already discussed that your writing of qualitative results should be much more than a listing of the data you collected as they pertain to the questions you are asking. Nevertheless, some further discussion about results and findings is necessary in order for the beginning doctoral researcher to have a clear idea of the differences between them.

At their core, results inform your reader about the process and specific outcomes of your data collection. They should be neutrally presented as though you were laying out your cards on the table in such a manner as to explain what went on. The purpose of your report of findings is to efficiently present your data so that your reader can put it in context, ask their own questions, and evaluate it from a position at a distance away from the actual research.

Findings, on the other hand, make sense of your results and tie them back to the purpose and structure of your study. Put another way, findings answer your research questions.

The Development of Findings

We hope that throughout your qualitative analysis process you have looked at your data from many points of view. Perhaps you have created charts and graphs, coded them with software, and so forth, but definitely took your data out of the context from which they were originally collected and resorted them in order to tease out similarities and differences between ideas. If you used qualitative software, then you coded them and reread just the things associated with each code. Hopefully you repeated this process over and over until you began to see subtleties beneath the obvious. Whatever analysis processes you employed, you uncovered

- Themes, categories, or main topics within your data
- Percentages or quantifications of how many agreed with each of these themes
- How those themes compared and contrasted with the literature in your discussion of it
- Relationships between themes as they tracked back to people or how ideas and themes developed and clustered among individual participants

Rubin and Rubin (2012) tell us

As you think about your writing, ask yourself four questions. First, *what is the core idea or set of ideas that you want to communicate*? Are you trying to explain a technical concept, the only history of an important political event, share an oral history, work out an academic theory, resolve a policy problem, or something else? Second, *who is the audience you're trying to reach in your writings*? Are you addressing a thesis committee, fellow academics, policy makers, or a broader informed public? Third, *what outlets are available to disseminate your findings?* Fourth, *what style and form of writing communicates the central ideas that will reach the intended audience*? (p. 246)

While the answers to the last two questions are decided for you, merely because you are writing a doctoral dissertation or thesis, it still bodes well for you to consider the ramifications of that audience on how qualitative analyses should or are most commonly presented. After you have completed, often multiple times, all of these steps listed above for data analysis, and you believe you know the key core concepts you wish to discuss, then perhaps it is time to reread the qualitative dissertations you collected as models. An overview of how others have approached the areas that trouble you the most may save you hours of mucking around trying to figure out how to establish your ideas or illuminate them from your data.

Figure 11.3 Rereading the model qualitative dissertations you have collected can help you begin to develop your findings.

Source: Pixland/Pixland/Thinkstock

We should mention here the importance, as you work with your data, of keeping daily notes of what you did, the thoughts that developed, and so forth, in your research journal. This becomes your audit trail. It is much easier to write the paragraph or two that will establish the veracity of your data and analysis when you can write out the specifics of how many days, times, codes, instances, and so forth were recorded in your journal.

Tracesea asks: *What if I am not sure that my findings actually make sense in relation to my results? Is it appropriate to share my results with others to get their ideas to compare to my own? If so, who would be best to ask?*

Answer: Take this discussion immediately to your supervisor—lay out your data, your conclusions as they result from those data, and then ask for suggestions to improve clarity. We suggest you do this as a discussion rather than in written form because it will help the discussion stay on the topic without being waylaid by writing issues. Writing up data is a challenge all its own, but first you need to be convinced yourself that your data demonstrate credible results to others.

Having Enough Data

As we mentioned at the beginning of this chapter, one of the downfalls of qualitative research may be when a study does not collect enough data. What is enough? Generally you collect data until everything you are hearing seems redundant with ideas that have been put forth by other participants (as mentioned earlier, this is called saturation). At that time, if your questions probed deep enough into your subject, you should have a range of ideas through which the sorting and resorting process will allow those precious discoveries or new ideas to unfold.

Another aspect of deciding how much is enough has to do with tracking outliers to the main results and findings. In other words, in any body of data there will be ideas that are not contained within the general range. If we were to track these in a chart or Bell curve they would be the tail before and after the bell. Human experience is such that no topic will ever be completely contained within one set of ideas, but some of those ideas will be rare. Complexity theory, however, has taught us that these outlying ideas may give rise to new outcomes in the future. Therefore, it is very important that all qualitative researchers capture and identify them. Obviously, there is a certain quantity that indicates there is enough evidence of these outlying ideas to allow you to discuss them. One suggestion is that, as you hear ideas that immediately seem to be outside of the general norm, you track them further to get a handle on how prevalent they are, where they congregate, and under what conditions. These data will greatly enhance the richness of your discussion.

Laying Out Findings and Results

As you will see when you overview many qualitative research dissertations or theses, the way you structure your results and findings will largely determine the efficiency and ease with which your reader understands the importance you were trying to convey. A good place to start might be to take the general outlines of the headings for the results and findings chapters (as we presented them in Chapter 10) and then to compare them across all of the qualitative dissertations you have collected for review. Patterns will emerge, and you will be able to delineate which set of headings best serves your particular needs. This is where dissertation and thesis writing becomes an art form rather than a prescribed method of design.

From our award-winning dissertations, an example of a linear pattern comes from Lam (2007), who reported data from a qualitative case study, looking into how managerial leadership affects inclusive collaborative relationships with IT or, adversely, affects risks and profitability. Borrowing an analysis structure reminiscent of hypotheses in quantitative work, his review of literature coalesced into five propositions. For example, "IT executives can design organizational development roles to improve organizational effectiveness" (p. 73). After reminding his reader of the goal (his questions and propositions), he reviewed the data collection and analysis procedures he used and then revealed outcome data from each form of data. He concluded

Findings aligned with the literary review presented in chapter 2. As the horizontal integration has begun in transition from being separate toward becoming collaborative, the transformation of an inclusive and collaborative organization by A. Evans (2003), N. Evans (2004a, 2004b), N. Evans and Hoole (2005), Haes and Grembergen (2005, 2006), and Coughlan et al. (2004) was confirmed. Related conclusions, implications, and recommendations for the beginning of this transformation are advanced in the summary and recommendations that follow in chapter 5. (Lam, 2007, p. 101)

Wakefield (2012), on the other hand, allowed the findings to emerge. Her purpose was to look for fractal patterns within human relationships in nonprofit or nongovernment administration and workers. Her initial data were open coded and patterns emerged, her second set of data were collected in the midst of a huge fire threatening her city and deeper levels of connection between organizations emerged. Finally, she went back for a member check and her participants added depth to her results through their explanations and insights. Her results chapter is laid out with a relatively quick overview of those events, the stories in aggregate, and then a taxonomy of each result as it is seen in a fractal pattern within and relating to self, others, and ecosystem. She concluded by answering the research question with yes, fractals can be found.

What Makes an Outstanding Qualitative Discussion?

In our analyses of award-winning dissertations and how they compared to solid and commendable doctoral research that did not reach that pinnacle of success, we found that amount of data and amount of critical analyses correlated directly with what made the award winners outstanding. Of course, there was a range in both populations, and there will be examples where a normal study and an award-winning study had similar numbers of interviews and pages of analysis. In general though, award winners are likely to have collected at least 50% more data and, in all cases, wrote more in their analysis section. While it is simplistic to say, more is better, it builds on an obvious truth that, as you have gotten more deeply into a subject, you have more to say about it. As we will see in the next chapter, this does not hold true for quantitative data analyses and discussion. The dissertations included in our analyses are referenced in Appendix E. The second and equally important distinction between an outstanding dissertation and one which sufficiently passes the rigors of examination will always be seen in the quality of the argument presented, which we will discuss next.

Figure 11.4 More is sometimes better; in award-winning qualitative dissertations we found more data and longer analysis sections.

Source: ©iStockphoto.com/artefy

Building a Qualitative Argument

Although we discussed argumentation in Chapter 7, as it related to literature reviews, we will look at those components again, from a different angle here. Likely at this stage of your analysis you either "feel" you've learned something from your data gathering or think you have. The next step is to objectively go back into your data, structure firm arguments, and then compare your outcomes to the work of others as you outlined them in your review of literature.

Argumentation

Looking again at the structure of Stephen Toulmin (1958, later cited and redefined by Hart, 1998), as we did in Chapter 7, an argument can be divided into four types of information:

1. A claim is an arguable statement. It is not, in and of itself, proven to be true. *What claims do you believe you can make based upon your data? As an example, Wakefield claims that there are fractal patterns in human relationship.*

2. Evidence is the word used to connote data that are being employed to back up the claim. *What evidence do you have for what you think or feel you have learned? Wakefield's evidence is based on an exhaustive data collection and analysis process that showed similarities in pattern between self, others, and the ecosystem.*

3. A warrant is the link between the evidence and the claim (since A is true then B must be true also). *How will you structure the warrants needed as you move towards your findings and discussions or conclusions? Since Wakefield found these patterns which held true and were verified as being true by participants, then her warrant is that there are fractal patterns in human endeavors and the new strategic manager will do well to look for them in this rather than or at least as well as in the more usual linear approach.*

4. Backing includes the context and the assumptions that support the validity of the warrant and the evidence (because). *With backing you now have established a basic argument for your findings. Wakefield backs her ideas with her discussion of complexity thinking and cybernetics (Wakefield, 2012).*

As you complete your analysis, you will likely have an idea of the claims you would like to make. You then look for the evidence within your data that back up that claim. Whether or not your reader will believe your claim will hinge on the degree to which you (a) link your claims to evidence and are able to (b) back up those with clear warrants or linkages.

Figure 11.5 Make sure there is a strong clear link between your evidence and your claim.

Source: Stockbyte/Stockbyte/Thinkstock

During and after construction of your arguments, you need to consider what graphic organizers, figures, tables, illustrations, and/ or examples might be used to back up your findings and to make their construction easier for your reader to understand. Qualitative data, by its nature, rarely can be considered irrefutable, so you will need to back up every assertion. As Hart (1998) pointed out, a generalized or hypothetical scenario is less convincing than concrete illustrations using the various methods mentioned above to back up findings. Qualitative researchers do well to frequently augment their arguments with direct quotes from their participants.

Dos and Don'ts in Qualitative Research

Do

- Be clear on the *difference between your results and your findings.*
- Tell your reader at the beginning of each section *how the results and findings will be presented and then follow that order.*
- *Superimpose a routine on your explanation of results,* repeating that routine throughout your argumentation in order for your reader to understand the sequence of thoughts and how they develop.
- *Consistently report your findings* so that your reader understands
  - From whom they were derived.
  - How the themes related to your questions.
  - The relative numerical justification for quantification of the idea within your larger body of data. As an example, if the majority of your study participants agreed with A then it should be discussed first and should be quantified with the percentage of people who mentioned something similar. The other results should follow in an obvious fashion.
  - The logical order that you maintain throughout all your arguments leading to your findings.
  - The role played by disparate data or outliers in your study. These should include a quantification of the significance of these other ideas within your whole collection of data.
- *Use graphic organizers,* different coding tools, concept maps, or new technologies. Use whatever helps you think outside of your own (and possibly your professor's) box to enliven your creative analysis and present new ideas.
- *Analyze the coherence of your data,* findings, and discussion or conclusion and *cross-check with participants,* if at all possible, for the validity of your findings. You will likely find that they can help your ideas go even deeper, thus saving you time writing.
- Include a substantive conversation about *how these data were analyzed, categorized, sorted, and re-sorted* to arrive at the findings.

> From an anonymous reviewer:
>
> *"What I need to see is a full and rigorous qualitative analysis that makes her findings credible and without question. For me to have that faith, I need to see her technique, the way the % worked out as to how many fell on one side or another of a discussion, and how she derived the themes she says emerged. Were they the only themes or just the convenient ones that answered her questions? What were the probes she took to assure a full depth of understanding, etc."*

- *Conclude with a summary* through which the reader is convinced that you completely understand your whole population, where they agreed and disagreed, and the mechanisms that influenced that variety.

Don't

- *Focus on your participants,* unless required by your methodology, such as case studies or narrative inquiry. Thinking in terms of, "this person said this" gets in the way of your seeing the big picture of your data across the wider population. A neutral research position considers the whole, compares it to the literature, and then tests it in ways that address your research questions.
- *Forget to consider the validity* of your findings, discussion or conclusions, and arguments as well as *credibility and reliability,* in your final discussion.

Chapter 11 Checklist

- ❏ I understand the main challenges my advisor may see within my qualitative data analysis.
- ❏ My data analysis will include a nonlinear approach.
- ❏ I have used reflection and reflexion as part of my ongoing data analysis structure.
- ❏ I understand the differences between results and findings.
- ❏ I have considered my data from all angles in order to develop my findings.
- ❏ I have enough data to adequately discuss both the majority and outlier positions.
- ❏ My argumentation is sound.
- ❏ I have considered my work in light of the differences inherent in award-winning qualitative dissertations.

Where Should I Go to Dig Deeper? Suggested Resources to Consider

Bloomberg, L. D., & Volpe, M. (2012). *Completing your qualitative dissertation: A road map from beginning to end* (2nd ed.). Thousand Oaks, CA: Sage. Contains a fabulous checklist for presentations of findings, analysis, and synthesis of findings to discussion or conclusions and final dissertation or thesis closure.

Creswell, J. W. (2009). *Research design: Qualitative, quantitative, and mixed methods approaches* (3rd ed.). Thousand Oaks, CA: Sage; Maxwell, J. A. (2013). *Qualitative research design: An interactive approach* (3rd ed.). Thousand Oaks: Sage. This updated version of a qualitative classic text has a great chapter (6 on page 121) dealing with issues of qualitative validity. It is also a very readable discussion of all the basic considerations.

Ortlipp, M. (2008). Keeping and using reflective journals in the qualitative research process. *The Qualitative Report, 13*(4), 695–705. This is a useful discussion on how to use reflective journaling to enhance your qualitative analysis.

Piantanida, M., & Garman, N. B. (1999). *The qualitative dissertation: A guide for students and faculty*. Thousand Oaks, CA: Corwin Press. These authors have excellent chapters on the details of analysis through portrayals and deliberation. While outside of the purview of this text these topics should be understood and considered by all qualitative researchers.

Rubin, H. J., & Rubin, I. (2012). *Qualitative interviewing: The art of hearing data* (3rd ed.). Thousand Oaks, CA: Sage. Not only does this text help the research get the most out of qualitative data collection, its final discussion on writing is well worth looking into.

Yin, R. K. (2011). *Qualitative research from start to finish*. New York: The Guilford Press. This book is excellent for two reasons: (a) It offers vignettes throughout to help researchers clarify some of the more subtle aspects they might encounter, and (b) trustworthiness and validity are discussed from many angles, helping researchers sort out the pros and cons of the choices they make.

12

Are You Ready to Write Up Your Quantitative Data?

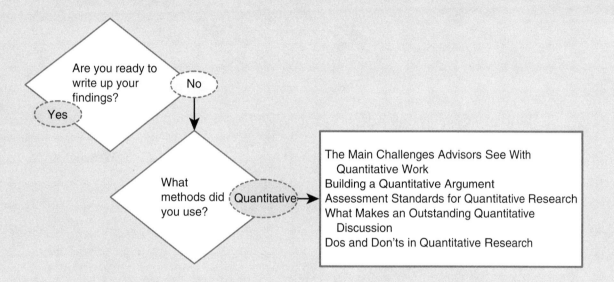

The purpose of this chapter is to help you write an outstanding doctoral dissertation or thesis using quantitative data. That said, it is outside of the purview of a single chapter to do that, especially when considering the intricacies of quantitative data analysis and the principles behind it. For that reason, we highly recommend the book *IBM SPSS for Introductory Statistics: Use and Interpretation* by G. A. Morgan, N. L. Leech, G. W. Gloeckner, and K. C.Barrett.

This chapter will discuss the main challenges seen by advisors, the basics about how you can decide which statistical analysis you need to undertake, and what builds a convincing quantitative argument. We close this chapter with the discussion of the differences seen between and within quantitative dissertations and theses, as we have reviewed them, comparing those which have received awards from those which have not.

The Questions Answered in This Chapter:

1. What are the main challenges advisors see with quantitative work?

2. How do I know I am using the right tool?

3. How do I organize my quantitative evidence?

4. How do I use tables and figures?

5. What builds a convincing quantitative argument?

6. What are the assessment standards for quantitative research?

7. What makes the difference between an average and an outstanding quantitative discussion?

The Main Challenges Advisors See With Quantitative Work

Because neither one of us is a quantitative researcher, we looked to a wider audience of professors/advisors around the world to help us with the questions presented in this chapter. We asked, what are the most common mistakes made by beginner researchers and quantitative analysis? The answers that we received indicated that students often make the mistake of thinking that complex statistical models and tests are preferable or necessary, when this is not always the case. Nieuwen-huis (2012) from *Universiteit Twente* responded that the most common mistake made by students was trying to examine their data using really complex models, such as multivariate regressions. It was Nieuwenhuis's argument that if a researcher is looking for an association between variables and this association is not to be found in a simple contingency table, the researcher should be able to provide very good reasons for trying to estimate using a more complex model. Quantitative analysis hinges on researchers understanding the assumptions inherent within different statistical models (Sanchez-Patino, 2012).

Figure 12.1   One of the most common mistakes made by students doing quantitative studies is that they use complex statistical models and tests, thinking this automatically makes for a better analysis.

Source: Jupiterimages, Brand X Pictures/Brand X Pictures/Thinkstock

Using the Right Tools

Several factors determine what tools to employ as the correct data analysis techniques for your study: your purpose, research questions, the number of independent and dependent variables, and the types of instruments you have used. As stated earlier, if you wish to observe and describe, then simple frequencies and basic descriptive statistics may be all the tools you need, but you will need to dig deeper into your evidence, perhaps with a mixed methods study to uncover aspects of the human experience involved in your study, as a study relying on descriptive statistics alone will seldom meet the standards for doctoral research. You would know this is appropriate because your questions would quantify what is going on or what exists now.

Better for studies at a graduate level is research that compares characteristics and/or behaviors. For these, you will be asking comparative questions, determining the differences between two or more groups, and you will be studying variance. When the aim of your study is to identify how two or more variables are associated, you ask relational questions and employ inferential statistics. Cause and effect questions are very difficult to prove and can only be addressed if you have used a randomized sample selection in an experimental study. Relational statistics are also employed for these types of questions, although multiple regressions may be employed as well. "Causation implies a study in which the affected variable is controlled statistically; therefore it is relational because it establishes the existence and direction of that relationship, but the difference as with other correlational studies is on the type of analysis done" (Sanchez-Patino, 2012, p. 12).

Digging deeper into what type of questions are answered by which type of statistics, let's look at descriptive questions. They might include

- Questions about existence: Is X a real problem in Y situation?
- Questions about description and classification: What are the characteristics of X?
- Questions about composition: What are the factors involved in X?
- Questions about distribution: Is this variable distributed approximately normally? Or, What percentage of participants displayed this characteristic?
- Questions related to statistical descriptions might also ask: What are the mean, mode, and median of this variable?

Questions that deal with two or more variables but do not require inferential statistics may be cross tabulated with or against each other. Examples might include: What percentages of the first and second group displayed similar characteristics?

For questions such as these you would use frequencies, percentages, proportions, measures of central tendency, such as mean, mode, and median, and measures of spread or dispersion, such as range, quartiles, standard deviation, and variance. Again, doctoral research will include descriptive questions, but not be limited to them.

Comparative questions attempt to describe differences or similarities between groups, among groups, within a variety of effects, or about the effect of an interaction. Comparative questions include

- Are there statistically significant differences between X and Y?
- Is there a statistically difference between the performance of these two groups?
- Which is more significantly more effective, A, B, or C, in a given circumstance?
- What is the difference in statistically derived measures of effectiveness between one method and another when it is used either alone or within a group?

As an example, Hinnerichs (2011) asked, "Can IRT in a mass screening shipboard environment statistically differentiate between afebrile participants without ILI exposure and febrile participants with ILI exposure" (p. 6)? Another question in the same study queries, "Does the relationship between oral and IRB surface temperatures vary by gender; in other words, does the efficacy of IRT for screening and identifying subjects with ILI differ between males and females" (p. 7)?

Researchers asking statistical questions need to look into which of the following might be appropriate statistical tests: t-test, Mann-Whitney U test, Analysis of Variance (ANOVA), Analysis of Covariance (ANCOVA), chi-square test, or the factorial analysis of variance (FANOVA).

Relational questions inquire into the association between two variables or among several variables. They can also look into the cause and effect relationship between two or more variables. Researchers should consider correlation coefficients, Z-tests and/or F-tests, regressions, or multiple regressions (Sanchez-Patino, 2012). Note—for a more in-depth discussion of quantitative problems, questions, and analytical tools see Appendix B in Morgan et al. (2011, pp. 217–220). Broomes (2010), as an example, asks the question, "How much variation in student achievement can be attributed to immigration, home language, school mobility or the interaction of all three factors" (p. 79)? Pershing (2003) asked, "Do beliefs about the appropriate degree of directiveness in the managerial relationship differ systematically according to demographic characteristics, education and organizational position?" This researcher also asked, "What is the relative strength of the relationship between demographic characteristics, education, organizational position, and beliefs about the appropriate degree of directiveness in the managerial relationship" (16)?

Organizing Quantitative Evidence

As with all results and findings, quantitative evidence that resides within a clear pattern, obvious to the reader, allows for easy digestion of both data and resulting conclusions. Joyner, Rouse, and Glatthorn (2013) suggest you step back and look at the patterns which have emerged as you have written your different chapters. The way in which you state the problem in your introduction moves forward to explain your methodology and needs to surface again as you summarize everything in your conclusion. Therefore, certain ways in which you might develop your results chapter will make more sense than others to your readers. As an example, you may ask yourself whether variables are the thread that tie everything together or perhaps research questions or perhaps hypotheses. These may be the patterns on which to display your results to their best advantage.

There are three major items every researcher must be concerned with when writing up quantitative results. First, the research should explain if the results are significant or not. If not, then perhaps effect size can be stated, if the p or sig value is less than .10 then report effect size. Can you be confident that the result is not due to chance? Yes, if p is $<$ .05 then you reject the null hypothesis.

Tracesea asks: *What if none of my results are statistically significant? Is this something I need to worry about? Is there anything I can do to ensure I will get statistically significant results?*

Answer: If none of your results are statistically significant, then the null hypotheses are accepted. From the point of view of the research, you do not need to worry since you are testing hypotheses and they can be accepted or rejected. What you need to do is to interpret the findings using the literature review. You cannot ensure significant results because if you did it would be a biased study. What you can do is to design a solid study from the methodological point of view, and that means choosing a research method appropriate for gathering your data that lets you answer the research questions in a valid way, sampling the population adequately, and analyzing data properly. Then the results will be what they will be and as long as you write them up in a credible manner your work will be defensible.

Once the statistical variance and significance values are reported, then you need to interpret the direction of the findings (which group performed better, has the higher mean, or has a coefficient (e.g. r) that is + or -). This is commonly missed. You have worked with your data and know the various performance levels, but your reader does not, so you need to state them clearly.

The third step is to provide the effect size. The APA requires that if effect sizes are not reported, then the item is not accepted for publication for quantitative data. A common trend is also to require confidence intervals for effect sizes. "For associational inferential statistics (e.g., correlation) . . . you must indicate whether the association or relationship is positive or negative" (Gloeckner, 2013; Morgan et al., 2011).

Quantitative work establishes the relationship between variables. As descriptive work is rarely sufficient for doctoral studies unless as part of a mixed method or more robust differential or associational study, you will be either comparing groups or finding strength in the associations between variables (Morgan et al., 2011; Thompson, 2006). Therefore, it is important that as you write up your findings, you don't get lost in the mathematics or reporting but instead on helping your reader understand those relationships and how they help you answer the questions on which your study is focused.

You should expect your analysis of your data to take many iterations. Aptly caught in the comic below, doctoral candidates should not believe that they will work through their data once, find the "true" answer and proceed easily to writing it all up.

Using Tables and Figures

As we will see in our discussion about the differences between an average and an outstanding qualitative dissertation or thesis, the use of tables and figures is paramount for quantitative researchers.

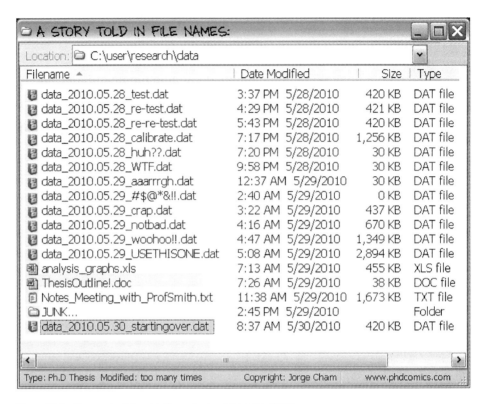

Figure 12.2   Be prepared to work through your data many times.

Source: From Jorge Cham's *A Story Told In File Names,* PhD Comic. Originally published by www.phdcomics.com.

Because of their importance, we suggest that you develop your tables and figures first and then write your first draft of the resulting chapters. Next, dig deeper into your analysis, as others question your results or findings, and then update your tables and figures to bear the maximum weight of your evidence. As you will see in our concluding discussion on award-winning quantitative dissertations, more tables with less writing is the highest standard for academic writing.

The purpose for using visual representations, such as charts or graphs, is to ease the mental load on your reader, which may be presented by the statistical analysis of large quantities of data as is common in quantitative research (Tufte, 1998). "When the data are few and simple, readers can grasp them as easily in a sentence is in the table, but if you present more than a few numbers, readers will struggle to keep them straight" (Booth et al., 2008, p. 213). How then do you choose the most effective graphic representation of your figures? These authors go on to say that when you graphically present complex data, likely you will consider tables, bar charts, or line graphs. While tables may allow you to offer a large quantity of exact numbers, charts and graphs present a visual image that may communicate more easily to the average reader. A bar chart might be used when you need to emphasize contrast, where a line graph might be more appropriate for consideration when you need to discuss continuous change over time (pp. 213–215).

Building a Quantitative Argument

As with our previous discussions on argumentation on pages 139 and 196, a convincing quantitative argument contains a claim or conclusion you are making that directly links to numerical evidence, derived from your statistical analysis. In this case, statistics stand in for the warrant and provide the mathematical linkages between your discussion or conclusions and the evidence in your data. Mathematical treatise or assumptions, upon which your quantitative methodology is based, back your argument. When you know the purpose of each component of both your data and analysis, within the arguments, discussion, or conclusions you are trying to draw, you can more easily structure them in such a way as to ensure that they are easily understood by your readers. It is important, therefore, that when you use tables and figures to stand in for any particular section of your argument—for example, your evidence—that your reader understands the linkages between graphic and written elements in order to make your argument complete.

Assessment Standards for Quantitative Research

Quantitative dissertations and theses require coherence or what Albertyn et al. (2007) call "the golden thread" as a minimum standard (p. 1214). In other words, any variable (as an example) which is mentioned anywhere in your study needs to be drawn out and discussed through your results, findings, discussion, or conclusions.

Three standards apply to all doctoral research: "objectivity, clarity, and replicability" (Bryant, 2004, p. 117). The standard of objectivity not only implies that you present your data from the position of the neutral observer in relation to your subject but that you share your evidence in a way where others who are interested will be able to draw from it for use in their own research. Clarity ensures that others who review your data will draw the same conclusions. In other words, you need to be transparent in how you develop your thoughts so that they may be analyzed by others. And finally, replicability means that if others followed your data collection and analysis in the same context, they would collect similar evidence and reach the same relative conclusions.

Alana says: *One of my students calls finding another study that can be replicated in your environment "Doc in a box." We want our research to be so apparent, methodical, and clear, that another researcher could follow it step-by-step for their own reasons—becoming their "Doc in a box" exemplar.*

What Makes an Outstanding Quantitative Discussion?

When we analyzed the difference between standard and award-winning dissertations, quantitative work stood out as being an anomaly to the "more is better" assumptions in terms of written discussions. In general, the larger the number of study participants included in the data set, the lower the percentage of pages involved in the description of the analysis and reporting of results. The most outstanding case, perhaps, was that of Broomes (2010), who reduced the analysis of over 70,000 cases, through the use of charts and tables, to less than 10 pages of written results. While her work was the most dramatic reduction of analysis to discussion, it was not uncommon to see results such as those by Tao (2009), who reduced the analysis of over 31,000 cases to 50 pages of discussion of results, 24 of which centered on descriptive statistics and 26 of which discussed regressions.

Having read many first drafts of quantitative work, we understand the struggles involved in digesting quantitative data and explaining outcomes to readers with clarity. The propensity of doctoral students is to get lost in the data analysis and write out their own version of "data dumping." What is never wanted is a blow-by-blow explanation of each variable, what participant categories wielded which results. A key issue is to keep the readers awareness at all times of the questions being answered and to use the data descriptions to clarify the answers.

The general outcome of our analysis of the award-winning quantitative dissertations or theses concluded that more cases allowed for deeper analysis while mastery of quantitative results was evident when the researcher could reduce and yet effectively display complex results within figures or tables. As we discussed in the last section, masterful presentation of quantitative evidence moves easily through all the parts of a solid argument while using both written word and graphic descriptions.

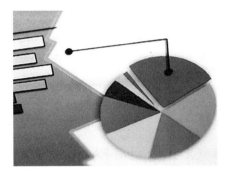

Figure 12.3 Award-winning dissertations often have tables and charts that display complex results that help the reader understand the data and analysis.

Source: Ryan McVay/ Photodisc/Thinkstock

Examples From Award Winners

We would like to help you understand both the idea of how to arrange your results chapter so that it guides your readers through your data easily, and the use of tables to encourage understanding of your data by examining parts of two award-winning dissertations.

While many quantitative studies focus their headings on the questions, analyzing appropriate data under each, Pershing (2003) chose to follow a somewhat chronological approach, leading the reader through the preliminary steps and then separating individual from ecological levels of analysis. As you will see in this excerpt from her table of contents (below), the ecological level was the most in depth and where this author placed the results that tested of the hypotheses around which the study was based. While we did not include all of her subheadings, it is useful to note as well her robust discussion of reliability and validity. Areas not included completely are marked with . . . .

CHAPTER 4: RESULTS

Preliminary Steps

Data Preparation

Reliability and Validity

    Internal Consistency Reliability

    Test Retest Reliability

    Convergent Validity

    Criterion—Related Validity

Summary (Pershing, 2003 p. vi)

We have discussed convincing use of tables as a means to engage your reader in your data. Figure 12.4 from (Broomes, 2010) is one such example. This award-winning dissertation from Canada focused on the difference in outcomes of students in the early grades who had immigrated to an area. As you will see in the table from page 942 of her study, she sets her reader up for understanding her comparison of likely grade proficiency of various student histories. She leads into this table stating:

The focus of this study is on whether students maintained proficiency between Grades 3 and 6 or achieved proficiency in Grade 6 if they did not in Grade 3, given that they may have experienced one or more of the following: been born outside of Canada, speak a language at home other than English, or changed schools. Table 4, therefore, shows the likelihood (the number of students who achieved proficiency over the number who did not) and the probability (the number of students who achieved proficiency out of the total number of students) of achieving proficiency at Grade 6 for students with different combinations of proficiency at Grade 3, country mobility, school mobility, and home language. (p. 90)

Dos and Don'ts in Quantitative Research

Do

- Be clear on the *difference between your results and your findings.*
- Tell your reader at the beginning of each section *how the results and findings will be presented* and then *follow that order.*
- *Superimpose a routine on your explanation of results,* repeating that routine throughout your argumentation in order for your reader to understand the sequence of thoughts and how they develop.
- *Use the tables and charts to present your data* to highlight and offer your reader more options for understanding your arguments rather than just written or formulaic descriptions
- *Clearly explain the statistical models and tests* you used and why they are best suited to your study
- *Include a substantive conversation about the statistical procedures* used to arrive at the findings.
- *Conclude with a summary* through which the reader can follow the course of your argument and will be convinced with the internal validity of your study.

Table 4

Likelihood and Probability of Grade 6 Proficiency by Grade 3 Proficiency, Immigration, School Mobility, and Home Language

Home Language	Proficient in Grade 3				Not Proficient in Grade 3			
	Born in Canada		Moved to Canada		Born in Canada		Moved to Canada	
	Did not change schools	Changed schools	Did not change schools	Changed schools	Did not change schools	Changed schools	Did not change schools	Changed schools
Proficient in Reading: Likelihood (Probability)								
English only	6.89 (0.87)	5.25 (0.84)	9.45 (0.90)	9.61 (0.91)	0.76 (0.43)	0.72 (0.42)	0.88 (0.47)	1.38 (0.58)
Another language instead of or in addition to English	7.05 (0.88)	6.17 (0.86)	12.69 (0.93)	12.13 (0.92)	0.83 (0.45)	0.88 (0.47)	1.18 (0.54)	1.28 (0.56)
Proficient in Writing: Likelihood (Probability)								
English only	6.11 (0.86)	4.60 (0.82)	11.94 (0.92)	9.41 (0.90)	0.80 (0.45)	0.75 (0.43)	1.14 (0.53)	1.41 (0.59)
Another language instead of or in addition to English	6.65 (0.87)	6.07 (0.86)	9.93 (0.91)	9.77 (0.91)	0.94 (0.48)	0.97 (0.49)	1.31 (0.57)	1.49 (0.60)
Proficient in Mathematics: Likelihood (Probability)								
English only	4.18 (0.81)	2.80 (0.74)	7.00 (0.88)	4.17 (0.81)	0.45 (0.31)	0.42 (0.30)	0.43 (0.30)	1.02 (0.51)
Another language instead of or in addition to English	4.88 (0.83)	3.88 (0.80)	8.41 (0.89)	8.28 (0.89)	0.54 (0.35)	0.59 (0.37)	0.80 (0.44)	1.33 (0.57)

Figure 12.4   Broomes Table of Likely Grade Proficiency

Source: Broomes (2010).

Don't

- *Spend too much space on written descriptions*, especially paragraph-long descriptions of frequencies of responses; instead organize quantitative evidence using tables and charts and show your readers how the qualitative data compare with quotations from that evidence.
- *Forget to consider the internal validity* of your findings, discussion or conclusions, and arguments in terms of both types of evidence. This discussion should be considered as part of your final chapter.

Figure 12.5 Long written descriptions of quantitative data aren't often effective; instead, focus on presenting your evidence using tables and charts.

Source: ©iStockphoto.com/shironosov

Chapter 12 Checklist

- ☐ I understand the most common challenges in quantitative reporting.
- ☐ I know which statistical tools to use in my research analysis.
- ☐ I have a solid organizational pattern through which to develop my quantitative evidence.
- ☐ I know both the challenges and potential outcomes in using tables and figures.
- ☐ I feel confident that I understand what is required to build a convincing quantitative argument.
- ☐ I can meet the assessment standards for quantitative analysis.
- ☐ I know how to interpret my results including direction and effect size.
- ☐ I have considered lessons learned from award-winning quantitative dissertations or theses.

Where Should I Go to Dig Deeper? Suggested Resources to Consider

Gliner, J. A., Morgan, G. A., & Leech, N. L. (2009). *Research methods in applied settings: An integrated approach to design and analysis* (2nd ed.). New York: Routledge/Psychology Press. This is an excellent text recommended by one of our reviewers as a great basic for quantitative research.

Huck, S. W. (2012). *Reading statistics and research* (6th ed.). Boston: Pearson. Also recommended by one of our reviewers, this book is known to be a "uniquely accessible text [that] shows precisely how to decipher and critique statistically-based research reports. Praised for its non-intimidating writing style, the text emphasizes concepts over formulas."

Morgan, G. A., Leech, N. L., Gloeckner, G. W., & Barrett, K. C. (2011). *IBM SPSS for introductory statistics: Use and interpretation*. New York: Routledge Taylor & Francis Group. Chapters 1, 3, and 6 respectively are a must read for quantitative researchers covering variables, research problems, questions, measurement, and descriptive statistics, and the selection of and interpretation of inferential statistics. Written in down-to-earth language and augmented by a thorough example that uses data from the High School and Beyond study. Appendix B has an especially good discussion of how to ask questions in quantitative studies.

Roberts, C. M. (2004). *The dissertation journey*. Thousand Oaks, CA: Corwin Press. Chapters 14 and 15 give a brief but useful description of the path from data gathering, through analysis, and on to the final discussion or conclusions. Many pullout boxes offer helpful hints and additional resources.

Rudestam, K. E., & Newton, R. R. (2007). *Surviving your dissertation: A comprehensive guide to content and process* (3rd ed.). Thousand Oaks, CA: Sage. This book contains an excellent set of appendices that discuss ways in which to present data in tables.

Salkind, N. J. (2012). *100 questions (and answers) about research methods*. Thousand Oaks, CA: SAGE. This book is laid out in, usually single-paged, questions and answers and has direct help for many of the most common challenges faced by the beginning quantitative researcher.

Thompson, B. (2006). *Foundations of behavioral statistics: An insight-based approach*. New York: Guilford Press. This book shows readers how to interpret research outcomes and make statistical decisions.

13

Are You Ready to Write Up Your Mixed Methods Data?

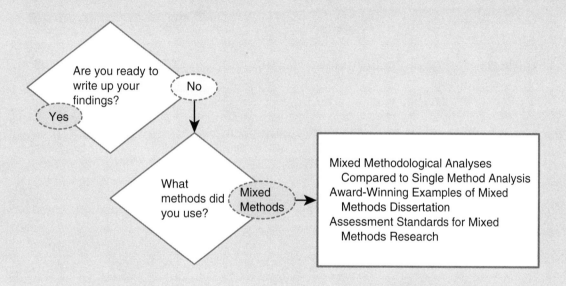

The purpose of this chapter is to help you sort through the similarities and differences between discussing your analysis of qualitative and quantitative methodologies singularly (as discussed in the last two chapters) and the discussion of similar data as part of a mixed methods study. We presuppose you have also read Chapters 11 and 12 and have a decent understanding of how you would approach qualitative and/or quantitative methodologies if you had done them individually. Mixed methods provide the researcher with more information from participants, allowing for the potential of relatively deep insights with perhaps less work than would be required by two separate studies, one qualitative and one quantitative. Even though they may involve less work than two independent studies, one employing each model, they require more mastery over the language of qualitative and quantitative methods and more synchronous discussion, so that each method enhances rather than detracts from the other (Creswell, 2009; Creswell & Plano Clark, 2011; Tashakkori & Teddlie, 2010; Thomas, 2003).

The Questions Answered in This Chapter:

1. Why and how are mixed methodological analyses similar to those by researchers employing either a qualitative or quantitative design?

2. Why and how are mixed method results different from single-method results and findings?

3. How can I start to build a convincing argument?

4. What makes the difference between an average and an outstanding mixed method discussion?

Mixed Methodological Analyses Compared to Single Method Analysis

Similarities

Figure 13.1 If you've collected data using different types of methodology, you should take some time to reflect on your original purpose before moving into analysis.

Source: Creatas Images/Creatas/Thinkstock

One major similarity between mixed methodologies and qualitative and quantitative taken separately is that researchers need to maintain focus on the original purpose behind their methodological choices. One purpose for using both qualitative and quantitative measures is to allow researchers to test out their theories and conclusions from one sort of method by using the other. Playing off of the requirement of different appropriate sample sizes, a researcher might choose to survey a large population, gather insight, and then question the smaller population through interviews or focus groups about the understanding derived from the initial survey.

An alternative approach entails a researcher asking a few people probing questions about the topic and then, when they think they have a handle on the full variety of likely responses, capturing these choices within an instrument and using quantitative methods to survey a much larger population (Creswell, 2009; Thomas, 2003). How you ask your questions in relation to time also becomes critical. Evaluation techniques rely heavily on time sequencing (Fitz-Gibbon & Morris, 1987) and required in your document will be a thorough discussion of relative sequential versus concurrent timing and why you chose the methods you did (Creswell, 2009).

The two examples above presuppose that a sequential approach was being used, where the researcher first uses one kind of data and then uses the other kind to substantiate discussion or conclusions. Concurrent studies might ask populations similar things using two methodologies at the same time, or they might make use of analysis of archival evidence while concurrently collecting new data. Whichever way mixed methods are sliced and diced, one aspect of their beauty, which also greatly adds to their complexity, is their flexible nature and potential for laser-like precision.

Therefore, we suggest that, if you are a researcher who has collected data using very different types of methodology, you should reflect for a moment on the original purposes behind your design and what you hoped to gain from both. We suggest that you print out the purpose behind your work and post it at a high level within your office. This can help you keep a certain mental focus on where you intend to go as you travel down data analysis pathways, otherwise it is too easy to get lost. The potential to lose mental focus and confuse a reader as you write up your results and findings is the second way in which we see mixed and singular methodologies in a similar light.

A third similarity is in the difficulty of keeping solid organization to support vast quantities of data that can potentially arise from mixed methodologies. If we think of data analysis as the researcher's means to exploit the human story within their topic, then mixed methods require you, as a writer, to explain two similar but different stories at the same time. Much like a piece of fiction where there are two main characters, each of whom is considered individually as well as together, it is incumbent upon you as the author to make all things come out together at the end with a solid discussion or conclusion.

Differences

One way in which some authors differentiate qualitative from quantitative in a mixed methods study is by proposing that there is logic inherent in one that is different from the other. Creswell (2009) has perhaps the most definitive discussion of these differences, proposing that in a quantitative study the researcher starts with a problem statement, moving on to the hypothesis and null hypothesis, through the instrumentation into a discussion of data collection, population, and data analysis. Creswell proposes that for a qualitative study the flow of logic begins with the purpose for the study, moves through the research questions discussed as data collected from a smaller group and then voices how they will be analyzed. One means of discussing both types of methodologies would be to first discuss one side using its logical progressive flow and then comparing and contrasting it to the other side using the opposing or differentiated topics.

However it is done, it is incumbent upon the researcher to differentiate both the purposes and the outcomes of the use of qualitative versus quantitative methods (Creswell & Plano Clark, 2011; Tashakkori & Teddlie, 2010). Then, once discussed, this same study needs to help the reader understand how both sets of results play off of each other to the benefit of a deeper understanding of the topics and questions being addressed in the study. The resulting discussion will likely pull them apart, put them together, play them off of each other, and finally, merge their analysis into a deeper understanding.

Award-Winning Examples of Mixed Methods Dissertations

Examples from award-winning dissertations may spur some ideas as to how you might organize your study and clarify the uses and outcomes of each type of data analysis as they pertain to your research questions. It is not uncommon for doctoral candidates to separate their data into sections. For instance, Ruhi (2010), in a very rigorous study of the sociotechnical determinants of member participation in virtual communities, organized his work into eight chapters. The first three follow the normal five chapter model: (1) introduction, (2) essential facets of virtual communities, (3) conceptual framework and research design. Then he chose to highlight each methodology and the results that develop. In chapter 4 he covered qualitative methodology (grounded theory with several levels of coding across a series of methods) and moved directly onto chapter 5 for the qualitative analysis and findings. Chapters 6 and 7 covered the quantitative work in a similar fashion. The study concluded with a discussion that is divided into conclusions merging qualitative and quantitative as they pertain to his answers to the research questions, five in all, each with its own section.

A middle ground in the organizational continuum we are discussing here is the work of Rodenbaugh (2002). In her study on the effectiveness of experiential education in executive development, this author chose to separate her results chapter into two main sections corresponding first to the quantitative side of her study and then to the qualitative. She developed her arguments sequentially, allowing the basis and reasoning behind each method to build a natural case for understanding the answers to her questions as she discussed them in her final discussion chapter.

Perhaps your mixed methods study would be one that is much more heavily slanted to one method over the other. Such is the case in Scharff (2005), who chose to make light of the mixed methodology, not separating out the two types of methods in any way during his discussion of results. Instead he discussed each hypothesis in very specific terms as to all the data that pertain to that topic. In general, for a study that is slanted towards one or the other method, the mixture may be best used as a form of triangulation. Thus in chapter 1, a set of results from one method may be discussed in depth as it pertains to a topic while results from the other method are mentioned in relation to how those data agree with the general finding. For example a snippet of qualitative data may be used to elucidate the quantitative evidence just as frequencies in responses or tests of significance may add internal validity to qualitative findings.

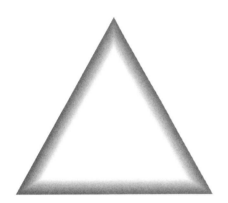

Figure 13.2   When using data from more than two sources, triangulation can be used to facilitate validation.

Building an Mixed Methods Argument

The question then becomes how you construct an argument that both highlights the differences in unique qualities of these two types of data and yet merges them to build a solid construct, a new understanding. As with quantitative data, tables, figures, and other means of graphic organizers may best serve your purposes. Wheeldon and Åhlberg (2012), in their text on visualizing social science research, propose adding concept mapping to the more standard tables and figures presented in qualitative and quantitative studies.

Figure 13.3 (below) was included in the ancillary materials for Creswell (2009) as an example of a concept map to be included in a mixed methods proposal. Taking this logic one step further, this same concept map could be used to highlight findings and begin to build the argument for a study's discussion or conclusions. You will see it follows a similar middle ground to the Rodenbaugh (2002) study mentioned above.

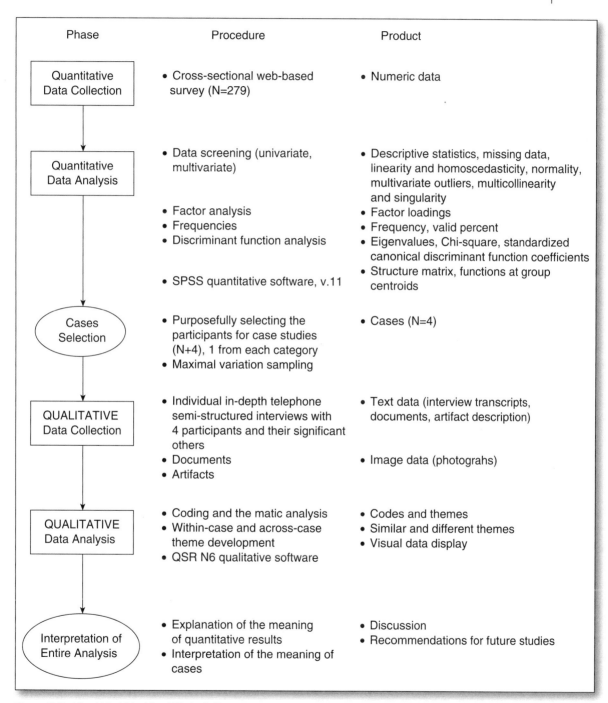

Figure 13.3   Visual Model for Mixed Methods Procedures

Source: From Nataliya Ivankova's *A Sample Mixed Methods Dissertation Proposa*l.

When we look at the table of contents of award-winning studies (discussed below), we see that it is not unusual to plot a course through data analysis in a very directive manner. As an example, both Konorti (2007) and Scharff (2005) laid out their chapters using the convention of listing the research questions and hypotheses with discussions of each type of data underneath.

Human beings follow different pathways to construct their ideas. It is not uncommon for a doctoral researcher to have the first version of their results turned back to them with comments indicating that they were just dumping their data on their reader rather than constructing findings. The most frequent response is, but what am I supposed to do? Employing the use of concept maps may help you move past this juncture. Starting with the concepts that you developed from your literature, consider your data and their analysis. Ask yourself what you have learned, and how and in what ways you have developed those new understandings. Then reflect upon how they will add to the previous literature. Initially you can record your reflections in any way you want to, but once they are in figure form, you will see the connections and groupings of concepts and ideas and have new ways of discussing them. After you have developed a discussion, go back and add tables and figures that will graphically display some of the more cumbersome parts (Maxwell, 2013; Ravitch & Riggan, 2012; Wheeldon & Åhlberg, 2012).

Figure 13.4   Sharing your ideas with stakeholders and responding to their questions can help your work progress and improve.

Source: Digital Vision/Digital Vision/Thinkstock

Because people follow different pathways to construct their ideas, the way in which your ideas develop most naturally may not be the easiest for others to follow. Nevertheless, once you have it sorted and can at least discuss your data, their relationship to each other and the literature, you will be on solid enough ground that you can ask for the opinion of others. We recommend that you show your ideas to your stakeholders, both those who are important to your study and to your university life. When your ideas are well developed and straightforward, the questions you receive in response will be less for clarification and more towards an enhancement of the concepts you were working with.

What Makes an Outstanding Mixed Method Discussion?

When we did an analysis of the differences between average mixed methods final dissertations or theses and those that won awards we noticed increased complexity, greater likelihood of larger numbers in the population and sample group, and a likelihood of multiple chapters being used to sort through and discuss data as they were analyzed in the study.

As to writing, organization, and composition, the award-winning mixed methods studies are exemplified by their authors' finding ways to make complex ideas clear to the reader. As mentioned previously in this chapter, quantitative and qualitative work have their own specific underlying logics, which will play off of each other in a myriad of ways dependent on the complexity of the topic and how they are managed chronologically to each other. As an example, a study using one method, analyzing it, and then moving to the other is very different from the one discussed below, which played the two off of each other throughout. Whether and to what extent you can separate your data and concisely discuss each component methodologically has as much to do with the complexity and the chronological order as to other considerations dependent on topic, and so forth.

Tracesea asks: *You mention that outstanding mixed method discussions are more complex. Does this mean that if I do a mixed methods study, I will likely be writing a longer dissertation?*

Answer: Are you concerned about length? Is that daunting? It shouldn't be, because when an author has a lot to say, the writing has greater length. Almost all of the award-winning dissertations we have studied are in the range of 250 to 300 pages. Mixed methods need a bit of explanation for your reader, but nothing that will inherently make the whole document much longer than others that employ either quantitative or qualitative methods by themselves.

Figure 13.5 (below) is a concept map from one of these award-winning studies (Konorti, 2007). When you compare this figure with the ancillary materials from Creswell in the last section, you begin to understand the complexities that drive the need for concept maps and other forms of graphic organizers. It also becomes completely understandable that, out of these four award winners, two of them used multiple chapters to discuss findings (three chapters in one case and four in another). It is likely that an exploratory study will require a longer explanation through data analysis to findings because of the inherent complexity in exploring new potential as it develops through data.

Assessment Standards for Mixed Methods Research

To conclude this chapter, we thought we would discuss the standards and assessment criteria of objectivity, clarity, and replicability. A clear and objective discussion of your mixed methods data would naturally include both the majority and minority opinions as well as a discussion of how they develop through each data set. The replicability of your study will be enhanced through the detail you give to your explanation of your instrumentation, your sample selection, and your outcomes (Bryant, 2004; Creswell & Plano Clark, 2011; Tashakkori & Teddlie, 2010).

Also, for more information on tips for doing a mixed methods study, make sure to look over the dos and don'ts lists for both qualitative (pp. 197–198) and quantitative (pp. 210–212) data collection and analysis.

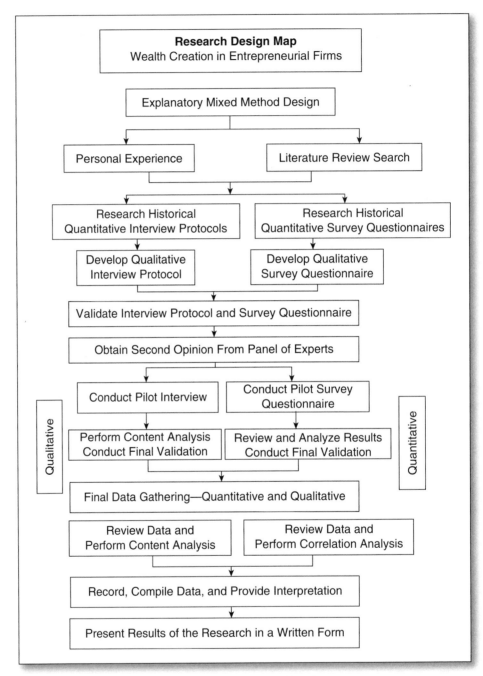

Figure 13.5   Concept Map as Reprinted by Permission by Eli Konorti

Source: Konorti (2007).

Chapter 13 Checklist

❐ I understand why and how mixed method analyses are similar to those employing either a qualitative or quantitative design.

❐ I understand why and how mixed method results are different from single-method results and findings.

❐ I understand how to begin to build a convincing argument in a mixed methods study.

❐ I understand what makes the difference between an average and an outstanding mixed method discussion.

Where Should I Go to Dig Deeper? Suggested Resources to Consider

Creswell, J. W., & Plano Clark, V. L. (2011). *Designing and conducting mixed methods research* (2nd ed.). Thousand Oaks, CA: Sage. This is an excellent discussion of mixed methods designs. Included as well is a wonderful, down-to-earth chapter on analyzing and interpreting data.

Ravitch, S. M., & Riggan, M. (2012). *Reason & rigor: How conceptual frameworks guide research*. Thousand Oaks, CA: Sage. This book has brilliantly illustrated and discussed examples of concept maps, including several that focus on the use of one-method supporting, confirming or denying the evidence of the other.

Roberts, C. M. (2004). *The dissertation journey*. Thousand Oaks, CA: Corwin Press. Chapters 14 and 15 give a brief but useful description of the path from data gathering, through analysis, and on to the final discussion or conclusions. Many pullout boxes offer helpful hints and additional resources.

Tashakkori, A., & Teddlie, C. (2010). *SAGE handbook of mixed methods in social & behavioral research* (2nd ed.). Thousand Oaks, CA: Sage. This is an excellent text on the subject, one that should be available through most university libraries.

Thomas, R. M. (2003). *Blending qualitative and quantitative research methods in theses and dissertations*. Thousand Oaks, CA: Corwin Press. Thomas offers many examples that will be helpful to students sorting out where and when to employ different writing patterns.

Yin, R. K. (2011). *Qualitative research from start to finish*. New York: The Guilford Press. This book contains excellent chapters pertaining to fieldwork and internal validity.

14

Are You Ready for
Your Final Defense?

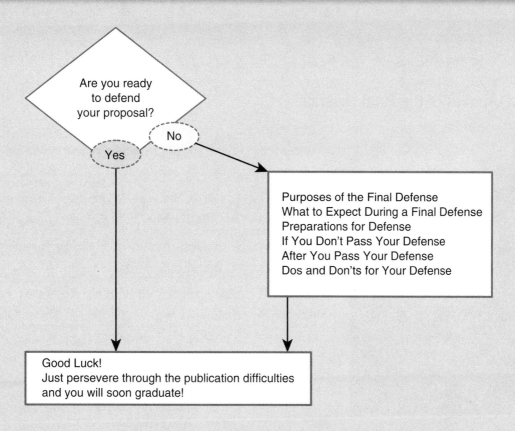

Are you ready
to defend
your proposal?

No

Yes

Purposes of the Final Defense
What to Expect During a Final Defense
Preparations for Defense
If You Don't Pass Your Defense
After You Pass Your Defense
Dos and Don'ts for Your Defense

Good Luck!
Just persevere through the publication difficulties
and you will soon graduate!

The purpose of this chapter is to help you feel comfortable as you prepare for your university's final defense of your doctoral dissertation or thesis.

The Questions Answered in This Chapter:

1. What are the purposes of the final defense?

2. What can I expect in my final defense?

3. What preparations do I need to make for defense once the final draft of my doctoral thesis has been turned in?

4. What claims am I making? Can I defend them?

5. What happens if I don't pass defense?

6. What comes after?

Purposes of the Final Defense

Figure 14.1 You and your university share the goal of your graduation, but your university also is concerned with protecting the integrity of the degrees it confers.

Source: Ryan McVay/Photodisc/Thinkstock

When we began this book, we stated that your research and your final dissertation or thesis was a rite of passage. While not a "test by fire," the final defense is the last significant step, marking the end of this journey. With it, the university agrees that you have completed your work and hold the right to call yourself doctor. Therefore, your purpose in the final defense is to pass and to have this title conferred upon you.

If your university follows a model where the professors sitting your defense are also those who have worked with you throughout the development of your research study, it is most likely that their purpose is closely aligned to yours. They have worked with you and are familiar with the choices you have made. They will be reading your final document looking for its level of mastery and consistency. It would be their goal to help you make your dissertation or thesis a completely congruent statement of your work. That being said, the university also will have one or more people who are required to look at your work from a very critical point of view, in order to protect the integrity of the university as pertains to the degrees that it offers.

Higher education, in many parts of the world, has grown in recent years to become big business. Private universities may have challenges keeping up their accreditation as opposed to their more staid public counterparts. The levels of minute guidance given to your final document may be influenced by the challenges of the university as a whole and should not be taken personally. As with any peer-reviewed document, your dissertation or thesis will progress as a result of the feedback you receive.

Keep in mind what the defense is and is not. It IS an argument or case related to a specified issue as developed through your research study. Notice that this puts the onus on you to develop your argument throughout your presentation. It IS NOT a presentation of your research in chronological or even written order.

What to Expect During a Final Defense

The final dissertation defense may be called many things: *dissertation hearing, orals, vitas,* and so forth. As with other aspects of the dissertation or thesis process, this final conversation may look quite different depending upon the historic tradition of the university that you attend. For example, at one end of the spectrum, in an asynchronous defense at an online university in the United States, students would present their final document to all the committee members first.

In this case the "defense" would be an asynchronous conversation between each committee member and the student about the work. Perhaps, when all committee members were agreed that the work was at an acceptable level, the same people might conduct a synchronous (live) event in the form of a conference call or web conference. It has been our experience that by this time, the live event is more a matter of form than would be experienced in the more European tradition. In this scenario, most of the difficult work of the defense will be completed by the time you meet as a group with your committee members.

A student who attends a traditional and perhaps conservative university might expect to meet in a room, standing in front of a panel of "judges" who represent different members of the university who are not previously known to the student. This panel will likely ask very difficult questions. They will expect the doctoral candidate to display evidence of already understanding the weaknesses within their study. They may also expect that the student has already gone through the process to improve these weaknesses. This is in contrast to the asynchronous example where the student is maneuvered towards a better and better document through what may seem like an endless series of comments and revisions.

There are several formats the synchronous defense may take. The doctoral candidate likely presents their work. It is important that the presentation rises above a mere chronological outline of their final document and rather follows the standard of argument that makes a credible case for their discussion based on data derived from a valid study. The defense may also be a completely open hearing where various departments or schools may attend during the process. Students might also have the opportunity to provide handouts, tripod boards to show a model, or PowerPoint slides to sequence information. If these aides are used, you should look to your chair or supervisor to outline any special guidelines that you need to be aware of.

Figure 14.2 Be prepared to face very tough questions during your final defense.

Source: Stockbyte/Stockbyte/Thinkstock

There are three common outcomes that you are likely to experience as a result of your defense. You may (a) pass with no revisions (almost never happens), (b) pass but with some level of substantive required changes, and (c) discover you do not pass and will be required to take another year or more to further investigate your study.

Because there are variations in the ways that universities require doctoral candidates to complete their work, it is strongly recommended that you carefully read all the handbooks and documentation provided by your university. You should also have discussions with students who have gone through the challenges before you in order to reap benefits from their experiences. Your advisors will also be able to tell you what to expect.

Variations also exist about the specifics of how your committee will "vote" on the outcome of your defense. For a face-to-face, synchronous meeting, you will likely have to leave the room while they discuss your immediate future. The best words you may hear when you come back into the room are, "Congratulations Dr. . . ." as this is likely to be the first time you are ever called by your new title. An asynchronous event that online universities may require means you will go all the way through the publication process before you get an email that confers that title for the first time. Whatever variation exists in your university, all the professors and academics there realize that the outcome you are hoping for and that for you it is a very loaded experience. The best way to ensure a positive outcome is to spend as much time in preparation for this last hurdle, as you did for any other section of your writing.

Tracesea asks: *You mention that in my defense I may be expected to know the weaknesses of my study and have already addressed them. Is this feedback that I will get from my advisor before my defense? How will I know if I have adequately acknowledged and addressed any weaknesses in my research before I have my final defense?*

Answer: If you attend a university that is known for its rigor in your subject, then we recommend that you go through a mock defense. Some supervisors may set this up. If that is not available then there are services (such as DoctoralNet) that provide this option.

Preparations for Defense

Once you have turned your paperwork over to your professors, you can get to work in preparation for your defense. Sometimes a slide presentation is required. If this is the case, be sure to ask how many slides are expected and how long you will be allowed to talk. When presenting, remember that the people in front of you have read your work, and so it is unnecessary for you to repeat the fine details of your study.

Defending Your Claims

To set the stage for a discussion on supporting your claims, we want you to consider the academic tradition from which the current defense of dissertation process evolved. Picture an auditorium filled with academics all in their robes and regalia. The most learned sit as a panel, separate from you, looking out at or down upon a single non-robed person. That person in the spotlight would be you. No one speaks as you present the case for your research. Then the people above you ask serious and pointed questions such as

- What is the purpose of your study as it is presented? Is your problem empirically verifiable? How have you have you delimited your scope?
- What are the assumptions of your study? Are they accepted in your field and to what extent?
- What scales operationalize your variables? How do you know that they are valid?
- What are your findings in terms of effect size? (Garson, 2002)

While few of our readers may have to face this degree of grilling at their final defense, it is a valid portion of the rite of passage, as it is not dissimilar to what your writing will go through when you present it to peer-reviewed journals. Don't let down your defenses and imagine that you have passed the last hurdle when you complete your analysis—hold on to the rigor throughout your discussion or conclusions, remember that the strength of your argument is the primary focus of your committee. Going back through your document and

Figure 14.3 Don't let your guard down after completing your analysis. Strong arguments are essential, and a solid credible document is the only type that is truly defensible.

Source: ©iStockphoto.com/bennyb

tying up any loose ends so that it consistently tells one single story of a research process from beginning to end, is the goal you need to shoot for. A solid and credible document is the only type that is truly defensible.

Be sure to include the limitations of your study as well. Like a statement of "truth in advertising," limitations denote that all was not perfect with the study. Just as there can never be no risk for your participants in your ethical review, there can be no perfect study. Limitations do not diminish your work but rather provide caution and direction for anyone who may wish to replicate it.

Start your focus by looking at the ideas from the literature you discussed at the beginning of your work. You may wish to start a graphic organizer as though you were drawing a tree and your literature and the ideas contained in the literature comprised the various roots. What are the key concepts, evidence, and warrants on which your claims are substantiated? These are the golden threads we have discussed throughout this book, the singular concepts or ideas that tie the whole together. These become the lifeblood of your final discussion or conclusions. If you cannot track such a logical progression throughout your document, you are not yet ready to defend your final work.

Tracesea asks: *What if I am petrified of public speaking? How can I convincingly defend my claims if I have a hard time getting up in front of others?*

Answer: Practice, practice, practice. Go through our sections on arguments again and then do your presentation over and over until you are comfortable doing it in front of a variety of audiences. Practice on your friends, family, hire strangers, coaches, and so forth until you can manage.

If You Don't Pass Your Defense

Figure 14.4   If you don't pass your final defense it may be a good time to get some help from outside of your university.

Source: ©iStockphoto.com/Palto

Most criticism that arises at the thesis or dissertation defense stage has to do with such fundamentals as the match of measured indicators to theoretical concepts, the match of research purposes to qualitative and quantitative methods, and the nature of the research design (Garson, 2002, p. 302).

Not everyone passes final defense. Some are sent away with a laundry list of things they need to do to complete their work. These students are often mystified, not understanding why they have failed. They believe that they followed every model and that surely by following these models they will have constructed a defensible set of ideas. Alas, if it were that easy, everyone would have become a doctor. The rite of passage is in whether and to what extent you can tease out a single argument. For any reader who may be faced with this challenge, go back to our previous chapters and really read every discussion about how to form your claims, warrants, and arguments. For any student who finds him- or herself in this confusing place, really realize that you are up against what some might call a glass ceiling, one in which you can break through if you are willing to reanalyze your work from the very beginning. If you do not do that, you are likely to keep spinning in revisions until you get so unhappy you simply go away. At this point, it is not the requirement of those in the academy to particularly help you. Simply by having gotten to this point, it can be expected that you have already achieved this mastery. Therefore, it may be useful to you to find outside help.

The personal and somewhat professional challenge you face should you have come close to or actually failed your final defense is one of resiliency. It is a sad moment for your advisor and committee, but a monumentally frustrating and upsetting one, of course, for you. The very basic challenge that you face is not only one of disappointment but of interior strength and courage. And this test, a rite of passage, gives everyone a chance to see the strength that you bring to this challenge.

However you do it, you will have been given a list of things that need to be done or attended to prior to bringing your document back for another defense. Do not assume that if you get everything done on that list you will pass the next time. Only by uncovering the key elements that caused the list will you have achieved the mastery that is being expected of you.

Most of our readers however will likely have passed with some level of revisions required. Hopefully, also as you were leaving the defense, you captured good notes on what those would be. Most colleges make it incumbent upon your advisor to see that these requirements are completed, but another full defense is not necessarily required. If that is the case, work closely with your advisor and get the work done as quickly as possible. This is analogous to getting your writing back from a peer-reviewed journal. Like it or not, the reviewers always find parts of your writing that would be improved by extra time and attention to detail. Painful work, but it always makes our writing and our ideas better.

After You Pass Your Defense

Once the research is done, the ideas are in place, and the discussion or conclusions drawn, it is useful to turn your attention towards the rigors of publication and dissemination. If you intend to follow an academic track, these become the continuous text of your work as it progresses across the rest of your career. Like all new challenges, each new challenge (presenting at conferences, publishing in journals, preparing displays of your work) has its own trajectory, guidelines, and stages or hierarchy of development.

Publishing

The first thing published will, of course, be your dissertation. Your university has developed strict guidelines that require you to adhere to the style as well as incorporate small variations, which suit their particular publication needs. You will need to concern yourself with issues such as margins, typeface, layout of various types of pages, how charts and tables are placed on the page, and so forth. This is no different than any other publication environment into which you will find yourself moving over the next years. Each has its own rules and regulations, which all authors who work for them must follow.

This is the time to consider issues of copyright. In most, if not all cases, a dissertation author maintains full rights of publication; however, first rights are given to the university or its database affiliate, which will present your dissertation to the world. After that presentation, you usually have full rights to rework or disseminate your work in any means that you would find pleasing or useful. There are a number of self-publishing houses that specialize in producing books from dissertations. They offer low-cost dissemination but no help when it comes to copy editing or final perfection of the finished document. Sometimes called "vanity" publications, consider how you intend to use them and whether they will advance your career prior to undergoing the expense. If you choose to use such a service, we recommend that you employ someone else to ensure all the references are in place, and so forth. Another mode of publishing your study and work is to divide it and parcel it out to different journals with slightly different spins on the material that you think is of greater interest to the wider academy. An example of this might be focusing on your methodology in one piece, written specifically for a journal focused on that type of methodology.

Alana says: *As an example, students using action research as the methodology have very good international journals to which they can submit their work, such as Educational Action Research, or Action Research, merely because of the methodology they chose.*

Oftentimes dissertation research has several threads or research questions it answers. These may be separated from the larger body and written up as individual smaller studies, of an appropriate size for academic journals. No matter what venue for publication you are interested in, be clear of its guidelines before you do much work on your document. The single biggest reason that journal articles are summarily turned down is that they contain too much verbiage as per the guidelines of that editorial board. Be prepared, as discussed in the previous section on what happens if you fail your dissertation, for a rigorous and sometimes painful review of how well you have put your research ideas together in a continuous or credible fashion. The purpose of the editors to the journal is to maintain a high standard of academic writing, and they rarely or never come back to a new or relatively untried author without a few suggestions for change.

If, after graduation, you hope to enter the academic world, there are several options for graduates that were not available even a few years ago. As university seats diminish, options grow for ad hoc influence through blogs, social media, forums for exchange, and so forth. A well-developed platform of influence in the modern world includes a wide variety and probably some coverage across all of the options. Always keep in mind that whatever you choose, part of the mix is likely to include some aspect that contains peer review. As mentioned elsewhere in this chapter, nothing hones skill development and enhances the final production of material as much as the gift of stern feedback. If you work in blogs and social media, consider being edited prior to publication.

Figure 14.5 There are many online options for getting your work out there, including blogs and social media.

Source: ©iStockphoto.com/atakan

However you go about it, many consider it an ethical responsibility for you to publish your research. This is seen as a benefit to the human subjects who contributed to your work, to ensure that their time was not wasted. It is also important that their feedback and your study contribute to your field. It is important that you do not work in isolation but that your ideas contribute to the stream of ideas in which your work resides.

Conferences

One of the most frequent questions in a defense of dissertation is, what do you intend to do next? An outcome of that discussion is almost always a suggestion that you consider presenting your work at professional and academic research-oriented conferences. One of the reasons these are a successful ground for new researchers, as well as anyone building a continuous body of work is that they are often peer reviewed, and even when the proposal is not looked at in such a strenuous fashion, the presentation at the conference at least brings this type of academic feedback. In most cases, a paper is presented for 20 minutes through a presentation and then questions are taken. The people sitting in the room have come to hear about your paper or those of your fellow presenters, which are usually grouped in general topic orientation. This means that you should receive interesting and probing questions through which your academic prowess should grow.

Look into whether and to what extent the large research conferences in your part of the world are of interest to you. They will contain Special Interest Groups (SIGs) that are made up of a group of researchers focused on whatever their topic is. Here you may find colleagues across your field of interest but outside of your local context. These people can become friends for life and even when this is not the case will provide valuable insight and input into your work.

Dos and Don'ts for Your Defense

For the defense itself, here are some things you should do:

Do

Figure 14.6   Color code 2 to 3 key points (golden threads) for reference during your defense.

Source: Jupiterimages/Photos.com/Thinkstock

- Consider searching out a *"mock defense"* service that gives you a full practice in front of professors and doctors from a variety of backgrounds. This will allow you to experience being drilled by people who bring their own differing contexts to your study.
- *Anticipate all the questions that may be asked of you.* If and to the extent you see areas requiring further development, feel free to either make handouts or extra slides to which you can refer should those questions arise.
- *Come early* to the room for a live defense to set up and get comfortable.
- See what the protocol is for inviting guests, but consider *having others there to witness and offer moral support.*
- Think beforehand what *two to three "takeaways" are the most important in your study.* Go through your dissertation/thesis in printed form and color code or mark the golden threads that lead to these claims. It is helpful to have passages marked that are, for you, the key points.
- *Practice your presentation in front of an audience* until you are completely comfortable both with the presentation and with answering questions.

- Remember that you can *exert some guidance to the way the conversation is going.* Should you feel that the context of others has taken things off track of your main premises, refer back to the passages you marked in number 5. This allows you to reference them and to draw the conversation back to those points should you feel the focus is straying.

Figure 14.7 Try not to give long rambling answers; you can always follow up if something wasn't understood.

Source: ©iStockphoto.com/id-work

Don't

- *Allow nervousness or adrenaline responses to cut off your ability to breath.* Long slow breaths oxygenate the body and relax your muscles. Roberts (2004) suggests a short answer first and then a more detailed response after confirming that more information on the topic is desired.
- *Give long-winded answers.* Give the best response you can but know that these people are not against you and will be willing to probe if you ask them—Is that what you meant? or Did that answer your question?"
- *Be afraid to say that you have not thought about that question,* could see how it would be relevant, but would like to come back to that person after doing a little bit more research. This is appropriate when the question is not endemic to your study. It also allows for you to bring a conversation that is straight off-topic back to a clear focus on your work.
- *Try to come up with answers about which you have little knowledge.*
- *Stray from being 100% authentic.*

Chapter 14 Checklist

- ❏ I understand the purposes of the final defense.
- ❏ I know what to expect.
- ❏ I have made all my preparations.
- ❏ I have outlined the claims I make in my study and can easily track the points that make them through the document.
- ❏ I am prepared for what I must do if I fail defense.
- ❏ I am prepared for publishing, conferences, papers, and books.

Where Should I Go to Dig Deeper? Suggested Resources to Consider

Joyner, R. L., Rouse, W. A., & Glatthorn, A. A. (2013). *Writing the winning thesis or dissertation: A step-by-step guide* (3rd ed.). Thousand Oaks, CA: Corwin Press. These authors include other topics of interest including finalizing your appendices, how to set up and complete your abstract, and how to plan for a book.

Mauch, J. E., & Park, N. (2003). *Guide to the successful thesis and dissertation: A handbook for students and faculty*. New York: Marcel Dekker. The end of this book contains an excellent list of unusual scholarly publications in electronic format, which you may consider for your first publications. Page 292 follows that up with some useful guidelines for academic publication.

Roberts, C. M. (2004). *The dissertation journey*. Thousand Oaks, CA: Corwin Press. Page 188 lists questions typically heard during a dissertation defense. The two that are our favorites are, what is your assessment of the strengths and weaknesses of your study? and what was the most significant aspect of the work you have done?

APPENDIX A
Generic Headings Template

NOTE: Chapters 3, 4, and 5 will vary according to methodology—refer also to Chapters 6, 11, 12, and 13.

CHAPTER 1: INTRODUCTION TO THE STUDY

Introduction

Background

Statement of the Problem

Purpose of the Study

Conceptual Framework

Research Questions

Research Propositions

Definition of Terms

Assumptions and Limitations

Significance of the Study

Summary and Transition

CHAPTER 2: LITERATURE REVIEW

Introduction

Overview of the Topic

   Subtopics

   Subtopics

   Subtopics

Discussion of Previous Research

Analysis of Gaps in the Literature

Methodological Lit

Summary and Transition

CHAPTER 3: METHODOLOGY

Introduction

Research Design

Research Question

Methodology

Methods

Conceptual Design

Data Collection

Procedures/Instrumentation

Population and Sample

Ethical Considerations

Data Analysis

Procedures

Validity

Limitations and Assumptions

Significance

Summary and Transition

CHAPTER 4: RESULTS

Purpose of the Research

Participants

Description of the Data Set

Analysis

Subtopics of Analysis

Subtopics continued . . .

Summary and Transition

CHAPTER 5: DISCUSSION

Introduction

Discussion of the Topic/Review of the Study

Discussion of the Results

Addressing the Research Questions

Implications for the Context/Practitioners

Implications for the Field of Study

Areas for Further Study

Summary and Transition

APPENDIX B
Checklist for Literature

Keep this checklist close by and refer to it to ensure you catch all the important aspects of the research you read.

- ✓ Have you captured the full bibliographic reference?
- ✓ Have you critically appraised their results?
- ✓ Was their methodology sound?
- ✓ If so, have you noted it?
- ✓ Do the authors write in a credible manner?
- ✓ If so, are there quotations to make note of? Have you captured the page number?
- ✓ Do you like the way they write? Make note in your journal of what is pleasing.
- ✓ Did you capture the DOI numbers?
- ✓ Are the statistics easy to follow and convincing?
- ✓ If so, did you make note of their process in case you want to use it.
- ✓ What else can you learn from this author, not only in the work they did but in the way they completed it and wrote it up?

APPENDIX C

Student Example From 5.1 Research Logic

Thank you to Dr. Jennifer Williams for use of her study for this example (2012)

Research Design Framework

Topic
Phonetic and Phonological Awareness Deficits in Teachers

Indicators of Local Situation
An increasing number of second through fourth grade students who are being referred to an intervention team with reading difficulties

Problem Statement
In a small, Midwestern district, there are an increasing number of second through fourth grade students who are being referred to the intervention team with reading problems due to phonetic and phonological awareness deficits. Factors that may have contributed to the problem in this district include a lack of training in phonological awareness and phonics instruction for new teachers, teacher turnover, and an emphasis on whole group teaching

Purpose
The purpose of this study was to explore kindergarten and first grade teachers' levels of knowledge about dyslexia, phonological awareness, and phonics, and to describe how they used this knowledge during reading intervention groups

Questions or Hypotheses
1. What are kindergarten and first grade teachers' perceptions of dyslexia's causes and symptoms?
2. How do kindergarten and first grade teachers describe their pedagogical content knowledge of phonological awareness and phonics?
3. How do kindergarten and first grade teachers describe their instruction on phonological awareness and phonics during reading intervention groups?

Theoretical Stance Methods Methodology
Pragmatic use of an instrumental case study

Data Collection Instrumentation and Ethics
Data were interviews, a survey, lesson plan documents. None of the participants were supervised by the researchers

Data Analysis
All data were stored and analyzed in qualitative software. Data analysis involves inductive coding, categorical aggregation, and the creation of themes. Data were cross checked and validated with inter-rater reliability and triangulated with the lesson plan data

APPENDIX D

Assessment Rubric

Section in Dissertation or Thesis	Basic Required	Excellent/Top Quality
Topic/Title	Appropriate, clear focus, contains all key words.	Addresses real problem and gives concise view.
Presentation and Formulation of Problem	Adequate appropriate argumentation.	Clearly understands the complexity/records key issues.
Research Goal/Purpose/Hypothesis	Goals and justifications clear and easily identified.	Clearly stated—grounded and motivated.
Design and Methods	Good description and justification.	Clear theoretical framework/well-argued and properly justified.
Scientific Approach / Standards	Good systematic theoretical foundation. Thesis satisfies necessary conditions to be considered scientific work.	Clear framework well argued and justified. Work meets the necessary standards to be considered scientific and in fact exceeds the norms for doctoral work.
Literature Review	Widely researched. Well presented, adequately assessed and interpreted.	Significant both in who they discuss and the conceptual understanding.
Context	Claims substantiated. Good depth and flow in argument.	Logical argument tied to problem with an impressive context and lit.
Language and Style	Minor slips on grammar/style—coherent.	Scholarly and complex in narrative while readable.
Clarity	Contents are presented in a clear and concise way. The style is appropriate and structure adequate. Tables, data, graphs, figures, and so forth are easily understood.	Contents are presented with clarity and finesse. The style and structure, including use of charts and graphs, uplifts the readability of the document.

(Continued)

(Continued)

Section in Dissertation or Thesis	Basic Required	Excellent/Top Quality
Precision	There is internal consistency between theory and practice and the report is thorough.	The thesis is not only internally consistent but rises above through its use of critical analysis. Writing is concise.
Documentation	Writing is well cited and referenced.	Citations and references are used appropriately, and discussion of literature is an apparent thread throughout the document.
Technical Aspects	Layout, graphics, good.	Good report writing with graphics that enhance.
References	Good range, key materials noted.	Wide range and some unexpected. Show keen understanding.
Data Analysis and Interpretation/Results	Clear mastery of data and interpretation—depth of research.	Analysis and interpretation, well grounded with theoretical underpinnings/ develops the literature in review.
Understandable Results	Conclusions generated from findings are logical and without bias.	Conclusions drawn from findings are provocative.
Significant Results	Conclusions drawn from findings progress knowledge in the field, they reaffirm will contradict previous studies.	Conclusions drawn from findings move the field of study forward in new or unexpected pathways. Conclusions contribute to the resolution of specific problems.
Original Findings	From either a theoretical or methodological point of view findings, discussion, or conclusions are worth consideration. They are presented with some critical analysis and pose a few issues that others may wish to investigate.	From both a theoretical and methodological point of view findings and discussion or conclusions are unique or novel. They are presented with strong critical analysis. They pose other outstanding issues for investigation.
Usefulness	Findings, discussion, or conclusions appear to be	Findings, discussion, or conclusions appear to be extremely useful, perhaps

Section in Dissertation or Thesis	Basic Required	Excellent/Top Quality
	useful, if perhaps for a limited audience or specific circumstance. Recommendations are made for implementation.	to a wider or varied audience. Explicit recommendations are made for implementation or policy.
Summary and Conclusions	Good understanding of concepts and methodology. Ties it all together.	Meaningful synthesis with conclusions linked to findings and to literature—meets significance level.
Recommendations	Appropriate and logically linked to findings/conclusions.	Justifiable, realistic, completely linked.
Contribution	Shows evidence of originality and independent thought. Contributes to either topic or methodology. There is intent to publish outside of the arena of the university.	Significant originality and independent thought. New lines of research naturally develop that will enhance the field. Valuable models are tools at the generated. Work has been disseminated on a scientific level including publication, seminars, and so forth.
Publishable	With minor editing.	Ready to go.
Effective Wrap Around Functions Between Chapters	There are obvious ties between chapters. The significance in the introduction chapter is played out in the conclusion. The literature discussed in your literature review is alluded to and brought in again during conclusions.	Redundancy is avoided by cross-referencing throughout so that the reader knows where to find important material and all those threads of logic follow cohesively.
Coherence Between Chapters "Golden Thread"	There is coherence and focus between chapters.	Every section of the entire work not only maintains focus and coherence but rises above that to be highly readable. Ideas are critically analyzed at every step and the reader remains engaged.

Sources: Albertyn et al. (2007); de-Miguel (2010).

APPENDIX E

Dissertations and Theses Included in Our Analysis of Outstanding, Award-Winning Work and Its Similarities and Differences From Those That Did Not Win Awards

Akkerman, S., Admiraal, W., Brekelmans, M., & Oost, H. (2008). Auditing quality of research in social sciences. *Quality & Quantity, 42*(2), 257–274. Retrieved from 10.1007/s11135-006-9044-4.

Albertyn, R. M., Kapp, C. A., & Frick, B. L. (2007). Taking the sting out of evaluations: Rating scales for thesis examination. *South African Journal of Higher Education,* (8), 1207–1221.

Amaladas, S. M. (2004). *A narrative inquiry into the experiences of individuals in the midst of organizational change: A shift from systems to stories* (Doctoral dissertation, Walden University).

Apori-Nkansah, L. (2008). *Transitional justice in postconflict contexts: The case of Sierra Leone's dual accountability mechanisms* (Doctoral dissertation, Walden University).

Brenner-Camp, S. (August 2011). *Student voice in educational decision-making processes: A key component for change in school models for the future* (Doctoral dissertation, Jones International University).

Broomes, O. (2010). *More than a new country: Effects of immigration, home language, and school mobility on elementary students' academic development* (Doctoral dissertation, University of Toronto).

Christopher, P. (2008). *Interaction within individualized education program meetings: Conversation analysis of a collective case study* (Doctoral dissertation, Walden University).

Cruse, T. (2012). *Relationship between adolescent gifted girls' attitudes and their value-added performance score* (Doctoral dissertation, Walden University).

de-Miguel, M. (2010). The evaluation of doctoral thesis. A model proposal. *RELIEVE: e-Journal of Educational Research, Assessment and Evaluation.* Retrieved from http://www.uv.es/RELIEVE/v16n1/RELIEVEv16n1_4 .htm website: http://www.uv.es/RELIEVE/v16n1/RELIEVEv16n1_4eng.htm

Deal, S. (2009). *The relationship between pragmatic language skills and behavior* (Doctoral dissertation, Walden University).

Duffy, L. (2002). *HIV/AIDS in Context: The culture of health promotion among Ndau women in rural Zimbabwe* (Doctoral dissertation, Walden University).

Eckrode, C. (2010). *Periodicity of epidemics of invasive disease due to infection with streptococcus pneumoniae in the United States* (Doctoral dissertation, Walden University).

Espino, M. M. (2008). *Master narratives and counter-narratives: An analysis of Mexican American life stories of oppression and resistance along the journeys to the doctorate* (Doctoral dissertation, the University of Arizona).

Finch, D. (2010). *The stakeholder scorecard: Evaluating the influence of stakeholder relationships on corporate performance* (Doctoral dissertation, Walden University).

Freund, L. S. (2008). *Exploiting task-document relations in support of information retrieval in the workplace* (Doctoral dissertation, University of Toronto).

Gatuz, C. R. (2009). *Mentoring the leader: The role of peer mentoring in the leadership development of students-of-color in higher education* (Doctoral dissertation, Michigan State University).

Hamilton, B. (2012). [Conversation during September virtual retreat].

Hinnerichs, C. (2011). *Efficacy of fixed infrared thermography for identification of subjects with influenza-like illness* (Doctoral dissertation, Walden University).

Hughes, R. (2010). *The process of choosing science, technology, engineering, and mathematics careers by undergraduate women: A narrative life history analysis* (Doctoral dissertation, Florida State University).

Jirik, S. (2011). *Teacher perceptions on the implementation of response to intervention and its impact on student achievement* (Doctoral dissertation, Jones International University).

Johnson, E. (2011). *A study of language deficits and math skills* (Doctoral dissertation, Jones International University).

Konorti, E. (2007). *The relationship between wealth creation and professional management in entrepreneurial enterprises* (Doctoral dissertation, University of Phoenix).

Lam, T. N. (2007). *Strategies for promoting business-IT fusion to meet organizational demands: A case study* (Doctoral dissertation, University of Phoenix).

Long, K. (2011). *A critical evaluation of participatory action research in curriculum design* (Doctoral dissertation, Colorado Technical University, Bangkok, Thailand).

MacMullen, J. (2007). *Contextual analysis of variation and quality in human-curated gene ontology annotations* (Doctoral dissertation, University of North Carolina at Chapel Hill, Chapel Hill).

McMickens, T. L. (2011). *Racism readiness as an educational outcome for graduates of historically black colleges and universities: A multi-campus grounded theory study* (Doctoral dissertation, University of Pennsylvania).

McNeal, T. (2011). [Conversation during doctoral defense].

McNeal, T. (2011). *The impact of African American womanist culture on organizational sensemaking* (Doctoral dissertation, Colorado Technical University).

Meyer, E. T. (2007). *Socio-technical perspectives on digital photography: Scientific digital photography use by marine mammal researchers* (Doctoral dissertation, Indiana University).

Mongkolkunwat, T. (2011). *Succession motives: Understanding succession in family business* (Doctoral dissertation, Colorado Technical University, Bangkok, Thailand).

Paige, R. (2007). *The relationship between self-directed informal learning and the career development process of technology users* (Doctoral dissertation, Walden University).

Pershing, J. L. (2003). *Beliefs about the appropriate degree of directiveness in the management relationship, as related to demographic characteristics, education background and organizational position* (Doctoral dissertation, Walden University).

Rodenbaugh, M. H. (2002). *The effectiveness of experiential education in executive development* (Doctoral dissertation, Walden University).

Ruhi, U. (2010). *Socio-technical determinants of member participation in virtual communities: An exploratory mixed methods investigation* (Doctoral dissertation, McMaster University, Canada).

Scharff, M. (2005). *A study of the dyadic relationships between managers and virtual employees* (Doctoral dissertation, University of Phoenix).

Shaker, G. (2008). *Off the track: The full-time nontenure-track faculty experience in English* (Doctoral dissertation, Indiana University).

Shelton, K. (2010). *A quality scorecard for the administration of online education programs: A delphi study* (Doctoral dissertation, University of Nebraska).

Speckels, H. (2011). *The impact of project-based learning on academic achievement for students with academic challenges at K-5 grade levels: A grounded theory revelation* (Doctoral dissertation, Jones International University).

Tao, Y. (2009). *The earning of Asian computer scientists and engineers in the United States* (Doctoral dissertation, Georgia Institute of Technology).

Vuttanont, U. (2010). *"Smart boys" and "sweet girls"—sex education needs in Thai teenagers: A mixed method study* (Doctoral dissertation, Royal Free and University College Medical School, University College London).

Wakefield, T. (2012). *An ontology of storytelling systemicity: Management, fractals and the Waldo Canyon fire* (Doctoral dissertation, Colorado Technical University).

Welch, P. (2011). *Teacher and administrator perceptions of professional learning communities and their effect on teaching practices and student achievement* (Doctoral dissertation, Jones International University).

Williams, J. (2012). *Teachers' perceptions and pedagogical content knowledge of phonological awareness* (Doctoral dissertation, Walden University).

Xiao, J. (2008). *Children's experience of the rituals of schooling: A case study* (Doctoral dissertation, University of Huddersfield).

References

Albertyn, R. M., Kapp, C. A., & Frick, B. L. (2007). Taking the sting out of evaluations: Rating scales for thesis examination. *South African Journal of Higher Education* (8), 1207–1221.

Argyris, C. (2002). Double-loop learning, teaching and research. *Academy of Management Learning and Education, 1*(2), 206.

Bataille, M., & Clanet, C. (1981). Elements contributing to a theory and a methodology of action research in education. *International Journal of Behavioral Development, 4* (1981), 271–291.

Bloomberg, L. D., & Volpe, M. (2012). *Completing your qualitative dissertation: A road map from beginning to end* (2nd ed.). Thousand Oaks, CA: Sage.

Bolker, J. (1998). *Writing your dissertation in fifteen minutes a day: A guide to starting, revising, and finishing your doctoral thesis* (1st ed.). New York: Henry Holt.

Booth, W. C., Colomb, G. G., & Williams, J. M. (2008). *The craft of research* (3rd ed.). Chicago: The University of Chicago Press.

Borg, S. (2001). The research journal: A tool for promoting and understanding the researcher development. *Language Teaching Research, 5*(2), 156–177.

Brause, R. S. (2000). *Writing your doctoral dissertation: Invisible rules for success.* London: Routledge Falmer.

Broomes, O. (2010). *More than a new country: Effects of immigration, home language, and school mobility on elementary students'academic development* (Doctor dissertation, University of Toronto, Toronto, CA).

Bryant, M. T. (2004). *The portable dissertation advisor.* Thousand Oaks, CA: Corwin Press.

Corbin, J. M., & Strauss, A. L. (2008). *Basics of qualitative research: Techniques and procedures for developing grounded theory* (3rd ed.). Thousand Oaks, CA: Sage.

Creswell, J. W. (2009). *Research design: Qualitative, quantitative, and mixed methods approaches* (3rd ed.). Thousand Oaks, CA: Sage.

Creswell, J. W. (2012). *Educational research: Planning, conducting, and evaluating quantitative and qualitative research.* London: Pearson Education.

Creswell, J. W., & Plano Clark, V. L. (2011). *Designing and conducting mixed methods research* (2nd ed.). Thousand Oaks, CA: Sage.

Cunliffe, A. L. (2004). On becoming a critically reflexive practitioner. *Journal of Management Education, 28*(4), 407–426.

Cunliffe, A. L. (2005). The need for reflexivity in public admininstration. *Administration & Society, 37*(2), 255–242.

Cyranoski, D., Gilbert, N., & Ledford, H. (2011, April). Education: The PhD Factory. *Nature: International Weekly Journal of Science, 20*(472), 276–279. doi: 10.1038/472276a.

de-Miguel, M. (2010). The evaluation of doctoral thesis. A model proposal. *RELIEVE: e-Journal of Educational Research, Assessment and Evaluation.* Retrieved from http://www.uv.es/RELIEVE/v16n1/RELIEVEv16n1_4 .htm website: http://www.uv.es/RELIEVE/v16n1/RELIEVEv16n1_4eng.htm.

DoctoralNet (2010–2013). *Student testimonials: Testimonials by student users.* Unpublished work format. County Cork, Ireland: DoctoralNet Ltd.

Elmore, R. M. (1979). Backward mapping: Implementation research and policy decisions. *Political Science Quarterly, 94*(4), 601–616.

Espino, M. M. (2008). *Master narratives and counter-narratives: An analysis of Mexican American life stories of oppression and resistance along the journeys to the doctorate* (Doctoral dissertation, The University of Arizona).

Finch, D. (2010). *The stakeholder scorecard: Evaluating the influence of stakeholder relationships on corporate performance* (Doctoral dissertation, Walden).

Fitz-Gibbon, C. T., & Morris, L. L. (1987). *How to design a program evaluation* (2nd ed.). Newbury Park, CA: Sage.

Garson, G. D. (2002). *Guide to writing empirical papers, theses, and dissertations.* New York: Marcel Dekker.

Glatthorn, A. A., & Joyner, R. L. (2005). *Writing the winning thesis or dissertation: A step-by-step guide* (2nd ed.). Thousand Oaks, CA: Corwin Press.

Gloeckner, G. W. (2013). *Reviewers comments.* Fort Collins, CO: Colorado State University.

Goodson, P. (2013). *Becoming an academic writer: 50 exercises for paced, productive, and powerful writing.* Thousand Oaks, CA: Sage.

Hamilton, B. (2012). [Conversation during September virtual retreat].

Hart, C. (1998). *Doing a literature review: Releasing social science research imagination.* Thousand Oaks, CA: Sage.

Hawking, S., & Mlodinow, L. (2010). *The grand design.* New York, NY, USA: Bantam Dell.

Herr, K., & Anderson, G. L. (2005). *The action research dissertation: A guide for students and faculty.* Thousand Oaks, CA: Sage.

Hinnerichs, C. (2011). *Efficacy of fixed infrared thermography for identification of subjects with influenza-like illness* (Doctoral dissertation, Walden).

Hoyle, R. H., Harris, M. J., & Judd, C. M. (2002). *Research methods in social relations* (7th ed.). New York: Wadsworth: Thomson Learning.

Hughes, R. (2010). *The process of choosing science, technology, engineering, and mathematics careers by undergraduate women: A narrative life history analysis* (Doctor dissertation, Florida State University).

James, E. A., Sanchez-Patino, M., & Banerji, A. (2013). *Setting up defensible research design.* Ireland: RL Enterprises.

James, E. A., Slater, T., & Bucknam, A. (2012). *Action research for business, nonprofits and public administration: A tool for complex times.* Thousand Oaks, CA: Sage.

James, W., & Gunn, G. (2000). *Pragmatism and Other Writings.* New York: Penguin Group.

Joyner, R. L., Rouse, W. A., & Glatthorn, A. A. (2013). *Writing the winning thesis or dissertation: A step-by-step guide* (3rd ed.). Thousand Oaks, CA: Corwin Press.

Kalmbach Phillips, D., & Carr, K. (2009). Dilemmas of trustworthiness in preservice teacher action research. *Action Research,* (7), 207–226.

Kildea, S., Barclay, L., Wardaguga, M., & Dawumal, M. (2009). Participative research in a remote Australian Aboriginal setting. *Action Research, 7*(2), 143–163.

King, R. (2002). Synthesis and evaluation of creativity. In T. Greenfield (Ed.), *Research Methods for Postgraduates* (pp. 126–136). London, New York: Oxford University Press.

Konorti, E. (2007). *The relationship between wealth creation and professional management in entrepreneurial enterprises.* (Doctoral dissertation, University of Phoenix).

Koprowski, E. J. (1972). Improving organization effectiveness through action research teams. *Training and Development Journal, 26*(6), 36–40.

Krathwohl, D. R., & Smith, N. L. (2005). *How to prepare a dissertation proposal: Suggestions for students in education and the social and behavioral sciences* (1st ed.). Syracuse, NY: Syracuse University Press.

Lam, T. N. (2007). *Strategies for promoting business-IT fusion to meet organizational demands: A case study.* (Doctor dissertation, University of Phoenix).

Leedy, P. D., & Ormrod, J. E. (2005). *Practical research: Planning and design* (8th ed.). Upper Saddle River, NJ: Pearson.

Libberton, B. (2011). 3 ways to structure your literature review. Retrieved from *Literature Review HQ* website: http://www.literaturereviewhq.com/youtube/

Loseke, D. R. (2013). *Methodological thinking: Basic principles of social research design*. Thousand Oaks, CA: Sage.

MacMullen, J. (2007). *Contextual analysis of variation and quality in human-curated gene ontology annotations* (Doctoral dissertation, University of North Carolina at Chapel Hill).

Mauch, J. E., & Park, N. (2003). *Guide to the successful thesis and dissertation: A handbook for students and faculty*. New York: Marcel Dekker.

Mauer, M., & Githens, R. P. (2009). Towards a reframing of action research for human resource and organization development: Moving beyond problem solving and toward dialogue. *Action Research, 8*(3), 267–292.

Maxwell, J. A. (2013). *Qualitative research design: An interactive approach* (3rd ed.). Thousand Oaks, CA: Sage.

McKenna, J., & Deunstan-Lewis, N. (2004). An action research approach to supporting elite student-athletes in higher education. *European Physical Education Review,* (10), 179–198.

McMickens, T. L. (2011). *Racism readiness as an educational outcome for graduates of historically black colleges and universities: A multi-campus grounded theory study* (Doctoral dissertation, University of Pennsylvania).

McNeal, T. (2011). [Conversation during doctoral defense].

Meyer, E. T. (2007). *Socio-technical perspectives on digital photography: Scientific digital photography use by marine mammal researchers* (Doctoral dissertation, Indiana University).

Morgan, G. A., Leech, N. L., Gloeckner, G. W., & Barrett, K. C. (2011). *IBM SPSS for introductory statistics: Use and interpretation*. New York: Routledge Taylor & Francis Group.

Nieuwenhuis, R. (2012). *Answer to question: What are the most common mistakes made by beginner researchers in quantitative analysis?* [Forum discussion between academics and researchers].

Ogden, E. H. (2007). *Complete your dissertation or thesis in two semesters or less*. Lanham, MD: Rowman & Littlefield Publishers: Distributed by National Book Network.

Ortlipp, M. (2008). Keeping and using reflective journals in the qualitative research process. *The Qualitative Report, 13*(4), 695–705.

Paige, R. (2007). *The relationship between self-directed informal learning and the career development process of technology users* (Doctoral dissertation, Walden).

Patton, M. Q. (2008). Literature Reviews. Retrieved from http://researchcenter.waldenu.edu/Literature-Reviews-Common-Errors-Made-When-Conducting-a-Literature-Review.htm.

Pease, N. (2009). Using action rsearch to implement a career development framework in facilities. *Journal of Facilities Management, 7*(1), 24–35.

Pershing, J. L. (2003). *Beliefs about the appropriate degree of directiveness in the management relationship, as related to demographic characteristics, education background and organizational position* (Doctor dissertation, Walden).

Piantanida, M., & Garman, N. B. (1999). *The qualitative dissertation: A guide for students and faculty*. Thousand Oaks, CA: Corwin Press.

Prasad, S., Rao, A., & Rehani, E. (2001). Developing hypothesis and research questions. *500 research methods*. Retrieved from http://www.public.asu.edu/ ~ kroel/www500/hypothesis.pdf.

Ravitch, S. M., & Riggan, M. (2012). *Reason & rigor: How conceptual frameworks guide research*. Thousand Oaks: Sage.

Roberts, C. M. (2004). *The dissertation journey*. Thousand Oaks, CA: Corwin Press.

Rodenbaugh, M. H. (2002). *The effectiveness of experiential education in excultive development* (Doctoral dissertation, Walden).

Rowlands, J. (2002). Problems of measurement. In T. Greenfield (Ed.), *Research Methods for Postgraduates* (pp. 218–225). London, New York: Oxford University Press.

Rubin, H. J., & Rubin, I. (2012). *Qualitative interviewing: The art of hearing data* (3rd ed.). Thousand Oaks, CA: Sage.

Rudestam, K. E., & Newton, R. R. (2007). *Surviving your dissertation: A comprehensive guide to content and process* (3rd ed.). Thousand Oaks, CA: Sage.

Ruhi, U. (2010). *Socio-technical determinants of member participation in virtual communities: An exploratory mixed methods investigation* (Doctoral dissertation, McMaster University, Canada).

Sanchez-Patino, M. (Producer). (2012, December 1. Quantitative data analysis: An introductory discussion on how to approach it. *Weekly Bigmarker DoctoralNet Conferences*. [Recorded video conference]

Sapsford, R., & Jupp, V. (1996). Validating evidence. In R. Sapsford & V. Jupp (Eds.), *Data collection and analysis* (pp. 3–35). London: Sage in association with Open University.

Scharff, M. (2005). *A study of the dyadic relationships between managers and virtual employees* (Doctoral dissertation, University of Phoenix, Arizona).

Scott-Ladd, B., & Chan, C. (2008). Using action research to teach students to manage team learning and improve teamwork satisfaction. *Active Learning in Higher Education, (9),* 231–248.

Single, P. B. (2009). *Demystifying dissertation writing: A streamlined process from choice of topic to final text* (1st ed.). Sterling, VA: Stylus.

Stewart, D., & Kamins, M. (1993). *Secondary research: Information sources and methods* (Vol. 4). Newbury Park, CA: Sage.

Tao, Y. (2009). *The earning of Asian computer scientists and engineers in the United States* (Doctoral dissertation, Georgia Institute of Technology).

Tashakkori, A., & Teddlie, C. (2010). *SAGE handbook of mixed methods in social & behavioral research* (2nd ed.). Thousand Oaks, CA: Sage.

Thomas, R. M. (2003). *Blending qualitative and quantitative research methods in theses and dissertations*. Thousand Oaks, CA: Corwin Press.

Thompson, B. (2006). *Foundations of behavioral statistics: An insight-based approach*. New York: Guilford Press.

Tufte, E. R. (1998). *The visual display of graphic information*. Cheshire, CT: Graphics Press.

Volk, K. S. (2009). Action research as a sustainable endeavor for teachers. *Action Research, 8*(3), 315–332.

Wakefield, T. (2012). *An ontology of storytelling systemicity: Management, fractals and the Waldo Canyon fire* (Doctoral dissertation, Colorado Technical University).

Walden University. (2010). Form and style recommendations for dissertation abstracts. Minneapolis, MN: Walden University.

Wheeldon, J., & Åhlberg, M. (2012). *Visualizing social science research: Maps, methods, & meaning*. Thousand Oaks, CA: Sage.

Whitfield, H. (2012). Answer to question from LinkedIn Group. Retrieved from http://www.linkedin.com/groupAnswers?viewQuestionAndAnswers=&discussionID=137155845&gid=1941649&commentID=89347620&trk=view_disc&ut=1F126KhF09GRk1.

Whitfield, H., Krinberg, G., & Zenhausern, K. (2012). Answer to question from LinkedIn Group. Retrieved from http://www.linkedin.com/groupAnswers?viewQuestionAndAnswers=&discussionID=137155845&gid=1941649&commentID=89347620&trk=view_disc&ut=1F126KhF09GRk1.

Williams, J. (2012). *Phonological awareness, phonics, and dyslexia: Teachers' perceptions and pedagogical content knowledge* (Doctoral dissertation, Walden).

Wise, M., Pulvermacher, A., Shanovich, K. K., Gustafson, D. H., Sorkness, C., & Bhattacharya, A. (2009). Using action research to implement an integrated pediatric asthma case management and e-health intervention for low-income families. *Health Promotion Practice, 2009*(11), 798–806.

Wyse, D. (2012). *The good writing guide for education students* (3rd ed.). Thousand Oaks, CA: Sage.

Index

⑤SAGE research**methods**

The essential online tool for researchers from the world's leading methods publisher

Find exactly what you are looking for, from basic explanations to advanced discussion

More content and new features added this year!

"*I have never really seen anything like this product before, and I think it is really valuable.*"

John Creswell, University of Nebraska–Lincoln

Discover **Methods Lists**—methods readings suggested by other users

Watch video interviews with leading methodologists

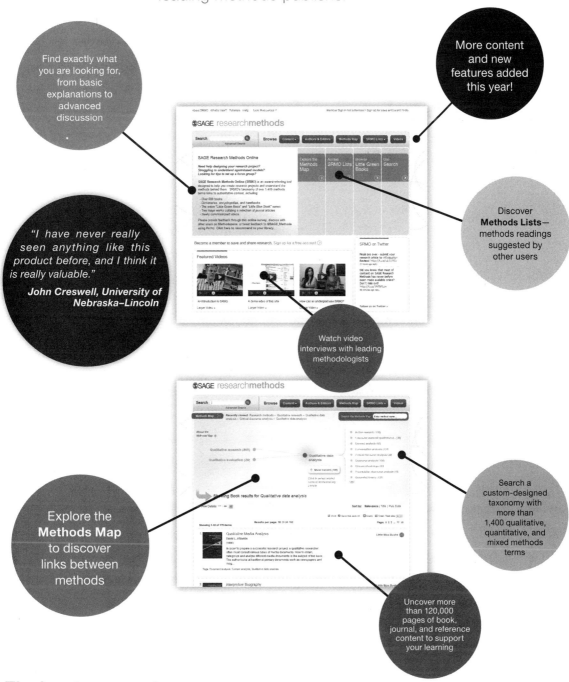

Explore the **Methods Map** to discover links between methods

Search a custom-designed taxonomy with more than 1,400 qualitative, quantitative, and mixed methods terms

Uncover more than 120,000 pages of book, journal, and reference content to support your learning

Find out more at
www.sageresearchmethods.com